CW00959925

Character

Samuel Smiles

Esprios.com

CHAPTER I. —INFLUENCE OF CHARACTER.

"Unless above himself he can Erect himself, how poor a thing is man"—DANIEL.

"Character is moral order seen through the medium, of an individual nature.... Men of character are the conscience of the society to which they belong. "—EMERSON.

"The prosperity of a country depends, not on the abundance of its revenues, nor on the strength of its fortifications, nor on the beauty of its public buildings; but it consists in the number of its cultivated citizens, in its men of education, enlightenment, and character; here are to be found its true interest, its chief strength, its real power. "—MARTIN LUTHER.

Character is one of the greatest motive powers in the world. In its noblest embodiments, it exemplifies human nature in its highest forms, for it exhibits man at his best.

Men of genuine excellence, in every station of life—men of industry, of integrity, of high principle, of sterling honesty of purpose—command the spontaneous homage of mankind. It is natural to believe in such men, to have confidence in them, and to imitate them. All that is good in the world is upheld by them, and without their presence in it the world would not be worth living in.

Although genius always commands admiration, character most secures respect. The former is more the product of brain-power, the latter of heart-power; and in the long run it is the heart that rules in life. Men of genius stand to society in the relation of its intellect, as men of character of its conscience; and while the former are admired, the latter are followed.

Great men are always exceptional men; and greatness itself is but comparative. Indeed, the range of most men in life is so limited, that very few have the opportunity of being great. But each man can act his part honestly and honourably, and to the best of his ability. He can use his gifts, and not abuse them. He can strive to make the best of life. He can be true, just, honest, and faithful, even in small things. In a word, he can do his Duty in that sphere in which Providence has placed him.

1

Commonplace though it may appear, this doing of one's Duty embodies the highest ideal of life and character. There may be nothing heroic about it; but the common lot of men is not heroic. And though the abiding sense of Duty upholds man in his highest attitudes, it also equally sustains him in the transaction of the ordinary affairs of everyday existence. Man's life is "centred in the sphere of common duties. " The most influential of all the virtues are those which are the most in request for daily use. They wear the best, and last the longest. Superfine virtues, which are above the standard of common men, may only be sources of temptation and danger. Burke has truly said that "the human system which rests for its basis on the heroic virtues is sure to have a superstructure of weakness or of profligacy. "

When Dr. Abbot, afterwards Archbishop of Canterbury, drew the character of his deceased friend Thomas Sackville, (1) he did not dwell upon his merits as a statesman, or his genius as a poet, but upon his virtues as a man in relation to the ordinary duties of life. "How many rare things were in him! " said he. "Who more loving unto his wife? Who more kind unto his children? —Who more fast unto his friend? —Who more moderate unto his enemy? —Who more true to his word? " Indeed, we can always better understand and appreciate a man's real character by the manner in which he conducts himself towards those who are the most nearly related to him, and by his transaction of the seemingly commonplace details of daily duty, than by his public exhibition of himself as an author, an orator, or a statesman.

At the same time, while Duty, for the most part, applies to the conduct of affairs in common life by the average of common men, it is also a sustaining power to men of the very highest standard of character. They may not have either money, or property, or learning, or power; and yet they may be strong in heart and rich in spirit— honest, truthful, dutiful. And whoever strives to do his duty faithfully is fulfilling the purpose for which he was created, and building up in himself the principles of a manly character. There are many persons of whom it may be said that they have no other possession in the world but their character, and yet they stand as firmly upon it as any crowned king.

Intellectual culture has no necessary relation to purity or excellence of character. In the New Testament, appeals are constantly made to the heart of man and to "the spirit we are of, " whilst allusions to the intellect are of very rare occurrence. "A handful of good life, " says George Herbert, "is worth a bushel of learning. " Not that learning is to be despised, but that it must be allied to goodness. Intellectual capacity is sometimes found associated with the meanest moral character with abject servility to those in high places, and arrogance to those of low estate. A man may be accomplished in art, literature, and science, and yet, in honesty, virtue, truthfulness, and the spirit of duty, be entitled to take rank after many a poor and illiterate peasant.

"You insist, " wrote Perthes to a friend, "on respect for learned men. I say, Amen! But, at the same time, don't forget that largeness of mind, depth of thought, appreciation of the lofty, experience of the world, delicacy of manner, tact and energy in action, love of truth, honesty, and amiability—that all these may be wanting in a man who may yet be very learned. " (2)

When some one, in Sir Walter Scott's hearing, made a remark as to the value of literary talents and accomplishments, as if they were above all things to be esteemed and honoured, he observed, "God help us! what a poor world this would be if that were the true doctrine! I have read books enough, and observed and conversed with enough of eminent and splendidly-cultured minds, too, in my time; but I assure you, I have heard higher sentiments from the lips of poor UNEDUCATED men and women, when exerting the spirit of severe yet gentle heroism under difficulties and afflictions, or speaking their simple thoughts as to circumstances in the lot of friends and neighbours, than I ever yet met with out of the Bible. We shall never learn to feel and respect our real calling and destiny, unless we have taught ourselves to consider everything as moonshine, compared with the education of the heart. " (3)

Still less has wealth any necessary connection with elevation of character. On the contrary, it is much more frequently the cause of its corruption and degradation. Wealth and corruption, luxury and vice, have very close affinities to each other. Wealth, in the hands of men of weak purpose, of deficient self-control, or of ill-regulated passions, is only a temptation and a snare—the source, it may be, of infinite mischief to themselves, and often to others.

On the contrary, a condition of comparative poverty is compatible with character in its highest form. A man may possess only his industry, his frugality, his integrity, and yet stand high in the rank of true manhood. The advice which Burns's father gave him was the best:

"He bade me act a manly part, though I had ne'er a farthing,
For without an honest manly heart no man was worth regarding."

One of the purest and noblest characters the writer ever knew was a labouring man in a northern county, who brought up his family respectably on an income never amounting to more than ten shillings a week. Though possessed of only the rudiments of common education, obtained at an ordinary parish school, he was a man full of wisdom and thoughtfulness. His library consisted of the Bible, 'Flavel, ' and 'Boston'—books which, excepting the first, probably few readers have ever heard of. This good man might have sat for the portrait of Wordsworth's well-known 'Wanderer. ' When he had lived his modest life of work and worship, and finally went to his rest, he left behind him a reputation for practical wisdom, for genuine goodness, and for helpfulness in every good work, which greater and richer men might have envied.

When Luther died, he left behind him, as set forth in his will, "no ready money, no treasure of coin of any description. " He was so poor at one part of his life, that he was under the necessity of earning his bread by turning, gardening, and clockmaking. Yet, at the very time when he was thus working with his hands, he was moulding the character of his country; and he was morally stronger, and vastly more honoured and followed, than all the princes of Germany.

Character is property. It is the noblest of possessions. It is an estate in the general goodwill and respect of men; and they who invest in it— though they may not become rich in this world's goods—will find their reward in esteem and reputation fairly and honourably won. And it is right that in life good qualities should tell—that industry, virtue, and goodness should rank the highest—and that the really best men should be foremost.

Simple honesty of purpose in a man goes a long way in life, if founded on a just estimate of himself and a steady obedience to the rule he knows and feels to be right. It holds a man straight, gives him strength and sustenance, and forms a mainspring of vigorous action. 'No man, " once said Sir Benjamin Rudyard, "is bound to be rich or great, —no, nor to be wise; but every man is bound to be honest. "(4)

But the purpose, besides being honest, must be inspired by sound principles, and pursued with undeviating adherence to truth, integrity, and uprightness. Without principles, a man is like a ship without rudder or compass, left to drift hither and thither with every wind that blows. He is as one without law, or rule, or order, or government. "Moral principles, " says Hume, "are social and universal. They form, in a manner, the PARTY of humankind against vice and disorder, its common enemy. "

Epictetus once received a visit from a certain magnificent orator going to Rome on a lawsuit, who wished to learn from the stoic something of his philosophy. Epictetus received his visitor coolly, not believing in his sincerity. "You will only criticise my style, " said he; "not really wishing to learn principles. "— "Well, but, " said the orator, "if I attend to that sort of thing; I shall be a mere pauper, like you, with no plate, nor equipage, nor land. "—"I don't WANT such things, " replied Epictetus; "and besides, you are poorer than I am, after all. Patron or no patron, what care I? You DO care. I am richer than you. I don't care what Caesar thinks of me. I flatter no one. This is what I have, instead of your gold and silver plate. You have silver vessels, but earthenware reasons, principles, appetites. My mind to me a kingdom is, and it furnishes me with abundant and happy occupation in lieu of your restless idleness. All your possessions seem small to you; mine seem great to me. Your desire is insatiate— mine is satisfied. " (5)

Talent is by no means rare in the world; nor is even genius. But can the talent be trusted? —can the genius? Not unless based on truthfulness—on veracity. It is this quality more than any other that commands the esteem and respect, and secures the confidence of others. Truthfulness is at the foundation of all personal excellence. It exhibits itself in conduct. It is rectitude—truth in action, and shines through every word and deed. It means reliableness, and convinces other men that it can be trusted. And a man is already of consequence in the world when it is known that he can be relied on, —that when he says he knows a thing, he does know it, —that when be says he will do a thing, he can do, and does it. Thus reliableness becomes a passport to the general esteem and confidence of mankind.

In the affairs of life or of business, it is not intellect that tells so much as character, —not brains so much as heart, —not genius so much as self-control, patience, and discipline, regulated by judgment. Hence there is no better provision for the uses of either private or public life, than a fair share of ordinary good sense guided by rectitude. Good sense, disciplined by experience and inspired by goodness, issues in practical wisdom. Indeed, goodness in a measure implies wisdom—the highest wisdom—the union of the worldly with the spiritual. "The correspondences of wisdom and goodness, " says Sir Henry Taylor, "are manifold; and that they will accompany each other is to be inferred, not only because men's wisdom makes them good, but because their goodness makes them wise. " (6)

It is because of this controlling power of character in life that we often see men exercise an amount of influence apparently out of all proportion to their intellectual endowments. They appear to act by means of some latent power, some reserved force, which acts secretly, by mere presence. As Burke said of a powerful nobleman of the last century, "his virtues were his means. " The secret is, that the aims of such men are felt to be pure and noble, and they act upon others with a constraining power.

Though the reputation of men of genuine character may be of slow growth, their true qualities cannot be wholly concealed. They may be misrepresented by some, and misunderstood by others; misfortune and adversity may, for a time, overtake them but, with patience and endurance, they will eventually inspire the respect and command the confidence which they really deserve.

It has been said of Sheridan that, had he possessed reliableness of character, he might have ruled the world; whereas, for want of it, his splendid gifts were comparatively useless. He dazzled and amused, but was without weight or influence in life or politics. Even the poor pantomimist of Drury Lane felt himself his superior. Thus, when Delpini one day pressed the manager for arrears of salary, Sheridan sharply reproved him, telling him he had forgotten his station. "No, indeed, Monsieur Sheridan, I have not, " retorted Delpini; "I know the difference between us perfectly well. In birth, parentage, and education, you are superior to me; but in life, character, and behaviour, I am superior to you. "

Unlike Sheridan, Burke, his countryman, was a great man of character. He was thirty-five before be gained a seat in Parliament, yet he found time to carve his name deep in the political history of England. He was a man of great gifts, and of transcendent force of character. Yet he had a weakness, which proved a serious defect—it was his want of temper; his genius was sacrificed to his irritability. And without this apparently minor gift of temper, the most splendid endowments may be comparatively valueless to their possessor.

Character is formed by a variety of minute circumstances, more or less under the regulation and control of the individual. Not a day passes without its discipline, whether for good or for evil. There is no act, however trivial, but has its train of consequences, as there is no hair so small but casts its shadow. It was a wise saying of Mrs. Schimmelpenninck's mother, never to give way to what is little; or by that little, however you may despise it, you will be practically governed.

Every action, every thought, every feeling, contributes to the education of the temper, the habits, and understanding; and exercises an inevitable influence upon all the acts of our future life. Thus character is undergoing constant change, for better or for worse—either being elevated on the one hand, or degraded on the other. "There is no fault nor folly of my life, " says Mr. Ruskin, "that does not rise up against me, and take away my joy, and shorten my power of possession, of sight, of understanding. And every past effort of my life, every gleam of rightness or good in it, is with me now, to help me in my grasp of this art and its vision. " (7)

The mechanical law, that action and reaction are equal, holds true also in morals. Good deeds act and react on the doers of them; and so do evil. Not only so: they produce like effects, by the influence of example, on those who are the subjects of them. But man is not the creature, so much as he is the creator, of circumstances: (8) and, by the exercise of his freewill, he can direct his actions so that they shall be productive of good rather than evil. "Nothing can work me damage but myself, " said St. Bernard; "the harm that I sustain I carry about with me; and I am never a real sufferer but by my own fault. "

The best sort of character, however, cannot be formed without effort. There needs the exercise of constant self-watchfulness, self-discipline, and self-control. There may be much faltering, stumbling, and temporary defeat; difficulties and temptations manifold to be battled with and overcome; but if the spirit be strong and the heart be upright, no one need despair of ultimate success. The very effort to advance—to arrive at a higher standard of character than we have reached—is inspiring and invigorating; and even though we may fall short of it, we cannot fail to be improved by every, honest effort made in an upward direction.

And with the light of great examples to guide us—representatives of humanity in its best forms—every one is not only justified, but bound in duty, to aim at reaching the highest standard of character: not to become the richest in means, but in spirit; not the greatest in worldly position, but in true honour; not the most intellectual, but the most virtuous; not the most powerful and influential, but the most truthful, upright, and honest.

It was very characteristic of the late Prince Consort—a man himself of the purest mind, who powerfully impressed and influenced others by the sheer force of his own benevolent nature —when drawing up the conditions of the annual prize to be given by Her Majesty at Wellington College, to determine that it should be awarded, not to the cleverest boy, nor to the most bookish boy, nor to the most precise, diligent, and prudent boy, —but to the noblest boy, to the boy who should show the most promise of becoming a large-hearted, high-motived man. (9)

Character exhibits itself in conduct, guided and inspired by principle, integrity, and practical wisdom. In its highest form, it is the individual will acting energetically under the influence of religion, morality, and reason. It chooses its way considerately, and pursues it steadfastly; esteeming duty above reputation, and the approval of conscience more than the world's praise. While respecting the personality of others, it preserves its own individuality and independence; and has the courage to be morally honest, though it may be unpopular, trusting tranquilly to time and experience for recognition.

Although the force of example will always exercise great influence upon the formation of character, the self-originating and sustaining force of one's own spirit must be the mainstay. This alone can hold up the life, and give individual independence and energy. "Unless man can erect himself above himself, " said Daniel, a poet of the Elizabethan era, "how poor a thing is man! " Without a certain degree of practical efficient force—compounded of will, which is the root, and wisdom, which is the stem of character—life will be indefinite and purposeless—like a body of stagnant water, instead of a running stream doing useful work and keeping the machinery of a district in motion.

When the elements of character are brought into action by determinate will, and, influenced by high purpose, man enters upon and courageously perseveres in the path of duty, at whatever cost of worldly interest, he may be said to approach the summit of his being. He then exhibits character in its most intrepid form, and embodies the highest idea of manliness. The acts of such a man become repeated in the life and action of others. His very words live and become actions. Thus every word of Luther's rang through Germany like a trumpet. As Richter said of him, "His words were half-battles. " And thus Luther's life became transfused into the life of his country, and still lives in the character of modern Germany.

On the other hand, energy, without integrity and a soul of goodness, may only represent the embodied principle of evil. It is observed by Novalis, in his 'Thoughts on Morals, ' that the ideal of moral perfection has no more dangerous rival to contend with than the ideal of the highest strength and the most energetic life, the maximum of the barbarian—which needs only a due admixture of pride, ambition, and selfishness, to be a perfect ideal of the devil. Amongst men of such stamp are found the greatest scourges and devastators of the world—those elect scoundrels whom Providence, in its inscrutable designs, permits to fulfil their mission of destruction upon earth. (10)

Very different is the man of energetic character inspired by a noble spirit, whose actions are governed by rectitude, and the law of whose life is duty. He is just and upright, —in his business dealings, in his public action, and in his family life—justice being as essential in the government of a home as of a nation. He will be honest in all things—in his words and in his work. He will be generous and merciful to his opponents, as well as to those who are weaker than himself. It was truly said of Sheridan —who, with all his improvidence, was generous, and never gave pain—that

"His wit in the combat, as gentle as bright,
Never carried a heart-stain away on its blade."

Such also was the character of Fox, who commanded the affection and service of others by his uniform heartiness and sympathy. He was a man who could always be most easily touched on the side of his honour. Thus, the story is told of a tradesman calling upon him one day for the payment of a promissory note which he presented. Fox was engaged at the time in counting out gold. The tradesman asked to be paid from the money before him. "No, " said Fox, "I owe this money to Sheridan; it is a debt of honour; if any accident happened to me, he would have nothing to show. " "Then, " said the tradesman, "I change MY debt into one of honour; " and he tore up the note. Fox was conquered by the act: he thanked the man for his confidence, and paid him, saying, "Then Sheridan must wait; yours is the debt of older standing. "

The man of character is conscientious. He puts his conscience into his work, into his words, into his every action. When Cromwell asked the Parliament for soldiers in lieu of the decayed serving-men and tapsters who filled the Commonwealth's army, he required that they should be men "who made some conscience of what they did; " and such were the men of which his celebrated regiment of "Ironsides" was composed.

The man of character is also reverential. The possession of this quality marks the noblest, and highest type of manhood and womanhood: reverence for things consecrated by the homage of generations—for high objects, pure thoughts, and noble aims— for the great men of former times, and the highminded workers amongst our contemporaries. Reverence is alike indispensable to the happiness of individuals, of families, and of nations. Without it there can be no trust, no faith, no confidence, either in man or God— neither social peace nor social progress. For reverence is but another word for religion, which binds men to each other, and all to God.

"The man of noble spirit, " says Sir Thomas Overbury, "converts all occurrences into experience, between which experience and his reason there is marriage, and the issue are his actions. He moves by affection, not for affection; he loves glory, scorns shame, and governeth and obeyeth with one countenance, for it comes from one consideration. Knowing reason to be no idle gift of nature, he is the steersman of his own destiny. Truth is his goddess, and he takes pains to get her, not to look like her. Unto the society of men he is a sun, whose clearness directs their steps in a regular motion. He is the wise man's friend, the example of the indifferent, the medicine of the vicious. Thus time goeth not from him, but with him, and he feels age more by the strength of his soul than by the weakness of his body. Thus feels he no pain, but esteems all such things as friends, that desire to file off his fetters, and help him out of prison. " (11)

Energy of will—self-originating force—is the soul of every great character. Where it is, there is life; where it is not, there is faintness, helplessness, and despondency. "The strong man and the waterfall, " says the proverb, "channel their own path. " The energetic leader of noble spirit not only wins a way for himself, but carries others with him. His every act has a personal significance, indicating vigour, independence, and self- reliance, and unconsciously commands respect, admiration, and homage. Such intrepidity of character characterised Luther, Cromwell, Washington, Pitt, Wellington, and all great leaders of men.

"I am convinced, " said Mr. Gladstone, in describing the qualities of the late Lord Palmerston in the House of Commons, shortly after his death—"I am convinced that it was the force of will, a sense of duty, and a determination not to give in, that enabled him to make himself a model for all of us who yet remain and follow him, with feeble and unequal steps, in the discharge of our duties; it was that force of will that in point of fact did not so much struggle against the infirmities of old age, but actually repelled them and kept them at a distance. And one other quality there is, at least, that may be noticed without the smallest risk of stirring in any breast a painful emotion. It is this, that Lord Palmerston had a nature incapable of enduring anger or any sentiment of wrath. This freedom from wrathful sentiment was not the result of painful effort, but the spontaneous fruit of the mind. It was a noble gift of his original nature—a gift which beyond all others it was delightful to observe, delightful also to remember in connection with him who has left us, and with whom we have no longer to do, except in endeavouring to profit by his example wherever it can lead us in the path of duty and of right, and of bestowing on him those tributes of admiration and affection which he deserves at our hands. "

The great leader attracts to himself men of kindred character, drawing them towards him as the loadstone draws iron. Thus, Sir John Moore early distinguished the three brothers Napier from the crowd of officers by whom he was surrounded, and they, on their part, repaid him by their passionate admiration. They were captivated by his courtesy, his bravery, and his lofty disinterestedness; and he became the model whom they resolved to imitate, and, if possible, to emulate. "Moore's influence, " says the biographer of Sir William Napier, "had a signal effect in forming and maturing their characters; and it is no small glory to have been the hero of those three men, while his early discovery of their mental and moral qualities is a proof of Moore's own penetration and judgment of character. "

There is a contagiousness in every example of energetic conduct. The brave man is an inspiration to the weak, and compels them, as it were, to follow him. Thus Napier relates that at the combat of Vera, when the Spanish centre was broken and in flight, a young officer, named Havelock, sprang forward, and, waving his hat, called upon the Spaniards within sight to follow him. Putting spurs to his horse, he leapt the abbatis which protected the French front, and went headlong against them. The Spaniards were electrified; in a moment they dashed after him, cheering for "EL CHICO BLANCO! " (the fair boy), and with one shock they broke through the French and sent them flying downhill. (12)

And so it is in ordinary life. The good and the great draw others after them; they lighten and lift up all who are within reach of their influence. They are as so many living centres of beneficent activity. Let a man of energetic and upright character be appointed to a position of trust and authority, and all who serve under him become, as it were, conscious of an increase of power. When Chatham was appointed minister, his personal influence was at once felt through all the ramifications of office. Every sailor who served under Nelson, and knew he was in command, shared the inspiration of the hero.

When Washington consented to act as commander-in-chief, it was felt as if the strength of the American forces had been more than doubled. Many years late; in 1798, when Washington, grown old, had withdrawn from public life and was living in retirement at Mount Vernon, and when it seemed probable that France would declare war against the United States, President Adams wrote to him, saying, "We must have your name, if you will permit us to use it; there will be more efficacy in it than in many an army. " Such was the esteem in which the great President's noble character and eminent abilities were held by his countrymen! (13)

An incident is related by the historian of the Peninsular War, illustrative of the personal influence exercised by a great commander over his followers. The British army lay at Sauroren, before which Soult was advancing, prepared to attack, in force. Wellington was absent, and his arrival was anxiously looked for. Suddenly a single horseman was seen riding up the mountain alone. It was the Duke, about to join his troops. One of Campbell's Portuguese battalions first descried him, and raised a joyful cry; then the shrill clamour, caught up by the next regiment, soon swelled as it ran along the line into that appalling shout which the British soldier is wont to give upon the edge of battle, and which no enemy ever heard unmoved. Suddenly he stopped at a conspicuous point, for he desired both armies should know he was there, and a double spy who was present pointed out Soult, who was so near that his features could be distinguished. Attentively Wellington fixed his eyes on that formidable man, and, as if speaking to himself, he said: "Yonder is a great commander; but he is cautious, and will delay his attack to ascertain the cause of those cheers; that will give time for the Sixth Division to arrive, and I shall beat him" — which he did. (14)

In some cases, personal character acts by a kind of talismanic influence, as if certain men were the organs of a sort of supernatural force. "If I but stamp on the ground in Italy, " said Pompey, "an army will appear. " At the voice of Peter the Hermit, as described by the historian, "Europe arose, and precipitated itself upon Asia. " It was said of the Caliph Omar that his walking-stick struck more terror into those who saw it than another man's sword. The very names of some men are like the sound of a trumpet. When the Douglas lay mortally wounded on the field of Otterburn, he ordered his name to be shouted still louder than before, saying there was a tradition in his family that a dead Douglas should win a battle. His followers, inspired by the sound, gathered fresh courage, rallied, and conquered; and thus, in the words of the Scottish poet: -

"The Douglas dead, his name hath won the field. " (15)

There have been some men whose greatest conquests have been achieved after they themselves were dead. "Never, " says Michelet, "was Caesar more alive, more powerful, more terrible, than when his old and worn-out body, his withered corpse, lay pierced with blows; he appeared then purified, redeemed, —that which he had been, despite his many stains—the man of humanity. " (16) Never did the great character of William of Orange, surnamed the Silent, exercise greater power over his countrymen than after his assassination at Delft by the emissary of the Jesuits. On the very day of his murder the Estates of Holland resolved "to maintain the good cause, with God's help, to the uttermost, without sparing gold or blood; " and they kept their word.

The same illustration applies to all history and morals. The career of a great man remains an enduring monument of human. energy. The man dies and disappears; but his thoughts and acts survive, and leave an indelible stamp upon his race. And thus the spirit of his life is prolonged and perpetuated, moulding the thought and will, and thereby contributing to form the character of the future. It is the men that advance in the highest and best directions, who are the true beacons of human progress. They are as lights set upon a hill, illumining the moral atmosphere around them; and the light of their spirit continues to shine upon all succeeding generations.

It is natural to admire and revere really great men. They hallow the nation to which they belong, and lift up not only all who live in their time, but those who live after them. Their great example becomes the common heritage of their race; and their great deeds and great thoughts are the most glorious of legacies to mankind. They connect the present with the past, and help on the increasing purpose of the future; holding aloft the standard of principle, maintaining the dignity of human character, and filling the mind with traditions and instincts of all that is most worthy and noble in life.

Character, embodied in thought and deed, is of the nature of immortality. The solitary thought of a great thinker will dwell in the minds of men for centuries until at length it works itself into their daily life and practice. It lives on through the ages, speaking as a voice from the dead, and influencing minds living thousands of years apart. Thus, Moses and David and Solomon, Plato and Socrates and Xenophon, Seneca and Cicero and Epictetus, still speak to us as from their tombs. They still arrest the attention, and exercise an influence upon character, though their thoughts be conveyed in languages unspoken by them and in their time unknown. Theodore Parker has said that a single man like Socrates was worth more to a country than many such states as South Carolina; that if that state went out of the world to-day, she would not have done so much for the world as Socrates. (17)

Great workers and great thinkers are the true makers of history, which is but continuous humanity influenced by men of character— by great leaders, kings, priests, philosophers, statesmen, and patriots—the true aristocracy of man. Indeed, Mr. Carlyle has broadly stated that Universal History is, at bottom, but the history of Great Men. They certainly mark and designate the epochs of national life. Their influence is active, as well as reactive. Though their mind is, in a measure; the product of their age, the public mind is also, to a great extent, their creation. Their individual action identifies the cause—the institution. They think great thoughts, cast them abroad, and the thoughts make events. Thus the early Reformers initiated the Reformation, and with it the liberation of modern thought. Emerson has said that every institution is to be regarded as but the lengthened shadow of some great man: as Islamism of Mahomet, Puritanism of Calvin, Jesuitism of Loyola, Quakerism of Fox, Methodism of Wesley, Abolitionism of Clarkson.

Great men stamp their mind upon their age and nation—as Luther did upon modern Germany, and Knox upon Scotland. (18) And if there be one man more than another that stamped his mind on modern Italy, it was Dante. During the long centuries of Italian degradation his burning words were as a watchfire and a beacon to all true men. He was the herald of his nation's liberty—braving persecution, exile, and death, for the love of it. He was always the most national of the Italian poets, the most loved, the most read. From the time of his death all educated Italians had his best passages by heart; and the sentiments they enshrined inspired their lives, and eventually influenced the history of their nation. "The Italians, " wrote Byron in 1821, "talk Dante, write Dante, and think and dream Dante, at this moment, to an excess which would be ridiculous, but that he deserves their admiration. " (19)

A succession of variously gifted men in different ages—extending from Alfred to Albert—has in like manner contributed, by their life and example, to shape the multiform character of England. Of these, probably the most influential were the men of the Elizabethan and Cromwellian, and the intermediate periods— amongst which we find the great names of Shakspeare, Raleigh, Burleigh, Sidney, Bacon, Milton, Herbert, Hampden, Pym, Eliot, Vane, Cromwell, and many more—some of them men of great force, and others of great dignity and purity of character. The lives of such men have become part of the public life of England, and their deeds and thoughts are regarded as among the most cherished bequeathments from the past.

So Washington left behind him, as one of the greatest treasures of his country, the example of a stainless life—of a great, honest, pure, and noble character—a model for his nation to form themselves by in all time to come. And in the case of Washington, as in so many other great leaders of men, his greatness did not so much consist in his intellect, his skill, and his genius, as in his honour, his integrity, his truthfulness, his high and controlling sense of duty—in a word, in his genuine nobility of character.

Men such as these are the true lifeblood of the country to which they belong. They elevate and uphold it, fortify and ennoble it, and shed a glory over it by the example of life and character which they have bequeathed. "The names and memories of great men, " says an able writer, "are the dowry of a nation. Widowhood, overthrow, desertion, even slavery, cannot take away from her this sacred inheritance.... Whenever national life begins to quicken.... the dead heroes rise in the memories of men, and appear to the living to stand by in solemn spectatorship and approval. No country can be lost which feels herself overlooked by such glorious witnesses. They are the salt of the earth, in death as well as in life. What they did once, their descendants have still and always a right to do after them; and their example lives in their country, a continual stimulant and encouragement for him who has the soul to adopt it. " (20)

But it is not great men only that have to be taken into account in estimating the qualities of a nation, but the character that pervades the great body of the people. When Washington Irving visited Abbotsford, Sir Walter Scott introduced him to many of his friends and favourites, not only amongst the neighbouring farmers, but the labouring peasantry. "I wish to show you, " said Scott, "some of our really excellent plain Scotch people. The character of a nation is not to be learnt from its fine folks, its fine gentlemen and ladies; such you meet everywhere, and they are everywhere the same. " While statesmen, philosophers, and divines represent the thinking power of society, the men who found industries and carve out new careers, as well as the common body of working-people, from whom the national strength and spirit are from time to time recruited, must necessarily furnish the vital force and constitute the real backbone of every nation.

Nations have their character to maintain as well as individuals; and under constitutional governments—where all classes more or less participate in the exercise of political power—the national character will necessarily depend more upon the moral qualities of the many than of the few. And the same qualities which determine the character of individuals, also determine the character of nations. Unless they are highminded, truthful, honest, virtuous, and courageous, they will be held in light esteem by other nations, and be without weight in the world. To have character, they must needs also be reverential, disciplined, self- controlling, and devoted to duty. The nation that has no higher god than pleasure, or even dollars or calico, must needs be in a poor way. It were better to revert to Homer's gods than be devoted to these; for the heathen deities at least imaged human virtues, and were something to look up to.

As for institutions, however good in themselves, they will avail but little in maintaining the standard of national character. It is the individual men, and the spirit which actuates them, that determine the moral standing and stability of nations. Government, in the long run, is usually no better than the people governed. Where the mass is sound in conscience, morals, and habit, the nation will be ruled honestly and nobly. But where they are corrupt, self-seeking, and dishonest in heart, bound neither by truth nor by law, the rule of rogues and wirepullers becomes inevitable.

The only true barrier against the despotism of public opinion, whether it be of the many or of the few, is enlightened individual freedom and purity of personal character. Without these there can be no vigorous manhood, no true liberty in a nation. Political rights, however broadly framed, will not elevate a people individually depraved. Indeed, the more complete a system of popular suffrage, and the more perfect its protection, the more completely will the real character of a people be reflected, as by a mirror, in their laws and government. Political morality can never have any solid existence on a basis of individual immorality. Even freedom, exercised by a debased people, would come to be regarded as a nuisance, and liberty of the press but a vent for licentiousness and moral abomination.

Nations, like individuals, derive support and strength from the feeling that they belong to an illustrious race, that they are the heirs of their greatness, and ought to be the perpetuators of their glory. It is of momentous importance that a nation should have a great past (21) to look back upon. It steadies the life of the present, elevates and upholds it, and lightens and lifts it up, by the memory of the great deeds, the noble sufferings, and the valorous achievements of the men of old. The life of nations, as of men, is a great treasury of experience, which, wisely used, issues in social progress and improvement; or, misused, issues in dreams, delusions, and failure. Like men, nations are purified and strengthened by trials. Some of the most glorious chapters in their history are those containing the record of the sufferings by means of which their character has been developed. Love of liberty and patriotic feeling may have done much, but trial and suffering nobly borne more than all.

A great deal of what passes by the name of patriotism in these days consists of the merest bigotry and narrow-mindedness; exhibiting itself in national prejudice, national conceit, amid national hatred. It does not show itself in deeds, but in boastings—in howlings, gesticulations, and shrieking helplessly for help—in flying flags and singing songs—and in perpetual grinding at the hurdy-gurdy of long-dead grievances and long- remedied wrongs. To be infested by SUCH a patriotism as this is, perhaps, amongst the greatest curses that can befall any country.

But as there is an ignoble, so is there a noble patriotism—the patriotism that invigorates and elevates a country by noble work— that does its duty truthfully and manfully—that lives an honest, sober, and upright life, and strives to make the best use of the opportunities for improvement that present themselves on every side; and at the same time a patriotism that cherishes the memory and example of the great men of old, who, by their sufferings in the cause of religion or of freedom, have won for themselves a deathless glory, and for their nation those privileges of free life and free institutions of which they are the inheritors and possessors.

Nations are not to be judged by their size any more than individuals:

"it is not growing like a tree
In bulk, doth make Man better be."

For a nation to be great, it need not necessarily be big, though bigness is often confounded with greatness. A nation may be very big in point of territory and population and yet be devoid of true greatness. The people of Israel were a small people, yet what a great life they developed, and how powerful the influence they have exercised on the destinies of mankind! Greece was not big: the entire population of Attica was less than that of South Lancashire. Athens was less populous than New York; and yet how great it was in art, in literature, in philosophy, and in patriotism! (22)

But it was the fatal weakness of Athens that its citizens had no true family or home life, while its freemen were greatly outnumbered by its slaves. Its public men were loose, if not corrupt, in morals. Its women, even the most accomplished, were unchaste. Hence its fall became inevitable, and was even more sudden than its rise.

In like manner the decline and fall of Rome was attributable to the general corruption of its people, and to their engrossing love of pleasure and idleness—work, in the later days of Rome, being regarded only as fit for slaves. Its citizens ceased to pride themselves on the virtues of character of their great forefathers; and the empire fell because it did not deserve to live. And so the nations that are idle and luxurious—that "will rather lose a pound of blood, " as old Burton says, "in a single combat, than a drop of sweat in any honest labour"—must inevitably die out, and laborious energetic nations take their place.

When Louis XIV. asked Colbert how it was that, ruling so great and populous a country as France, he had been unable to conquer so small a country as Holland, the minister replied: "Because, Sire, the greatness of a country does not depend upon the extent of its territory, but on the character of its people. It is because of the industry, the frugality, and the energy of the Dutch that your Majesty has found them so difficult to overcome. "

It is also related of Spinola and Richardet, the ambassadors sent by the King of Spain to negotiate a treaty at the Hague in 1608, that one day they saw some eight or ten persons land from a little boat, and, sitting down upon the grass, proceed to make a meal of bread-and-cheese and beer. "Who are those travellers asked the ambassadors of a peasant. "These are worshipful masters, the deputies from the States, " was his reply. Spinola at once whispered to his companion, "We must make peace: these are not men to be conquered. "

In fine, stability of institutions must depend upon stability of character. Any number of depraved units cannot form a great nation. The people may seem to be highly civilised, and yet be ready to fall to pieces at first touch of adversity. Without integrity of individual character, they can have no real strength, cohesion, soundness. They may be rich, polite, and artistic; and yet hovering on the brink of ruin. If living for themselves only, and with no end but pleasure—each little self his own little

—such a nation is doomed, and its decay is inevitable.

Where national character ceases to be upheld, a nation may be regarded as next to lost. Where it ceases to esteem and to practise the virtues of truthfulness, honesty, integrity, and justice, it does not deserve to live. And when the time arrives in any country when wealth has so corrupted, or pleasure so depraved, or faction so infatuated the people, that honour, order, obedience, virtue, and loyalty have seemingly become things of the past; then, amidst the darkness, when honest men—if, haply, there be such left—are groping about and feeling for each other's hands, their only remaining hope will be in the restoration and elevation of Individual Character; for by that alone can a nation be saved; and if character be irrecoverably lost, then indeed there will be nothing left worth saving.

NOTES

(1) Sackville, Lord Buckhurst, Lord High Treasurer under Elizabeth and James I.

(2) 'Life of Perthes, ' ii. 217.

(3) Lockhart's 'Life of Scott. '

(4) Debate on the Petition of Right, A.D. 1628.

(5) The Rev. F. W. Farrer's 'Seekers after God, ' p. 241.

(6) 'The Statesman, ' p. 30.

(7) 'Queen of the Air, ' p. 127

(8) Instead of saying that man is the creature of Circumstance, it would be nearer the mark to say that man is the architect of Circumstance. It is Character which builds an existence out of Circumstance. Our strength is measured by our plastic power. From the same materials one man builds palaces, another hovels: one warehouses, another villas. Bricks and mortar are mortar and bricks, until the architect can make them something else. Thus it is that in the same family, in the same circumstances, one man rears a stately edifice, while his brother, vacillating and incompetent, lives for ever amid ruins: the block of granite, which was an obstacle on the pathway of the weak, becomes a stepping-stone on the pathway of the strong. "—G. H. Lewes, LIFE OF GOETHE.

(9) Introduction to 'The Principal Speeches and Addresses of H. R.H. the Prince Consort' (1862), pp. 39-40.

(10) Among the latest of these was Napoleon "the Great, " a man of abounding energy, but destitute of principle. He had the lowest opinion of his fellowmen. "Men are hogs, who feed on gold, " he once said: "Well, I throw them gold, and lead them whithersoever I will. " When the Abbe de Pradt, Archbishop of Malines, was setting out on his embassy to Poland in 1812, Napoleon's parting instruction to him was, "Tenez bonne table et soignez les femmes, " —of which Benjamin Constant said that such an observation, addressed to a feeble priest of sixty, shows Buonaparte's profound contempt for the human race, without distinction of nation or sex.

(11) Condensed from Sir Thomas Overbury's 'Characters' (1614).

(12) 'History of the Peninsular War, ' v. 319. —Napier mentions another striking illustration of the influence of personal qualities in young Edward Freer, of the same regiment (the 43rd), who, when he fell at the age of nineteen, at the Battle of the Nivelle, had already seen more combats and sieges than he could count years. "So slight in person, and of such surpassing beauty, that the Spaniards often thought him a girl disguised in man's clothing, he was yet so vigorous, so active, so brave, that the most daring and experienced veterans watched his looks on the field of battle, and, implicitly following where he led, would, like children, obey his slightest sign in the most difficult situations. "

(13) When the dissolution of the Union at one time seemed imminent, and Washington wished to retire into private life, Jefferson wrote to him, urging his continuance in office. "The confidence of the whole Union, " he said, "centres in you. Your being at the helm will be more than an answer to every argument which can be used to alarm and lead the people in any quarter into violence and secession.... There is sometimes an eminence of character on which society has such peculiar claims as to control the predilection of the individual for a particular walk of happiness, and restrain him to that alone arising from the present and future benedictions of mankind. This seems to be your condition, and the law imposed on you by Providence in forming your character and fashioning the events on which it was to operate; and it is to motives like these, and not to personal anxieties of mine or others, who have no right to call on you for sacrifices, that I appeal from your former determination,

and urge a revisal of it, on the ground of change in the aspect of things. "—Sparks' Life of Washington, i. 480.

(14) Napier's 'History of the Peninsular War, ' v. 226.

(15) Sir W. Scott's 'History of Scotland, ' vol. i. chap. xvi.

(16) Michelet's 'History of Rome, ' p. 374.

(17) Erasmus so reverenced the character of Socrates that he said, when he considered his life and doctrines, he was inclined to put him in the calendar of saints, and to exclaim, "SANCTE SOCRATES, ORA PRO NOBIS. '" (Holy Socrates, pray for us!

(18) "Honour to all the brave and true; everlasting honour to John Knox one of the truest of the true! That, in the moment while he and his cause, amid civil broils, in convulsion and confusion, were still but struggling for life, he sent the schoolmaster forth to all corners, and said, 'Let the people be taught: ' this is but one, and, and indeed, an inevitable and comparatively inconsiderable item in his great message to men. This message, in its true compass, was, 'Let men know that they are men created by God, responsible to God who work in any meanest moment of time what will last through eternity... ' This great message Knox did deliver, with a man's voice and strength; and found a people to believe him. Of such an achievement, were it to be made once only, the results are immense. Thought, in such a country, may change its form, but cannot go out; the country has attained MAJORITY thought, and a certain manhood, ready for all work that man can do, endures there.... The Scotch national character originated in many circumstances: first of all, in the Saxon stuff there was to work on; but next, and beyond all else except that, is the Presbyterian Gospel of John Knox. "— (Carlyle' s MISCELLANIES, iv. 118.

(19) Moore's 'Life of Byron, ' 8vo. ed. p. 484. —Dante was a religious as well as a political reformer. He was a reformer three hundred years before the Reformation, advocating the separation of the spiritual from the civil power, and declaring the temporal government of the Pope to be a usurpation. The following memorable words were written over five hundred and sixty years ago, while Dante was still a member of the Roman Catholic Church: - "Every Divine law is found in one or other of the two Testaments; but in neither can I find that the care of temporal matters was given

to the priesthood. On the contrary, I find that the first priests were removed from them by law, and the later priests, by command of Christ, to His disciples. "—DE MONARCHIA, lib. iii. cap. xi.

Dante also, still clinging to 'the Church he wished to reform, ' thus anticipated the fundamental doctrine of the Reformation: - "Before the Church are the Old and New Testament; after the Church are traditions. It follows, then, that the authority of the Church depends, not on traditions, but traditions on the Church. "

(20) 'Blackwood's Magazine, ' June, 1863, art. 'Girolamo Savonarola.'

(21) One of the last passages in the Diary of Dr. Arnold, written the year before his death, was as follows: - "It is the misfortune of France that her 'past' cannot be loved or respected—her future and her present cannot be wedded to it; yet how can the present yield fruit, or the future have promise, except their roots be fixed in the past? The evil is infinite, but the blame rests with those who made the past a dead thing, out of which no healthful life could be produced. "—LIFE, ii. 387-8, Ed. 1858.

(22) A public orator lately spoke with contempt of the Battle of Marathon, because only 192 perished on the side of the Athenians, whereas by improved mechanism and destructive chemicals, some 50,000 men or more may now be destroyed within a few hours. Yet the Battle of Marathon, and the heroism displayed in it, will probably continue to be remembered when the gigantic butcheries of modern times have been forgotten.

CHAPTER II. —HOME POWER.

"So build we up the being that we are,
Thus deeply drinking in the soul of things,
We shall be wise perforce." WORDSWORTH.

"The millstreams that turn the clappers of the world
arise in solitary places."—HELPS.

"In the course of a conversation with Madame Campan, Napoleon Buonaparte remarked: 'The old systems of instruction seem to be worth nothing; what is yet wanting in order that the people should be properly educated? ' 'MOTHERS, ' replied Madame Campan. The reply struck the Emperor. 'Yes! ' said he 'here is a system of education in one word. Be it your care, then, to train up mothers who shall know how to educate their children. '"—AIME MARTIN.

"Lord! with what care hast Thou begirt us round!
Parents first season us. Then schoolmasters
Deliver us to laws. They send us bound
To rules of reason."—GEORGE HERBERT.

HOME is the first and most important school of character. It is there that every human being receives his best moral training, or his worst; for it is there that he imbibes those principles of conduct which endure through manhood, and cease only with life.

It is a common saying that "Manners make the man; " and there is a second, that "Mind makes the man; " but truer than either is a third, that "Home makes the man. " For the home-training includes not only manners and mind, but character. It is mainly in the home that the heart is opened, the habits are formed, the intellect is awakened, and character moulded for good or for evil.

From that source, be it pure or impure, issue the principles and maxims that govern society. Law itself is but the reflex of homes. The tiniest bits of opinion sown in the minds of children in private life afterwards issue forth to the world, and become its public opinion; for nations are gathered out of nurseries, and they who hold the leading-strings of children may even exercise a greater power than those who wield the reins of government. (1)

It is in the order of nature that domestic life should be preparatory to social, and that the mind and character should first be formed in the home. There the individuals who afterwards form society are dealt with in detail, and fashioned one by one. From the family they enter life, and advance from boyhood to citizenship. Thus the home may be regarded as the most influential school of civilisation. For, after all, civilisation mainly resolves itself into a question of individual training; and according as the respective members of society are well or ill- trained in youth, so will the community which they constitute be more or less humanised and civilised.

The training of any man, even the wisest, cannot fail to be powerfully influenced by the moral surroundings of his early years. He comes into the world helpless, and absolutely dependent upon those about him for nurture and culture. From the very first breath that he draws, his education begins. When a mother once asked a clergyman when she should begin the education of her child, then four years old, he replied: "Madam, if you have not begun already, you have lost those four years. From the first smile that gleams upon an infant's cheek, your opportunity begins. "

But even in this case the education had already begun; for the child learns by simple imitation, without effort, almost through the pores of the skin. "A figtree looking on a figtree becometh fruitful, " says the Arabian proverb. And so it is with children; their first great instructor is example.

However apparently trivial the influences which contribute to form the character of the child, they endure through life. The child's character is the nucleus of the man's; all after-education is but superposition; the form of the crystal remains the same. Thus the saying of the poet holds true in a large degree, "The child is father of the man; " or, as Milton puts it, "The childhood shows the man, as morning shows the day. " Those impulses to conduct which last the longest and are rooted the deepest, always have their origin near our birth. It is then that the germs of virtues or vices, of feelings or sentiments, are first implanted which determine the character for life.

The child is, as it were, laid at the gate of a new world, and opens his eyes upon things all of which are full of novelty and wonderment. At first it is enough for him to gaze; but by-and-by he begins to see, to observe, to compare, to learn, to store up impressions and ideas; and under wise guidance the progress which he makes is really wonderful. Lord Brougham has observed that between the ages of eighteen and thirty months, a child learns more of the material world, of his own powers, of the nature of other bodies, and even of his own mind and other minds, than he acquires in all the rest of his life. The knowledge which a child accumulates, and the ideas generated in his mind, during this period, are so important, that if we could imagine them to be afterwards obliterated, all the learning of a senior wrangler at Cambridge, or a first-classman at Oxford, would be as nothing to it, and would literally not enable its object to prolong his existence for a week.

It is in childhood that the mind is most open to impressions, and ready to be kindled by the first spark that falls into it. Ideas are then caught quickly and live lastingly. Thus Scott is said to have received, his first bent towards ballad literature from his mother's and grandmother's recitations in his hearing long before he himself had learned to read. Childhood is like a mirror, which reflects in after-life the images first presented to it. The first thing continues for ever with the child. The first joy, the first sorrow, the first success, the first failure, the first achievement, the first misadventure, paint the foreground of his life.

All this while, too, the training of the character is in progress —of the temper, the will, and the habits—on which so much of the happiness of human beings in after-life depends. Although man is endowed with a certain self-acting, self-helping power of contributing to his own development, independent of surrounding circumstances, and of reacting upon the life around him, the bias given to his moral character in early life is of immense importance. Place even the highest-minded philosopher in the midst of daily discomfort, immorality, and vileness, and he will insensibly gravitate towards brutality. How much more susceptible is the impressionable and helpless child amidst such surroundings! It is not possible to rear a kindly nature, sensitive to evil, pure in mind and heart, amidst coarseness, discomfort, and impurity.

Thus homes, which are the nurseries of children who grow up into men and women, will be good or bad according to the power that governs them. Where the spirit of love and duty pervades the home —where head and heart bear rule wisely there—where the daily life is honest and virtuous—where the government is sensible, kind, and loving, then may we expect from such a home an issue of healthy, useful, and happy beings, capable, as they gain the requisite strength, of following the footsteps of their parents, of walking uprightly, governing themselves wisely, and contributing to the welfare of those about them.

On the other hand, if surrounded by ignorance, coarseness, and selfishness, they will unconsciously assume the same character, and grow up to adult years rude, uncultivated, and all the more dangerous to society if placed amidst the manifold temptations of what is called civilised life. "Give your child to be educated by a slave, " said an ancient Greek, "and instead of one slave, you will then have two. "

The child cannot help imitating what he sees. Everything is to him a model—of manner, of gesture, of speech, of habit, of character. "For the child, " says Richter, "the most important era of life is that of childhood, when he begins to colour and mould himself by companionship with others. Every new educator effects less than his predecessor; until at last, if we regard all life as an educational institution, a circumnavigator of the world is less influenced by all the nations he has seen than by his nurse. " (2) Models are therefore of every importance in moulding the nature of the child; and if we would have fine characters, we must necessarily present before them fine models. Now, the model most constantly before every child's eye is the Mother.

One good mother, said George Herbert, is worth a hundred schoolmasters. In the home she is "loadstone to all hearts, and loadstar to all eyes. " Imitation of her is constant—imitation, which Bacon likens to "a globe of precepts. " But example is far more than precept. It is instruction in action. It is teaching without words, often exemplifying more than tongue can teach. In the face of bad example, the best of precepts are of but little avail. The example is followed, not the precepts. Indeed, precept at variance with practice is worse than useless, inasmuch as it only serves to teach the most cowardly of vices—hypocrisy. Even children are judges of consistency, and the lessons of the parent who says one thing and does the opposite, are quickly seen through. The teaching of the friar was not worth much, who preached the virtue of honesty with a stolen goose in his sleeve.

By imitation of acts, the character becomes slowly and imperceptibly, but at length decidedly formed. The several acts may seem in themselves trivial; but so are the continuous acts of daily life. Like snowflakes, they. fall unperceived; each flake added to the pile produces no sensible change, and yet the accumulation of snowflakes makes the avalanche. So do repeated acts, one following another, at length become consolidated in habit, determine the action of the human being for good or for evil, and, in a word, form the character.

It is because the mother, far more than the father, influences the action and conduct of the child, that her good example is of so much greater importance in the home. It is easy to understand how this should be so. The home is the woman's domain—her kingdom, where she exercises entire control. Her power over the little subjects she rules there is absolute. They look up to her for everything. She is the example and model constantly before their eyes, whom they unconsciously observe and imitate.

Cowley, speaking of the influence of early example, and ideas early implanted in the mind, compares them to letters cut in the bark of a young tree, which grow and widen with age. The impressions then made, howsoever slight they may seem, are never effaced. The ideas then implanted in the mind are like seeds dropped into the ground, which lie there and germinate for a time, afterwards springing up in acts and thoughts and habits. Thus the mother lives again in her children. They unconsciously mould themselves after her manner, her speech, her conduct, and her method of life. Her habits become theirs; and her character is visibly repeated in them.

This maternal love is the visible providence of our race. Its influence is constant and universal. It begins with the education of the human being at the out-start of life, and is prolonged by virtue of the powerful influence which every good mother exercises over her children through life. When launched into the world, each to take part in its labours, anxieties, and trials, they still turn to their mother for consolation, if not for counsel, in their time of trouble and difficulty. The pure and good thoughts she has implanted in their minds when children, continue to grow up into good acts, long after she is dead; and when there is nothing but a memory of her left, her children rise up and call her blessed.

It is not saying too much to aver that the happiness or misery, the enlightenment or ignorance, the civilisation or barbarism of the world, depends in a very high degree upon the exercise of woman's power within her special kingdom of home. Indeed, Emerson says, broadly and truly, that "a sufficient measure of civilisation is the influence of good women. " Posterity may be said to lie before us in the person of the child in the mother's lap. What that child will eventually become, mainly depends upon the training and example which he has received from his first and most influential educator.

Woman, above all other educators, educates humanly. Man is the brain, but woman is the heart of humanity; he its judgment, she its feeling; he its strength, she its grace, ornament, and solace. Even the understanding of the best woman seems to work mainly through her affections. And thus, though man may direct the intellect, woman cultivates the feelings, which mainly determine the character. While he fills the memory, she occupies the heart. She makes us love what he can only make us believe, and it is chiefly through her that we are enabled to arrive at virtue.

The respective influences of the father and the mother on the training and development of character, are remarkably illustrated in the life of St. Augustine. While Augustine's father, a poor freeman of Thagaste, proud of his son's abilities, endeavoured to furnish his mind with the highest learning of the schools, and was extolled by his neighbours for the sacrifices he made with that object "beyond the ability of his means"—his mother Monica, on the other hand, sought to lead her son's mind in the direction of the highest good, and with pious care counselled him, entreated him, advised him to chastity, and, amidst much anguish and tribulation, because of his wicked life, never ceased to pray for him until her prayers were heard and answered. Thus her love at last triumphed, and the patience and goodness of the mother were rewarded, not only by the conversion of her gifted son, but also of her husband. Later in life, and after her husband's death, Monica, drawn by her affection, followed her son to Milan, to watch over him; and there she died, when he was in his thirty- third year. But it was in the earlier period of his life that her example and instruction made the deepest impression upon his mind, and determined his future character.

There are many similar instances of early impressions made upon a child's mind, springing up into good acts late in life, after an intervening period of selfishness and vice. Parents may do all that they can to develope an upright and virtuous character in their children, and apparently in vain. It seems like bread cast upon the waters and lost. And yet sometimes it happens that long after the parents have gone to their Rest—it may be twenty years or more—the good precept, the good example set before their sons and daughters in childhood, at length springs up and bears fruit.

One of the most remarkable of such instances was that of the Reverend John Newton of Olney, the friend of Cowper the poet. It was long subsequent to the death of both his parents, and after leading a vicious life as a youth and as a seaman, that he became suddenly awakened to a sense of his depravity; and then it was that the lessons which his mother had given him when a child sprang up vividly in his memory. Her voice came to him as it were from the dead, and led him gently back to virtue and goodness.

Another instance is that of John Randolph, the American statesman, who once said: "I should have been an atheist if it had not been for one recollection—and that was the memory of the time when my departed mother used to take my little hand in hers, and cause me on my knees to say, 'Our Father who art in heaven! '"

But such instance must, on the whole, be regarded as exceptional. As the character is biassed in early life, so it generally remains, gradually assuming its permanent form as manhood is reached. "Live as long as you may, " said Southey, "the first twenty years are the longest half of your life, " and they are by far the most pregnant in consequences. When the worn-out slanderer and voluptuary, Dr. Wolcot, lay on his deathbed, one of his friends asked if he could do anything to gratify him. "Yes, " said the dying man, eagerly, "give me back my youth. " Give him but that, and he would repent—he would reform. But it was all too late! His life had become bound and enthralled by the chains of habit. ' (3)

Gretry, the musical composer, thought so highly of the importance of woman as an educator of character, that he described a good mother as "Nature's CHEF-D'OEUVRE. " And he was right: for good mothers, far more than fathers, tend to the perpetual renovation of mankind, creating, as they do, the moral atmosphere of the home, which is the nutriment of man's moral being, as the physical atmosphere is of his corporeal frame. By good temper, suavity, and kindness, directed by intelligence, woman surrounds the indwellers with a pervading atmosphere of cheerfulness, contentment, and peace, suitable for the growth of the purest as of the manliest natures.

The poorest dwelling, presided over by a virtuous, thrifty, cheerful, and cleanly woman, may thus be the abode of comfort, virtue, and happiness; it may be the scene of every ennobling relation in family life; it may be endeared to a man by many delightful associations; furnishing a sanctuary for the heart, a refuge from the storms of life, a sweet resting-place after labour, a consolation in misfortune, a pride in prosperity, and a joy at all times.

The good home is thus the best of schools, not only in youth but in age. There young and old best learn cheerfulness, patience, self-control, and the spirit of service and of duty. Izaak Walton, speaking of George Herbert's mother, says she governed her family with judicious care, not rigidly nor sourly, "but with such a sweetness and compliance with the recreations and pleasures of youth, as did incline them to spend much of their time in her company, which was to her great content. "

The home is the true school of courtesy, of which woman is always the best practical instructor. "Without woman, " says the Provencal proverb, "men were but ill-licked cubs. " Philanthropy radiates from the home as from a centre. "To love the little platoon we belong to in society, " said Burke, "is the germ of all public affections. " The wisest and the best have not been ashamed to own it to be their greatest joy and happiness to sit "behind the heads of children" in the inviolable circle of home. A life of purity and duty there is not the least effectual preparative for a life of public work and duty; and the man who loves his home will not the less fondly love and serve his country. But while homes, which are the nurseries of character, may be the best of schools, they may also be the worst. Between childhood and manhood how incalculable is the mischief which ignorance in the home has the power to cause! Between the drawing of the first breath and the last, how vast is the moral suffering and disease occasioned by incompetent mothers and nurses! Commit a child to the care of a worthless ignorant woman, and no culture in after- life will remedy the evil you have done. Let the mother be idle, vicious, and a slattern; let her home be pervaded by cavilling, petulance, and discontent, and it will become a dwelling of misery — a place to fly from, rather than to fly to; and the children whose misfortune it is to be brought up there, will be morally dwarfed and deformed—the cause of misery to themselves as well as to others.

Napoleon Buonaparte was accustomed to say that "the future good or bad conduct of a child depended entirely on the mother. " He himself attributed his rise in life in a great measure to the training of his will, his energy, and his self-control, by his mother at home. "Nobody had any command over him, " says one of his biographers, "except his mother, who found means, by a mixture of tenderness, severity, and justice, to make him love, respect, and obey her: from her he learnt the virtue of obedience. "

A curious illustration of the dependence of the character of children on that of the mother incidentally occurs in one of Mr. Tufnell's school reports. The truth, he observes, is so well established that it has even been made subservient to mercantile calculation. "I was informed, " he says, "in a large factory, where many children were employed, that the managers before they engaged a boy always inquired into the mother's character, and if that was satisfactory they were tolerably certain that her children would conduct themselves creditably. NO ATTENTION WAS PAID TO THE CHARACTER OF THE FATHER. " (4)

It has also been observed that in cases where the father has turned out badly—become a drunkard, and "gone to the dogs"— provided the mother is prudent and sensible, the family will be kept together, and the children probably make their way honourably in life; whereas in cases of the opposite sort, where the mother turns out badly, no matter how well-conducted the father may be, the instances of after-success in life on the part of the children are comparatively rare.

The greater part of the influence exercised by women on the formation of character necessarily remains unknown. They accomplish their best work in the quiet seclusion of the home and the family, by sustained effort and patient perseverance in the path of duty. Their greatest triumphs, because private and domestic, are rarely recorded; and it is not often, even in the biographies of distinguished men, that we hear of the share which their mothers have had in the formation of their character, and in giving them a bias towards goodness. Yet are they not on that account without their reward. The influence they have exercised, though unrecorded, lives after them, and goes on propagating itself in consequences for ever.

We do not often hear of great women, as we do of great men. It is of good women that we mostly hear; and it is probable that by determining the character of men and women for good, they are doing even greater work than if they were to paint great pictures, write great books, or compose great operas. "It is quite true, " said Joseph de Maistre, "that women have produced no CHEFS-DOEUVRE. They have written no 'Iliad, ' nor 'Jerusalem Delivered, ' nor 'Hamlet, ' nor 'Phaedre, ' nor 'Paradise Lost, ' nor 'Tartuffe; ' they have designed no Church of St. Peter's, composed no 'Messiah,' carved no 'Apollo Belvidere, ' painted no 'Last Judgment; ' they have invented neither algebra, nor telescopes, nor steam-engines; but they have done something far greater and better than all this, for it is at their knees that upright and virtuous men and women have been trained—the most excellent productions in the world. "

De Maistre, in his letters and writings, speaks of his own mother with immense love and reverence. Her noble character made all other women venerable in his eyes. He described her as his "sublime mother"—"an angel to whom God had lent a body for a brief season." To her he attributed the bent of his character, and all his bias towards good; and when he had grown to mature years, while acting as ambassador at the Court of St. Petersburg, he referred to her noble example and precepts as the ruling influence in his life.

One of the most charming features in the character of Samuel Johnson, notwithstanding his rough and shaggy exterior, was the tenderness with which he invariably spoke of his mother (5)—a woman of strong understanding, who firmly implanted in his mind, as he himself acknowledges, his first impressions of religion. He was accustomed, even in the time of his greatest difficulties, to contribute largely, out of his slender means, to her comfort; and one of his last acts of filial duty was to write 'Rasselas' for the purpose of paying her little debts and defraying her funeral charges.

George Washington was only eleven years of age—the eldest of five children—when his father died, leaving his mother a widow. She was a woman of rare excellence—full of resources, a good woman of business, an excellent manager, and possessed of much strength of character. She had her children to educate and bring up, a large household to govern, and extensive estates to manage, all of which she accomplished with complete success. Her good sense, assiduity, tenderness, industry, and vigilance, enabled her to overcome every obstacle; and as the richest reward of her solicitude and toil, she had the happiness to see all her children come forward with a fair promise into life, filling the spheres allotted to them in a manner equally honourable to themselves, and to the parent who had been the only guide of their, principles, conduct, and habits. (6)

The biographer of Cromwell says little about the Protector's father, but dwells upon the character of his mother, whom he describes as a woman of rare vigour and decision of purpose: "A woman, " he says, "possessed of the glorious faculty of self-help when other assistance failed her; ready for the demands of fortune in its extremest adverse turn; of spirit and energy equal to her mildness and patience; who, with the labour of her own hands, gave dowries to five daughters sufficient to marry them into families as honourable but more wealthy than their own; whose single pride was honesty, and whose passion was love; who preserved in the gorgeous palace at Whitehall the simple tastes that distinguished her in the old brewery at Huntingdon; and whose only care, amidst all her splendour, was for the safety of her son in his dangerous eminence. " (7)

We have spoken of the mother of Napoleon Buonaparte as a woman of great force of character. Not less so was the mother of the Duke of Wellington, whom her son strikingly resembled in features, person, and character; while his father was principally distinguished as a musical composer and performer. (8) But, strange to say, Wellington's mother mistook him for a dunce; and, for some reason or other, he was not such a favourite as her other children, until his great deeds in after-life constrained her to be proud of him.

The Napiers were blessed in both parents, but especially in their mother, Lady Sarah Lennox, who early sought to inspire her sons' minds with elevating thoughts, admiration of noble deeds, and a chivalrous spirit, which became embodied in their lives, and continued to sustain them, until death, in the path of duty and of honour.

Among statesmen, lawyers, and divines, we find marked mention made of the mothers of Lord Chancellors Bacon, Erskine, and Brougham— all women of great ability, and, in the case of the first, of great learning; as well as of the mothers of Canning, Curran, and President Adams—of Herbert, Paley, and Wesley. Lord Brougham speaks in terms almost approaching reverence of his grandmother, the sister of Professor Robertson, as having been mainly instrumental in instilling into his mind a strong desire for information, and the first principles of that persevering energy in the pursuit of every kind of knowledge which formed his prominent characteristic throughout life.

Canning's mother was an Irishwoman of great natural ability, for whom her gifted son entertained the greatest love and respect to the close of his career. She was a woman of no ordinary intellectual power. "Indeed, " says Canning's biographer, "were we not otherwise assured of the fact from direct sources, it would be impossible to contemplate his profound and touching devotion to her, without being led to conclude that the object of such unchanging attachment must have been possessed of rare and commanding qualities. She was esteemed by the circle in which she lived, as a woman of great mental energy. Her conversation was animated and vigorous, and marked by a distinct originality of manner and a choice of topics fresh and striking, and out of the commonplace routine. To persons who were but slightly acquainted with her, the energy of her manner had even something of the air of eccentricity."(9)

Curran speaks with great affection of his mother, as a woman of strong original understanding, to whose wise counsel, consistent piety, and lessons of honourable ambition, which she diligently enforced on the minds of her children, he himself principally attributed his success in life. "The only inheritance, " he used to say, "that I could boast of from my poor father, was the very scanty one of an unattractive face and person; like his own; and if the world has ever attributed to me something more valuable than face or person, or than earthly wealth, it was that another and a dearer parent gave her child a portion from the treasure of her mind. " (10)

When ex-President Adams was present at the examination of a girls' school at Boston, he was presented by the pupils with an address which deeply affected him; and in acknowledging it, he took the opportunity of referring to the lasting influence which womanly training and association had exercised upon his own life and character. "As a child, " he said, "I enjoyed perhaps the greatest of blessings that can be bestowed on man—that of a mother, who was anxious and capable to form the characters of her children rightly. From her I derived whatever instruction (religious especially, and moral) has pervaded a long life—I will not say perfectly, or as it ought to be; but I will say, because it is only justice to the memory of her I revere, that, in the course of that life, whatever imperfection there has been, or deviation from what she taught me, the fault is mine, and not hers. "

The Wesleys were peculiarly linked to their parents by natural piety, though the mother, rather than the father, influenced their minds and developed their characters. The father was a man of strong will, but occasionally harsh and tyrannical in his dealings with his family; (11) while the mother, with much strength of understanding and ardent love of truth, was gentle, persuasive, affectionate, and simple. She was the teacher and cheerful companion of her children, who gradually became moulded by her example. It was through the bias given by her to her sons' minds in religious matters that they acquired the tendency which, even in early years, drew to them the name of Methodists. In a letter to her son, Samuel Wesley, when a scholar at Westminster in 1709, she said: "I would advise you as much as possible to throw your business into a certain METHOD, by which means you will learn to improve every precious moment, and find an unspeakable facility in the performance of your respective duties. " This "method" she went on to describe, exhorting her son "in all things to act upon principle; " and the society which the brothers John and Charles afterwards founded at Oxford is supposed to have been in a great measure the result of her exhortations.

In the case of poets, literary men, and artists, the influence of the mother's feeling and taste has doubtless had great effect in directing the genius of their sons; and we find this especially illustrated in the lives of Gray, Thomson, Scott, Southey, Bulwer, Schiller, and Goethe. Gray inherited, almost complete, his kind and loving nature from his mother, while his father was harsh and unamiable. Gray was, in fact, a feminine man—shy, reserved, and wanting in energy, —but thoroughly irreproachable in life and character. The poet's mother maintained the family, after her unworthy husband had deserted her; and, at her death, Gray placed on her grave, in Stoke Pogis, an epitaph describing her as "the careful tender mother of many children, one of whom alone had the misfortune to survive her. " The poet himself was, at his own desire, interred beside her worshipped grave.

Goethe, like Schiller, owed the bias of his mind and character to his mother, who was a woman of extraordinary gifts. She was full of joyous flowing mother-wit, and possessed in a high degree the art of stimulating young and active minds, instructing them in the science of life out of the treasures of her abundant experience. (12) After a lengthened interview with her, an enthusiastic traveller said, "Now do I understand how Goethe has become the man he is. " Goethe himself affectionately cherished her memory. "She was worthy of life! " he once said of her; and when he visited Frankfort, he sought out every individual who had been kind to his mother, and thanked them all.

It was Ary Scheffer's mother—whose beautiful features the painter so loved to reproduce in his pictures of Beatrice, St. Monica, and others of his works—that encouraged his study of art, and by great self-denial provided him with the means of pursuing it. While living at Dordrecht, in Holland, she first sent him to Lille to study, and afterwards to Paris; and her letters to him, while absent, were always full of sound motherly advice, and affectionate womanly sympathy. "If you could but see me, " she wrote on one occasion, "kissing your picture, then, after a while, taking it up again, and, with a tear in my eye, calling you 'my beloved son, ' you would comprehend what it costs me to use sometimes the stern language of authority, and to occasion to you moments of pain. * * * Work diligently—be, above all, modest and humble; and when you find yourself excelling others, then compare what you have done with Nature itself, or with the 'ideal' of your own mind, and you will be secured, by the contrast which will be apparent, against the effects of pride and presumption. "

Long years after, when Ary Scheffer was himself a grandfather, he remembered with affection the advice of his mother, and repeated it to his children. And thus the vital power of good example lives on from generation to generation, keeping the world ever fresh and young. Writing to his daughter, Madame Marjolin, in 1846, his departed mother's advice recurred to him, and he said: "The word MUST—fix it well in your memory, dear child; your grandmother seldom had it out of hers. The truth is, that through our lives nothing brings any good fruit except what is earned by either the work of the hands, or by the exertion of one's self- denial. Sacrifices must, in short, be ever going on if we would obtain any comfort or happiness. Now that I am no longer young, I declare that few passages in my life afford me so much satisfaction as those in which I made sacrifices, or denied myself enjoyments. 'Das Entsagen' (the forbidden) is the motto of the wise man. Self-denial is the quality of which Jesus Christ set us the example. " (13)

The French historian Michelet makes the following touching reference to his mother in the Preface to one of his most popular books, the subject of much embittered controversy at the time at which it appeared: - "Whilst writing all this, I have had in my mind a woman, whose strong and serious mind would not have failed to support me in these contentions. I lost her thirty years ago (I was a child then)—nevertheless, ever living in my memory, she follows me from age to age.

"She suffered with me in my poverty, and was not allowed to share my better fortune. When young, I made her sad, and now I cannot console her. I know not even where her bones are: I was too poor then to buy earth to bury her! "

"And yet I owe her much. I feel deeply that I am the son of woman. Every instant, in my ideas and words (not to mention my features and gestures), I find again my mother in myself. It is my mother's blood which gives me the sympathy I feel for bygone ages, and the tender remembrance of all those who are now no more. "

"What return then could I, who am myself advancing towards old age, make her for the many things I owe her? One, for which she would have thanked me—this protest in favour of women and mothers. " (14)

But while a mother may greatly influence the poetic or artistic mind of her son for good, she may also influence it for evil. Thus the characteristics of Lord Byron—the waywardness of his impulses, his defiance of restraint, the bitterness of his hate, and the precipitancy of his resentments—were traceable in no small degree to the adverse influences exercised upon his mind from his birth by his capricious, violent, and headstrong mother. She even taunted her son with his personal deformity; and it was no unfrequent occurrence, in the violent quarrels which occurred between them, for her to take up the poker or tongs, and hurl them after him as he fled from her presence. (15) It was this unnatural treatment that gave a morbid turn to Byron's after-life; and, careworn, unhappy, great, and yet weak as he was, he carried about with him the mother's poison which he had sucked in his infancy. Hence he exclaims, in his 'Childe Harold': -

"Yet must I think less wildly:- I have thought
Too long and darkly, till my brain became,
In its own eddy boiling and o'erwrought,

38

A whirling gulf of phantasy and flame:
And thus, UNTAUGHT IN YOUTH MY HEART TO TAME,
MY SPRINGS OF LIFE WERE POISONED."

In like manner, though in a different way, the character of Mrs. Foote, the actor's mother, was curiously repeated in the life of her joyous, jovial-hearted son. Though she had been heiress to a large fortune, she soon spent it all, and was at length imprisoned for debt. In this condition she wrote to Sam, who had been allowing her a hundred a year out of the proceeds of his acting: - "Dear Sam, I am in prison for debt; come and assist your loving mother, E. Foote. " To which her son characteristically replied— "Dear mother, so am I; which prevents his duty being paid to his loving mother by her affectionate son, Sam Foote. "

A foolish mother may also spoil a gifted son, by imbuing his mind with unsound sentiments. Thus Lamartine's mother is said to have trained him in altogether erroneous ideas of life, in the school of Rousseau and Bernardin de St. -Pierre, by which his sentimentalism, sufficiently strong by nature, was exaggerated instead of repressed: (16) and he became the victim of tears, affectation, and improvidence, all his life long. It almost savours of the ridiculous to find Lamartine, in his 'Confidences, ' representing himself as a "statue of Adolescence raised as a model for young men. " (17) As he was his mother's spoilt child, so he was the spoilt child of his country to the end, which was bitter and sad. Sainte-Beuve says of him: "He was the continual object of the richest gifts, which he had not the power of managing, scattering and wasting them—all, excepting, the gift of words, which seemed inexhaustible, and on which he continued to play to the end as on an enchanted flute. "(18)

We have spoken of the mother of Washington as an excellent woman of business; and to possess such a quality as capacity for business is not only compatible with true womanliness, but is in a measure essential to the comfort and wellbeing of every properly- governed family. Habits of business do not relate to trade merely, but apply to all the practical affairs of life—to everything that has to be arranged, to be organised, to be provided for, to be done. And in all these respects the management of a family, and of a household, is as much a matter of business as the management of a shop or of a counting-house. It requires method, accuracy, organization, industry, economy, discipline, tact, knowledge, and capacity for adapting means to ends. All this is of the essence of business; and hence business habits are as necessary to be cultivated by women who would succeed in the affairs of home—in other words, who would make home happy—as by men in the affairs of trade, of commerce, or of manufacture.

The idea has, however, heretofore prevailed, that women have no concern with such matters, and that business habits and qualifications relate to men only. Take, for instance, the knowledge of figures. Mr. Bright has said of boys, "Teach a boy arithmetic thoroughly, and he is a made man. " And why? —Because it teaches him method, accuracy, value, proportions, relations. But how many girls are taught arithmetic well? —Very few indeed. And what is the consequence? —When the girl becomes a wife, if she knows nothing of figures, and is innocent of addition and multiplication, she can keep no record of income and expenditure, and there will probably be a succession of mistakes committed which may be prolific in domestic contention. The woman, not being up to her business—that is, the management of her domestic affairs in conformity with the simple principles of arithmetic— will, through sheer ignorance, be apt to commit extravagances, though unintentional, which may be most injurious to her family peace and comfort.

Method, which is the soul of business, is also of essential importance in the home. Work can only be got through by method. Muddle flies before it, and hugger-mugger becomes a thing unknown. Method demands punctuality, another eminently business quality. The unpunctual woman, like the unpunctual man, occasions dislike, because she consumes and wastes time, and provokes the reflection that we are not of sufficient importance to make her more prompt. To the business man, time is money; but to the business woman, method is more—it is peace, comfort, and domestic prosperity.

Prudence is another important business quality in women, as in men. Prudence is practical wisdom, and comes of the cultivated judgment. It has reference in all things to fitness, to propriety; judging wisely of the right thing to be done, and the right way of doing it. It calculates the means, order, time, and method of doing. Prudence learns from experience, quickened by knowledge.

For these, amongst other reasons, habits of business are necessary to be cultivated by all women, in order to their being efficient helpers in the world's daily life and work. Furthermore, to direct the power of the home aright, women, as the nurses, trainers, and educators of children, need all the help and strength that mental culture can give them.

Mere instinctive love is not sufficient. Instinct, which preserves the lower creatures, needs no training; but human intelligence, which is in constant request in a family, needs to be educated. The physical health of the rising generation is entrusted to woman by Providence; and it is in the physical nature that the moral and mental nature lies enshrined. It is only by acting in accordance with the natural laws, which before she can follow woman must needs understand, that the blessings of health of body, and health of mind and morals, can be secured at home. Without a knowledge of such laws, the mother's love too often finds its recompence only in a child's coffin. (19)

It is a mere truism to say that the intellect with which woman as well as man is endowed, has been given for use and exercise, and not "to fust in her unused. " Such endowments are never conferred without a purpose. The Creator may be lavish in His gifts, but he is never wasteful.

Woman was not meant to be either an unthinking drudge, or the merely pretty ornament of man's leisure. She exists for herself, as well as for others; and the serious and responsible duties she is called upon to perform in life, require the cultivated head as well as the sympathising heart. Her highest mission is not to be fulfilled by the mastery of fleeting accomplishments, on which so much useful time is now wasted; for, though accomplishments may enhance the charms of youth and beauty, of themselves sufficiently charming, they will be found of very little use in the affairs of real life.

The highest praise which the ancient Romans could express of a noble matron was that she sat at home and span—"DOMUM MANSIT, LANAM FECIT. " In our own time, it has been said that chemistry enough to keep the pot boiling, and geography enough to know the different rooms in her house, was science enough for any woman; whilst Byron, whose sympathies for woman were of a very imperfect kind, professed that he would limit her library to a Bible and a cookery-book. But this view of woman's character and culture is as absurdly narrow and unintelligent, on the one hand, as the opposite view, now so much in vogue, is extravagant and unnatural on the other—that woman ought to be educated so as to be as much as possible the equal of man; undistinguishable from him, except in sex; equal to him in rights and votes; and his competitor in all that makes life a fierce and selfish struggle for place and power and money.

Speaking generally, the training and discipline that are most suitable for the one sex in early life, are also the most suitable for the other; and the education and culture that fill the mind of the man will prove equally wholesome for the woman. Indeed, all the arguments which have yet been advanced in favour of the higher education of men, plead equally strongly in favour of the higher education of women. In all the departments of home, intelligence will add to woman's usefulness and efficiency. It will give her thought and forethought, enable her to anticipate and provide for the contingencies of life, suggest improved methods of management, and give her strength in every way. In disciplined mental power she will find a stronger and safer protection against deception and imposture than in mere innocent and unsuspecting ignorance; in moral and religious culture she will secure sources of influence more powerful and enduring than in physical attractions; and in due self-reliance and self-dependence she will discover the truest sources of domestic comfort and happiness.

But while the mind and character of women ought to be cultivated with a view to their own wellbeing, they ought not the less to be educated liberally with a view to the happiness of others. Men themselves cannot be sound in mind or morals if women be the reverse; and if, as we hold to be the case, the moral condition of a people mainly depends upon the education of the home, then the education of women is to be regarded as a matter of national importance. Not only does the moral character but the mental strength of man find their best safeguard and support in the moral purity and mental cultivation of woman; but the more completely the powers of both are developed, the more harmonious and well-ordered will society be—the more safe and certain its elevation and advancement.

When about fifty years since, the first Napoleon said that the great want of France was mothers, he meant, in other words, that the French people needed the education of homes, provided over by good, virtuous, intelligent women. Indeed, the first French Revolution presented one of the most striking illustrations of the social mischiefs resulting from a neglect of the purifying influence of women. When that great national outbreak occurred, society was impenetrated with vice and profligacy. Morals, religion, virtue, were swamped by sensualism. The character of woman had become depraved. Conjugal fidelity was disregarded; maternity was held in reproach; family and home were alike corrupted. Domestic purity no longer bound society together. France was motherless; the children broke loose; and the Revolution burst forth, "amidst the yells and the fierce violence of women. " (20)

But the terrible lesson was disregarded, and again and again France has grievously suffered from the want of that discipline, obedience, self-control, and self-respect which can only be truly learnt at home. It is said that the Third Napoleon attributed the recent powerlessness of France, which left her helpless and bleeding at the feet of her conquerors, to the frivolity and lack of principle of the people, as well as to their love of pleasure— which, however, it must be confessed, he himself did not a little to foster. It would thus seem that the discipline which France still needs to learn, if she would be good and great, is that indicated by the First Napoleon—home education by good mothers.

The influence of woman is the same everywhere. Her condition influences the morals, manners, and character of the people in all countries. Where she is debased, society is debased; where she is morally pure and enlightened, society will be proportionately elevated.

Hence, to instruct woman is to instruct man; to elevate her character is to raise his own; to enlarge her mental freedom is to extend and secure that of the whole community. For Nations are but the outcomes of Homes, and Peoples of Mothers.

But while it is certain that the character of a nation will be elevated by the enlightenment and refinement of woman, it is much more than doubtful whether any advantage is to be derived from her entering into competition with man in the rough work of business and politics. Women can no more do men's special work in the world than men can do women's. And wherever woman has been withdrawn from her home and family to enter upon other work, the result has been socially disastrous. Indeed, the efforts of some of the best philanthropists have of late years been devoted to withdrawing women from toiling alongside of men in coalpits, factories, nailshops, and brickyards.

It is still not uncommon in the North for the husbands to be idle at home, while the mothers and daughters are working in the factory; the result being, in many cases, an entire subversion of family order, of domestic discipline, and of home rule. (21) And for many years past, in Paris, that state of things has been reached which some women desire to effect amongst ourselves. The women there mainly attend to business—serving the BOUTIQUE, or presiding at the COMPTOIR—while the men lounge about the Boulevards. But the result has only been homelessness, degeneracy, and family and social decay.

Nor is there any reason to believe that the elevation and improvement of women are to be secured by investing them with political power. There are, however, in these days, many believers in the potentiality of "votes, " (22) who anticipate some indefinite good from the "enfranchisement" of women. It is not necessary here to enter upon the discussion of this question. But it may be sufficient to state that the power which women do not possess politically is far more than compensated by that which they exercise in private life—by their training in the home those who, whether as men or as women, do all the manly as well as womanly work of the world. The Radical Bentham has said that man, even if he would, cannot keep power from woman; for that she already governs the world "with the whole power of a despot, " (23) though the power that she mainly governs by is love. And to form the character of the whole human race, is certainly a power far greater than that which women could ever hope to exercise as voters for members of Parliament, or even as lawmakers.

There is, however, one special department of woman's work demanding the earnest attention of all true female reformers, though it is one which has hitherto been unaccountably neglected. We mean the better economizing and preparation of human food, the waste of which at present, for want of the most ordinary culinary knowledge, is little short of scandalous. If that man is to be regarded as a benefactor of his species who makes two stalks of corn to grow where only one grew before, not less is she to be regarded as a public benefactor who economizes and turns to the best practical account the food-products of human skill and labour. The improved use of even our existing supply would be equivalent to an immediate extension of the cultivable acreage of our country—not to speak of the increase in health, economy, and domestic comfort. Were our female reformers only to turn their energies in this direction with effect, they would earn the gratitude of all households, and be esteemed as among the greatest of practical philanthropists.

NOTES

(1) Civic virtues, unless they have their origin and consecration in private and domestic virtues, are but the virtues of the theatre. He who has not a loving heart for his child, cannot pretend to have any true love for humanity. —Jules Simon's LE DEVOIR.

(2) 'Levana; or, The Doctrine of Education. '

(3) Speaking of the force of habit, St. Augustine says in his 'Confessions' "My will the enemy held, and thence had made a chain for me, and bound me. For of a froward will was a lust made; and a lust served became custom; and custom not resisted became necessity. By which links, as it were, joined together (whence I called it a chain) a hard bondage held me enthralled. "

(4) Mr. Tufnell, in 'Reports of Inspectors of Parochial School Unions in England and Wales, ' 1850.

(5) See the letters (January 13th, 16th, 18th, 20th, and 23rd, 1759), written by Johnson to his mother when she was ninety, and he himself was in his fiftieth year. —Crokers BOSWELL, 8vo. Ed. pp. 113, 114.

(6) Jared Sparks' 'Life of Washington. '

(7) Forster's 'Eminent British Statesmen' (Cabinet Cyclop.) vi. 8.

(8) The Earl of Mornington, composer of 'Here in cool grot, ' &c.

(9) Robert Bell's 'Life of Canning, ' p. 37.

(10) 'Life of Curran, ' by his son, p. 4.

(11) The father of the Wesleys had even determined at one time to abandon his wife because her conscience forbade her to assent to his prayers for the then reigning monarch, and he was only saved from the consequences of his rash resolve by the accidental death of William III. He displayed the same overbearing disposition in dealing with his children; forcing his daughter Mehetabel to marry,

against her will, a man whom she did not love, and who proved entirely unworthy of her.

(12) Goethe himself says— "Vom Vater hab' ich die Statur, Des Lebens ernstes Fuhren; Von Mutterchen die Frohnatur Und Lust zu fabuliren. "

(13) Mrs. Grote's 'Life of Ary Scheffer, ' p. 154.

(14) Michelet, 'On Priests, Women, and Families. '

(15) Mrs. Byron is said to have died in a fit of passion, brought on by reading her upholsterer's bills.

(16) Sainte-Beuve, 'Causeries du Lundi, ' i. 23.

(17) Ibid. i. 22.

(18) Ibid. 1. 23.

(19) That about one-third of all the children born in this country die under five years of age, can only he attributable to ignorance of the natural laws, ignorance of the human constitution, and ignorance of the uses of pure air, pure water, and of the art of preparing and administering wholesome food. There is no such mortality amongst the lower animals.

(20) Beaumarchais' 'Figaro, ' which was received with such enthusiasm in France shortly before the outbreak of the Revolution, may be regarded as a typical play; it represented the average morality of the upper as well as the lower classes with respect to the relations between the sexes. "Label men how you please, " says Herbert Spencer, "with titles of 'upper' and 'middle' and 'lower, ' you cannot prevent them from being units of the same society, acted upon by the same spirit of the age, moulded after the same type of character. The mechanical law, that action and reaction are equal, has its moral analogue. The deed of one man to another tends ultimately to produce a like effect upon both, be the deed good or bad. Do but put them in relationship, and no division into castes, no differences of wealth, can prevent men from assimilating.... The same influences which rapidly adapt the individual to his society, ensure, though by a slower process, the general uniformity of a national character.... And so long as the assimilating influences productive of it continue

at work, it is folly to suppose any one grade of a community can be morally different from the rest. In whichever rank you see corruption, be assured it equally pervades all ranks—be assured it is the symptom of a bad social diathesis. Whilst the virus of depravity exists in one part of the body-politic, no other part can remain healthy. "—SOCIAL STATICS, chap. xx. 7.

(21) Some twenty-eight years since, the author wrote and published the following passage, not without practical knowledge of the subject; and notwithstanding the great amelioration in the lot of factory- workers, effected mainly through the noble efforts of Lord Shaftesbury, the description is still to a large extent true: — "The factory system, however much it may have added to the wealth of the country, has had a most deleterious effect on the domestic condition of the people. It has invaded the sanctuary of home, and broken up family and social ties. It has taken the wife from the husband, and the children from their parents. Especially has its tendency been to lower the character of woman. The performance of domestic duties is her proper office, —the management of her household, the rearing of her family, the economizing of the family means, the supplying of the family wants. But the factory takes her from all these duties. Homes become no longer homes. Children grow up uneducated and neglected. The finer affections become blunted. Woman is no more the gentle wife, companion, and friend of man, but his fellow- labourer and fellow-drudge. She is exposed to influences which too often efface that modesty of thought and conduct which is one of the best safeguards of virtue. Without judgment or sound principles to guide them, factory-girls early acquire the feeling of independence. Ready to throw off the constraint imposed on them by their parents, they leave their homes, and speedily become initiated in the vices of their associates. The atmosphere, physical as well as moral, in which they live, stimulates their animal appetites; the influence of bad example becomes contagious among them and mischief is propagated far and wide."— THE UNION, January, 1843.

(22)A French satirist, pointing to the repeated PLEBISCITES and perpetual voting of late years, and to the growing want of faith in anything but votes, said, in 1870, that we seemed to be rapidly approaching the period when the only prayer of man and woman would be, "Give us this day our daily vote! "

(23) "Of primeval and necessary and absolute superiority, the relation of the mother to the child is far more complete, though less seldom quoted as an example, than that of father and son.... By Sir Robert Filmer, the supposed necessary as well as absolute power of the father over his children, was taken as the foundation and origin, and thence justifying cause, of the power of the monarch in every political state. With more propriety he might have stated the absolute dominion of a woman as the only legitimate form of government. "—DEONTOLOGY, ii. 181.

CHAPTER III. —COMPANIONSHIP AND EXAMPLES

"Keep good company, and you shall be of the number."
—GEORGE HERBERT.

"For mine own part,
I Shall be glad to learn of noble men." —SHAKSPEARE

"Examples preach to th' eye—Care then, mine says,
Not how you end but how you spend your days."
HENRY MARTEN—'LAST THOUGHTS.'

"Dis moi qui t'admire, et je dirai qui tu es. "—SAINTE-BEUVE

He that means to be a good limner will be sure to draw after the most excellent copies and guide every stroke of his pencil by the better pattern that lays before him; so he that desires that the table of his life may be fair, will be careful to propose the best examples, and will never be content till he equals or excels them. "—OWEN FELTHAM

The natural education of the Home is prolonged far into life— indeed, it never entirely ceases. But the time arrives, in the progress of years, when the Home ceases to exercise an exclusive influence on the formation of character; and it is succeeded by the more artificial education of the school and the companionship of friends and comrades, which continue to mould the character by the powerful influence of example.

Men, young and old—but the young more than the old—cannot help imitating those with whom they associate. It was a saying of George Herbert's mother, intended for the guidance of her sons, "that as our bodies take a nourishment suitable to the meat on which we feed, so do our souls as insensibly take in virtue or vice by the example or conversation of good or bad company. "

Indeed, it is impossible that association with those about us should not produce a powerful influence in the formation of character. For men are by nature imitators, and all persons are more or less impressed by the speech, the manners, the gait, the gestures, and the very habits of thinking of their companions. "Is example nothing? " said Burke. "It is everything. Example is the school of mankind, and they will learn at no other. " Burke's grand motto, which he wrote for the tablet of the Marquis of Rockingham, is worth repeating: it was, "Remember—resemble— persevere. "

Imitation is for the most part so unconscious that its effects are almost unheeded, but its influence is not the less permanent on that account. It is only when an impressive nature is placed in contact with an impressionable one, that the alteration in the character becomes recognisable. Yet even the weakest natures exercise some influence upon those about them. The approximation of feeling, thought, and habit is constant, and the action of example unceasing.

Emerson has observed that even old couples, or persons who have been housemates for a course of years, grow gradually like each other; so that, if they were to live long enough, we should scarcely be able to know them apart. But if this be true of the old, how much more true is it of the young, whose plastic natures are so much more soft and impressionable, and ready to take the stamp of the life and conversation of those about them!

"There has been, " observed Sir Charles Bell in one of his letters, "a good deal said about education, but they appear to me to put out of sight EXAMPLE, which is all-in-all. My best education was the example set me by my brothers. There was, in all the members of the family, a reliance on self, a true independence, and by imitation I obtained it. " (1)

It is in the nature of things that the circumstances which contribute to form the character, should exercise their principal influence during the period of growth. As years advance, example and imitation become custom, and gradually consolidate into habit, which is of so much potency that, almost before we know it, we have in a measure yielded up to it our personal freedom.

It is related of Plato, that on one occasion he reproved a boy for playing at some foolish game. "Thou reprovest me, " said the boy, "for a very little thing. " "But custom, " replied Plato, "is not a little thing. " Bad custom, consolidated into habit, is such a tyrant that men sometimes cling to vices even while they curse them. They have become the slaves of habits whose power they are impotent to resist. Hence Locke has said that to create and maintain that vigour of mind which is able to contest the empire of habit, may be regarded as one of the chief ends of moral discipline.

Though much of the education of character by example is spontaneous and unconscious, the young need not necessarily be the passive followers or imitators of those about them. Their own conduct, far more than the conduct of their companions, tends to fix the purpose and form the principles of their life. Each possesses in himself a power of will and of free activity, which, if courageously exercised, will enable him to make his own individual selection of friends and associates. It is only through weakness of purpose that young people, as well as old, become the slaves of their inclinations, or give themselves up to a servile imitation of others.

It is a common saying that men are known by the company they keep. The sober do not naturally associate with the drunken, the refined with the coarse, the decent with the dissolute. To associate with depraved persons argues a low taste and vicious tendencies, and to frequent their society leads to inevitable degradation of character. "The conversation of such persons, " says Seneca, "is very injurious; for even if it does no immediate harm, it leaves its seeds in the mind, and follows us when we have gone from the speakers—a plague sure to spring up in future resurrection. "

If young men are wisely influenced and directed, and conscientiously exert their own free energies, they will seek the society of those better than themselves, and strive to imitate their example. In companionship with the good, growing natures will always find their best nourishment; while companionship with the bad will only be fruitful in mischief. There are persons whom to know is to love, honour, and admire; and others whom to know is to shun and despise, —"DONT LE SAVOIR N'EST QUE BETERIE, " as says Rabelais when speaking of the education of Gargantua. Live with persons of elevated characters, and you will feel lifted and lighted up in them: "Live with wolves, " says the Spanish proverb, "and you will learn to howl. "

Intercourse with even commonplace, selfish persons, may prove most injurious, by inducing a dry, dull reserved, and selfish condition of mind, more or less inimical to true manliness and breadth of character. The mind soon learns to run in small grooves, the heart grows narrow and contracted, and the moral nature becomes weak, irresolute, and accommodating, which is fatal to all generous ambition or real excellence.

On the other hand, association with persons wiser, better, and more experienced than ourselves, is always more or less inspiring and invigorating. They enhance our own knowledge of life. We correct our estimates by theirs, and become partners in their wisdom. We enlarge our field of observation through their eyes, profit by their experience, and learn not only from what they have enjoyed, but—which is still more instructive—from what they have suffered. If they are stronger than ourselves, we become participators in their strength. Hence companionship with the wise and energetic never fails to have a most valuable influence on the formation of character—increasing our resources, strengthening our resolves, elevating our aims, and enabling us to exercise greater dexterity and ability in our own affairs, as well as more effective helpfulness of others.

"I have often deeply regretted in myself, " says Mrs. Schimmelpenninck, "the great loss I have experienced from the solitude of my early habits. We need no worse companion than our unregenerate selves, and, by living alone, a person not only becomes wholly ignorant of the means of helping his fellow- creatures, but is without the perception of those wants which most need help. Association with others, when not on so large a scale as to make hours of retirement impossible, may be considered as furnishing to an individual a rich multiplied experience; and sympathy so drawn forth, though, unlike charity, it begins abroad, never fails to bring back rich treasures home. Association with others is useful also in strengthening the character, and in enabling us, while we never lose sight of our main object, to thread our way wisely and well. " (2)

An entirely new direction may be given to the life of a young man by a happy suggestion, a timely hint, or the kindly advice of an honest friend. Thus the life of Henry Martyn the Indian missionary, seems to have been singularly influenced by a friendship which he formed, when a boy, at Truro Grammar School. Martyn himself was of feeble frame, and of a delicate nervous temperament. Wanting in animal spirits, he took but little pleasure in school sports; and being of a somewhat petulant temper, the bigger boys took pleasure in provoking him, and some of them in bullying him. One of the bigger boys, however, conceiving a friendship for Martyn, took him under his protection, stood between him and his persecutors, and not only fought his battles for him, but helped him with his lessons. Though Martyn was rather a backward pupil, his father was desirous that he should have the advantage of a college education, and at the age of about fifteen he sent him to Oxford to try for a Corpus scholarship, in which he failed. He remained for two years more at the Truro Grammar School, and then went to Cambridge, where he was entered at St. John's College. Who should he find already settled there as a student but his old champion of the Truro Grammar School? Their friendship was renewed; and the elder student from that time forward acted as the Mentor, of the younger one. Martyn was fitful in his studies, excitable and petulant, and occasionally subject to fits of almost uncontrollable rage. His big friend, on the other hand, was a steady, patient, hardworking fellow; and he never ceased to watch over, to guide, and to advise for good his irritable fellow-student. He kept Martyn out of the way of evil company, advised him to work hard, "not for the praise of men, but for the glory of God; " and so successfully assisted him in his studies, that at the following Christmas examination he was the first of his year. Yet Martyn's kind friend and Mentor never achieved any distinction himself; he passed away into obscurity, leading, most probably, a useful though an unknown career; his greatest wish in life having been to shape the character of his friend, to inspire his soul with the love of truth, and to prepare him for the noble work, on which he shortly after entered, of an Indian missionary.

A somewhat similar incident is said to have occurred in the college career of Dr. Paley. When a student at Christ's College Cambridge, he was distinguished for his shrewdness as well as his clumsiness, and he was at the same time the favourite and the butt of his companions. Though his natural abilities were great, he was thoughtless, idle, and a spendthrift; and at the commencement of his third year be had made comparatively little progress. After one of his usual night-dissipations, a friend stood by his bedside on the following morning. "Paley, " said he, "I have not been able to sleep for thinking about you. I have been thinking what a fool you are! I have the means of dissipation, and can afford to be idle: YOU are poor, and cannot afford it. I could do nothing, probably, even were I to try: YOU are capable of doing anything. I have lain awake all night thinking about your folly, and I have now come solemnly to warn you. Indeed, if you persist in your indolence, and go on in this way, I must renounce your society altogether!

It is said that Paley was so powerfully affected by this admonition, that from that moment he became an altered man. He formed an entirely new plan of life, and diligently persevered in it. He became one of the most industrious of students. One by one he distanced his competitors, and at the end of the year be came out Senior Wrangler. What he afterwards accomplished as an author and a divine is sufficiently well known.

No one recognised more fully the influence of personal example on the young than did Dr. Arnold. It was the great lever with which he worked in striving to elevate the character of his school. He made it his principal object, first to put a right spirit into the leading boys, by attracting their good and noble feelings; and then to make them instrumental in propagating the same spirit among the rest, by the influence of imitation, example, and admiration. He endeavoured to make all feel that they were fellow-workers with himself, and sharers with him in the moral responsibility for the good government of the place. One of the first effects of this highminded system of management was, that it inspired the boys with strength and self-respect. They felt that they were trusted. There were, of course, MAUVAIS SUJETS at Rugby, as there are at all schools; and these it was the master's duty to watch, to prevent their bad example contaminating others. On one occasion he said to an assistant-master: "Do you see those two boys walking together? I never saw them together before. You should make an especial point of observing the company they keep: nothing so tells the changes in a boy's character. "

Dr. Arnold's own example was an inspiration, as is that of every great teacher. In his presence, young men learned to respect themselves; and out of the root of self-respect there grew up the manly virtues. "His very presence, " says his biographer, "seemed to create a new spring of health and vigour within them, and to give to life an interest and elevation which remained with them long after they had left him; and dwelt so habitually in their thoughts as a living image, that, when death had taken him away, the bond appeared to be still unbroken, and the sense of separation almost lost in the still deeper sense of a life and a Union indestructible. " (3) And thus it was that Dr. Arnold trained a host of manly and noble characters, who spread the influence of his example in all parts of the world.

So also was it said of Dugald Stewart, that he breathed the love of virtue into whole generations of pupils. "To me, " says the late Lord Cockburn, "his lectures were like the opening of the heavens. I felt that I had a soul. His noble views, unfolded in glorious sentences, elevated me into a higher world... They changed my whole nature."(4)

Character tells in all conditions of life. The man of good character in a workshop will give the tone to his fellows, and elevate their entire aspirations. Thus Franklin, while a workman in London, is said to have reformed the manners of an entire workshop. So the man of bad character and debased energy will unconsciously lower and degrade his fellows. Captain John Brown— the "marching-on Brown"—once said to Emerson, that "for a settler in a new country, one good believing man is worth a hundred, nay, worth a thousand men without character. " His example is so contagious, that all other men are directly and beneficially influenced by him, and he insensibly elevates and lifts them up to his own standard of energetic activity.

Communication with the good is invariably productive of good. The good character is diffusive in his influence. "I was common clay till roses were planted in me, " says some aromatic earth in the Eastern fable. Like begets like, and good makes good. "It is astonishing, " says Canon Moseley, "how much good goodness makes. Nothing that is good is alone, nor anything bad; it makes others good or others bad—and that other, and so on: like a stone thrown into a pond, which makes circles that make other wider ones, and then others, till the last reaches the shore.... Almost all the good that is in the world has, I suppose, thus come down to us traditionally from remote times, and often unknown centres of good. " (5) So Mr. Ruskin says, "That which is born of evil begets evil; and that which is born of valour and honour, teaches valour and honour. "

Hence it is that the life of every man is a daily inculcation of good or bad example to others. The life of a good man is at the same time the most eloquent lesson of virtue and the most severe reproof of vice. Dr. Hooker described the life of a pious clergyman of his acquaintance as "visible rhetoric, " convincing even the most godless of the beauty of goodness. And so the good George Herbert said, on entering upon the duties of his parish: "Above all, I will be sure to live well, because the virtuous life of a clergyman is the most powerful eloquence, to persuade all who see it to reverence and love, and—at least to desire to live like him. And this I will do, " he added, "because I know we live in an age that hath more need of good examples than precepts. " It was a fine saying of the same good priest, when reproached with doing an act of kindness to a poor man, considered beneath the dignity of his office, —that the thought of such actions "would prove music to him at midnight. " (6) Izaak Walton speaks of a letter written by George Herbert to Bishop Andrewes, about a holy life, which the latter "put into his bosom, " and after showing it to his scholars, "did always return it to the place where he first lodged it, and continued it so, near his heart, till the last day of his life. "

Great is the power of goodness to charm and to command. The man inspired by it is the true king of men, drawing all hearts after him. When General Nicholson lay wounded on his deathbed before Delhi, he dictated this last message to his equally noble and gallant friend, Sir Herbert Edwardes: - "Tell him, " said he, "I should have been a better man if I had continued to live with him, and our heavy public duties had not prevented my seeing more of him privately. I was always the better for a residence with him and his wife, however short. Give my love to them both! "

There are men in whose presence we feel as if we breathed a spiritual ozone, refreshing and invigorating, like inhaling mountain air, or enjoying a bath of sunshine. The power of Sir Thomas More's gentle nature was so great that it subdued the bad at the same time that it inspired the good. Lord Brooke said of his deceased friend, Sir Philip Sidney, that "his wit and understanding beat upon his heart, to make himself and others, not in word or opinion, but in life and action, good and great. "

The very sight of a great and good man is often an inspiration to the young, who cannot help admiring and loving the gentle, the brave, the truthful, the magnanimous! Cbateaubriand saw Washington only once, but it inspired him for life. After describing the interview, he says: "Washington sank into the tomb before any little celebrity had attached to my name. I passed before him as the most unknown of beings. He was in all his glory —I in the depth of my obscurity. My name probably dwelt not a whole day in his memory. Happy, however, was I that his looks were cast upon me. I have felt warmed for it all the rest of my life. There is a virtue even in the looks of a great man. "

When Niebuhr died, his friend, Frederick Perthes, said of him: "What a contemporary! The terror of all bad and base men, the stay of all the sterling and honest, the friend and helper of youth. " Perthes said on another occasion: "It does a wrestling man good to be constantly surrounded by tried wrestlers; evil thoughts are put to flight when the eye falls on the portrait of one in whose living presence one would have blushed to own them. " A Catholic money-lender, when about to cheat, was wont to draw a veil over the picture of his favourite saint. So Hazlitt has said of the portrait of a beautiful female, that it seemed as if an unhandsome action would be impossible in its presence. "It does one good to look upon his manly honest face, " said a poor German woman, pointing to a portrait of the great Reformer hung upon the wall of her humble dwelling.

Even the portrait of a noble or a good man, hung up in a room, is companionship after a sort. It gives us a closer personal interest in him. Looking at the features, we feel as if we knew him better, and were more nearly related to him. It is a link that connects us with a higher and better nature than our own. And though we may be far from reaching the standard of our hero, we are, to a certain extent, sustained and fortified by his depicted presence constantly before us.

Fox was proud to acknowledge how much he owed to the example and conversation of Burke. On one occasion he said of him, that "if he was to put all the political information he had gained from books, all that he had learned from science, or that the knowledge of the world and its affairs taught him, into one scale, and the improvement he had derived from Mr. Burke's conversation and instruction into the other, the latter would preponderate. "

Professor Tyndall speaks of Faraday's friendship as "energy and inspiration. " After spending an evening with him he wrote: "His work excites admiration, but contact with him warms and elevates the heart. Here, surely, is a strong man. I love strength, but let me not forget the example of its union with modesty, tenderness, and sweetness, in the character of Faraday. "

Even the gentlest natures are powerful to influence the character of others for good. Thus Wordsworth seems to have been especially impressed by the character of his sister Dorothy, who exercised upon his mind and heart a lasting influence. He describes her as the blessing of his boyhood as well as of his manhood. Though two years younger than himself, her tenderness and sweetness contributed greatly to mould his nature, and open his mind to the influences of poetry:

"She gave me eyes, she gave me ears,
And humble cares, and delicate fears;
A heart, the fountain of sweet tears,
And love and thought and joy."

Thus the gentlest natures are enabled, by the power of affection and intelligence, to mould the characters of men destined to influence and elevate their race through all time.

Sir William Napier attributed the early direction of his character, first to the impress made upon it by his mother, when a boy; and afterwards to the noble example of his commander, Sir John Moore, when a man. Moore early detected the qualities of the young officer; and he was one of those to whom the General addressed the encouragement, "Well done, my majors! " at Corunna. Writing home to his mother, and describing the little court by which Moore was surrounded, he wrote, "Where shall we find such a king? " It was to his personal affection for his chief that the world is mainly indebted to Sir William Napier for his great book, 'The History of the Peninsular War. ' But he was stimulated to write the book by the advice of another friend, the late Lord Langdale, while one day walking with him across the fields on which Belgravia is now built. "It was Lord Langdale, " he says, "who first kindled the fire within me. " And of Sir William Napier himself, his biographer truly says, that "no thinking person could ever come in contact with him without being strongly impressed with the genius of the man.

The career of the late Dr. Marshall Hall was a lifelong illustration of the influence of character in forming character. Many eminent men still living trace their success in life to his suggestions and assistance, without which several valuable lines of study and investigation might not have been entered on, at least at so early a period. He would say to young men about him, "Take up a subject and pursue it well, and you cannot fail to succeed. " And often he would throw out a new idea to a young friend, saying, "I make you a present of it; there is fortune in it, if you pursue it with energy. "

Energy of character has always a power to evoke energy in others. It acts through sympathy, one of the most influential of human agencies. The zealous energetic man unconsciously carries others along with him. His example is contagious, and compels imitation. He exercises a sort of electric power, which sends a thrill through every fibre—flows into the nature of those about him, and makes them give out sparks of fire.

Dr. Arnold's biographer, speaking of the power of this kind exercised by him over young men, says: "It was not so much an enthusiastic admiration for true genius, or learning, or eloquence, which stirred within them; it was a sympathetic thrill, caught from a spirit that was earnestly at work in the world— whose work was healthy, sustained, and constantly carried forward in the fear of God—a work that was founded on a deep sense of its duty and its value. " (7)

Such a power, exercised by men of genius, evokes courage, enthusiasm, and devotion. It is this intense admiration for individuals—such as one cannot conceive entertained for a multitude—which has in all times produced heroes and martyrs. It is thus that the mastery of character makes itself felt. It acts by inspiration, quickening and vivifying the natures subject to its influence.

Great minds are rich in radiating force, not only exerting power, but communicating and even creating it. Thus Dante raised and drew after him a host of great spirits—Petrarch, Boccacio, Tasso, and many more. From him Milton learnt to bear the stings of evil tongues and the contumely of evil days; and long years after, Byron, thinking of Dante under the pine-trees of Ravenna, was incited to attune his harp to loftier strains than he had ever attempted before. Dante inspired the greatest painters of Italy— Giotto, Orcagna, Michael Angelo, and Raphael. So Ariosto and Titian mutually inspired one another, and lighted up each other's glory.

Great and good men draw others after them, exciting the spontaneous admiration of mankind. This admiration of noble character elevates the mind, and tends to redeem it from the bondage of self, one of the greatest stumbling blocks to moral improvement. The recollection of men who have signalised themselves by great thoughts or great deeds, seems as if to create for the time a purer atmosphere around us: and we feel as if our aims and purposes were unconsciously elevated.

"Tell me whom you admire, " said Sainte-Beuve, "and I will tell you what you are, at least as regards your talents, tastes, and character. " Do you admire mean men? —your own nature is mean. Do you admire rich men? —you are of the earth, earthy. Do you admire men of title? —you are a toad-eater, or a tuft-hunter. (8) Do you admire honest, brave, and manly men? —you are yourself of an honest, brave, and manly spirit.

It is in the season of youth, while the character is forming, that the impulse to admire is the greatest. As we advance in life, we crystallize into habit; and "NIL ADMIRARI" too often becomes our motto. It is well to encourage the admiration of great characters while the nature is plastic and open to impressions; for if the good are not admired—as young men will have their heroes of some sort—most probably the great bad may be taken by them for models. Hence it always rejoiced Dr. Arnold to hear his pupils expressing admiration of great deeds, or full of enthusiasm for persons or even scenery. "I believe, " said he, "that "NIL ADMIRARI" is the devil's favourite text; and he could not choose a better to introduce his pupils into the more esoteric parts of his doctrine. And, therefore, I have always looked upon a man infected with the disorder of anti-romance as one who has lost the finest part of his nature, and his best protection against everything low and foolish. " (9)

It was a fine trait in the character of Prince Albert that he was always so ready to express generous admiration of the good deeds of others. "He had the greatest delight, " says the ablest delineator of his character, "in anybody else saying a fine saying, or doing a great deed. He would rejoice over it, and talk about it for days; and whether it was a thing nobly said or done by a little child, or by a veteran statesman, it gave him equal pleasure. He delighted in humanity doing well on any occasion and in any manner. " (10)

"No quality, " said Dr. Johnson, "will get a man more friends than a sincere admiration of the qualities of others. It indicates generosity of nature, frankness, cordiality, and cheerful recognition of merit. " It was to the sincere—it might almost be said the reverential—admiration of Johnson by Boswell, that we owe one of the best biographies ever written. One is disposed to think that there must have been some genuine good qualities in Boswell to have been attracted by such a man as Johnson, and to have kept faithful to his worship in spite of rebuffs and snubbings innumerable. Macaulay speaks of Boswell as an altogether contemptible person—as a coxcomb and a bore—weak, vain, pushing, curious, garrulous; and without wit, humour, or eloquence. But Carlyle is doubtless more just in his characterisation of the biographer, in whom—vain and foolish though he was in many respects—he sees a man penetrated by the old reverent feeling of discipleship, full of love and admiration for true wisdom and excellence. Without such qualities, Carlyle insists, the 'Life of Johnson' never could have been written. "Boswell wrote a good book, " he says, "because he had a heart and an eye to discern wisdom, and an utterance to render it forth; because of his free insight, his lively talent, and, above all, of his love and childlike openmindedness. "

Most young men of generous mind have their heroes, especially if they be book-readers. Thus Allan Cunningham, when a mason's apprentice in Nithsdale, walked all the way to Edinburgh for the sole purpose of seeing Sir Walter Scott as he passed along the street. We unconsciously admire the enthusiasm of the lad, and respect the impulse which impelled him to make the journey. It is related of Sir Joshua Reynolds, that when a boy of ten, he thrust his hand through intervening rows of people to touch Pope, as if there were a sort of virtue in the contact. At a much later period, the painter Haydon was proud to see and to touch Reynolds when on a visit to his native place. Rogers the poet used to tell of his ardent desire, when a boy, to see Dr. Johnson; but when his hand was on the knocker of the house in Bolt Court, his courage failed him, and he turned away. So the late Isaac Disraeli, when a youth, called at Bolt Court for the same purpose; and though be HAD the courage to knock, to his dismay he was informed by the servant that the great lexicographer had breathed his last only a few hours before.

On the contrary, small and ungenerous minds cannot admire heartily. To their own great misfortune, they cannot recognise, much less reverence, great men and great things. The mean nature admires meanly. The toad's highest idea of beauty is his toadess. The small snob's highest idea of manhood is the great snob. The slave-dealer values a man according to his muscles. When a Guinea trader was told by Sir Godfrey Kneller, in the presence of Pope, that he saw before him two of the greatest men in the world, he replied: "I don't know how great you may be, but I don't like your looks. I have often bought a man much better than both of you together, all bones and muscles, for ten guineas! "

Although Rochefoucauld, in one of his maxims, says that there is something that is not altogether disagreeable to us in the misfortunes of even our best friends, it is only the small and essentially mean nature that finds pleasure in the disappointment, and annoyance at the success of others. There are, unhappily, for themselves, persons so constituted that they have not the heart to be generous. The most disagreeable of all people are those who "sit in the seat of the scorner. " Persons of this sort often come to regard the success of others, even in a good work, as a kind of personal offence. They cannot bear to hear another praised, especially if he belong to their own art, or calling, or profession. They will pardon a man's failures, but cannot forgive his doing a thing better than they can do. And where they have themselves failed, they are found to be the most merciless of detractors. The sour critic thinks of his rival:

"When Heaven with such parts has blest him,
Have I not reason to detest him?"

The mean mind occupies itself with sneering, carping, and fault-finding; and is ready to scoff at everything but impudent effrontery or successful vice. The greatest consolation of such persons are the defects of men of character. "If the wise erred not, " says George Herbert, "it would go hard with fools. " Yet, though wise men may learn of fools by avoiding their errors, fools rarely profit by the example which, wise men set them. A German writer has said that it is a miserable temper that cares only to discover the blemishes in the character of great men or great periods. Let us rather judge them with the charity of Bolingbroke, who, when reminded of one of the alleged weaknesses of Marlborough, observed, —"He was so great a man that I forgot he had that defect. "

Admiration of great men, living or dead, naturally evokes imitation of them in a greater or less degree. While a mere youth, the mind of Themistocles was fired by the great deeds of his contemporaries, and he longed to distinguish himself in the service of his country. When the Battle of Marathon had been fought, he fell into a state of melancholy; and when asked by his friends as to the cause, he replied "that the trophies of Miltiades would not suffer him to sleep." A few years later, we find him at the head of the Athenian army, defeating the Persian fleet of Xerxes in the battles of Artemisium and Salamis, —his country gratefully acknowledging that it had been saved through his wisdom and valour.

It is related of Thucydides that, when a boy, he burst into tears on hearing Herodotus read his History, and the impression made upon his mind was such as to determine the bent of his own genius. And Demosthenes was so fired on one occasion by the eloquence of

Callistratus, that the ambition was roused within him of becoming an orator himself. Yet Demosthenes was physically weak, had a feeble voice, indistinct articulation, and shortness of breath— defects which he was only enabled to overcome by diligent study and invincible determination. But, with all his practice, he never became a ready speaker; all his orations, especially the most famous of them, exhibiting indications of careful elaboration, —the art and industry of the orator being visible in almost every sentence.

Similar illustrations of character imitating character, and moulding itself by the style and manner and genius of great men, are to be found pervading all history. Warriors, statesmen, orators, patriots, poets, and artists—all have been, more or less unconsciously, nurtured by the lives and actions of others living before them or presented for their imitation.

Great men have evoked the admiration of kings, popes, and emperors. Francis de Medicis never spoke to Michael Angelo without uncovering, and Julius III. made him sit by his side while a dozen cardinals were standing. Charles V. made way for Titian; and one day, when the brush dropped from the painter's hand, Charles stooped and picked it up, saying, "You deserve to be served by an emperor. " Leo X. threatened with excommunication whoever should print and sell the poems of Ariosto without the author's consent. The same pope attended the deathbed of Raphael, as Francis I. did that of Leonardo da Vinci.

Though Haydn once archly observed that he was loved and esteemed by everybody except professors of music, yet all the greatest musicians were unusually ready to recognise each other's greatness. Haydn himself seems to have been entirely free from petty jealousy. His admiration of the famous Porpora was such, that he resolved to gain admission to his house, and serve him as a valet. Having made the acquaintance of the family with whom Porpora lived, he was allowed to officiate in that capacity. Early each morning he took care to brush the veteran's coat, polish his shoes, and put his rusty wig in order. At first Porpora growled at the intruder, but his asperity soon softened, and eventually melted into affection. He quickly discovered his valet's genius, and, by his instructions, directed it into the line in which Haydn eventually acquired so much distinction.

Haydn himself was enthusiastic in his admiration of Handel. "He is the father of us all, " he said on one occasion. Scarlatti followed Handel in admiration all over Italy, and, when his name was mentioned, be crossed himself in token of veneration. Mozart's recognition of the great composer was not less hearty. "When he chooses, " said he, "Handel strikes like the thunderbolt. " Beethoven hailed him as "The monarch of the musical kingdom. " When Beethoven was dying, one of his friends sent him a present of Handel's works, in forty volumes. They were brought into his chamber, and, gazing on them with reanimated eye, be exclaimed, pointing at them with his finger, "There—there is the truth! "

Haydn not only recognised the genius of the great men who had passed away, but of his young contemporaries, Mozart and Beethoven. Small men may be envious of their fellows, but really great men seek out and love each other. Of Mozart, Haydn wrote "I only wish I could impress on every friend of music, and on great men in particular, the same depth of musical sympathy, and profound appreciation of Mozart's inimitable music, that I myself feel and enjoy; then nations would vie with each other to possess such a jewel within their frontiers. Prague ought not only to strive to retain this precious man, but also to remunerate him; for without this the history of a great genius is sad indeed.... It enrages me to think that the unparalleled Mozart is not yet engaged by some imperial or royal court. Forgive my excitement; but I love the man so dearly! "

Mozart was equally generous in his recognition of the merits of Haydn. "Sir, " said he to a critic, speaking of the latter, "if you and I were both melted down together, we should not furnish materials for one Haydn. " And when Mozart first heard Beethoven, he observed: "Listen to that young man; be assured that he will yet make a great name in the world. "

Buffon set Newton above all other philosophers, and admired him so highly that he had always his portrait before him while he sat at work. So Schiller looked up to Shakspeare, whom he studied reverently and zealously for years, until he became capable of comprehending nature at first-hand, and then his admiration became even more ardent than before.

Pitt was Canning's master and hero, whom he followed and admired with attachment and devotion. "To one man, while he lived, " said Canning, "I was devoted with all my heart and all my soul. Since the death of Mr. Pitt I acknowledge no leader; my political allegiance lies buried in his grave. " (11)

A French physiologist, M. Roux, was occupied one day in lecturing to his pupils, when Sir Charles Bell, whose discoveries were even better known and more highly appreciated abroad than at home, strolled into his class-room. The professor, recognising his visitor, at once stopped his exposition, saying: "MESSIEURS, C'EST ASSEZ POUR AUJOURD'HUI, VOUS AVEZ VU SIR CHARLES BELL! "

The first acquaintance with a great work of art has usually proved an important event in every young artist's life. When Correggio first gazed on Raphael's 'Saint Cecilia, ' he felt within himself an awakened power, and exclaimed, "And I too am a painter" So Constable used to look back on his first sight of Claude's picture of 'Hagar, ' as forming an epoch in his career. Sir George Beaumont's admiration of the same picture was such that he always took it with him in his carriage when he travelled from home.

The examples set by the great and good do not die; they continue to live and speak to all the generations that succeed them. It was very impressively observed by Mr. Disraeli, in the House of Commons, shortly after the death of Mr. Cobden: —"There is this consolation remaining to us, when we remember our unequalled and irreparable losses, that those great men are not altogether lost to us—that their words will often be quoted in this House—that their examples will often be referred to and appealed to, and that even their expressions will form part of our discussions and debates. There are now, I may say, some members of Parliament who, though they may not be present, are still members of this House—who are independent of dissolutions, of the caprices of constituencies, and even of the course of time. I think that Mr. Cobden was one of those men. "

It is the great lesson of biography to teach what man can be and can do at his best. It may thus give each man renewed strength and confidence. The humblest, in sight of even the greatest, may admire, and hope, and take courage. These great brothers of ours in blood and lineage, who live a universal life, still speak to us from their graves, and beckon us on in the paths which they have trod. Their example is still with us, to guide, to influence, and to direct us. For nobility of character is a perpetual bequest; living from age to age, and constantly tending to reproduce its like.

"The sage, " say the Chinese, "is the instructor of a hundred ages. When the manners of Loo are heard of, the stupid become intelligent, and the wavering determined. " Thus the acted life of a good man continues to be a gospel of freedom and emancipation to all who succeed him:

"To live in hearts we leave behind,
is not to die."

The golden words that good men have uttered, the examples they have set, live through all time: they pass into the thoughts and hearts of their successors, help them on the road of life, and often console them in the hour of death. "And the most miserable or most painful of deaths, " said Henry Marten, the Commonwealth man, who died in prison, "is as nothing compared with the memory of a well-spent life; and great alone is he who has earned the glorious privilege of bequeathing such a lesson and example to his successors!

NOTES.

(1) 'Letters of Sir Charles Bell, ' p. 10. (2) 'Autobiography of Mary Anne Schimmelpenninck, ' p. 179.

(3) Dean Stanley's 'Life of Dr. Arnold, ' i. 151 (Ed. 1858).

(4) Lord Cockburn's 'Memorials, ' pp. 25-6.

(5) From a letter of Canon Moseley, read at a Memorial Meeting held shortly after the death of the late Lord Herbert of Lea.

(6) Izaak Walton's 'Life of George Herbert. '

(7) Stanley's 'Life and Letters of Dr. Arnold, ' i. 33.

(8) Philip de Comines gives a curious illustration of the subservient, though enforced, imitation of Philip, Duke of Burgundy, by his courtiers. When that prince fell ill, and had his head shaved, he ordered that all his nobles, five hundred in number, should in like manner shave their heads; and one of them, Pierre de Hagenbach, to prove his devotion, no sooner caught sight of an unshaven nobleman, than he forthwith had him seized and carried off to the barber! —Philip de Comines (Bohn's Ed.), p. 243.

(9) 'Life, ' i. 344.

(10) Introduction to 'The Principal Speeches and Addresses of H. R.H. the Prince Consort, ' p. 33.

(11) Speech at Liverpool, 1812.

CHAPTER IV. —WORK.

"Arise therefore, and be doing, and the Lord be with thee."
—1 CHRONICLES xxii. 16.

"Work as if thou hadst to live for aye;
Worship as if thou wert to die to-day." —TUSCAN PROVERB.

"C'est par le travail qu'on regne." —LOUIS XIV

"Blest work! if ever thou wert curse of God,
What must His blessing be!" —J. B. SELKIRK.

"Let every man be OCCUPIED, and occupied in the highest employment of which his nature is capable, and die with the consciousness that he has done his best" —Sydney Smith.

WORK is one of the best educators of practical character. It evokes and disciplines obedience, self-control, attention, application, and perseverance; giving a man deftness and skill in his special calling, and aptitude and dexterity in dealing with the affairs of ordinary life.

Work is the law of our being—the living principle that carries men and nations onward. The greater number of men have to work with their hands, as a matter of necessity, in order to live; but all must work in one way or another, if they would enjoy life as it ought to be enjoyed.

Labour may be a burden and a chastisement, but it is also an honour and a glory. Without it, nothing can be accomplished. All that is great in man comes through work; and civilisation is its product. Were labour abolished, the race of Adam were at once stricken by moral death.

It is idleness that is the curse of man—not labour. Idleness eats the heart out of men as of nations, and consumes them as rust does iron. When Alexander conquered the Persians, and had an opportunity of observing their manners, he remarked that they did not seem conscious that there could be anything more servile than a life of pleasure, or more princely than a life of toil.

When the Emperor Severus lay on his deathbed at York, whither he had been borne on a litter from the foot of the Grampians, his final watchword to his soldiers was, "LABOREMUS" (we must work); and nothing but constant toil maintained the power and extended the authority of the Roman generals.

In describing the earlier social condition of Italy, when the ordinary occupations of rural life were considered compatible with the highest civic dignity, Pliny speaks of the triumphant generals and their men, returning contentedly to the plough. In those days the lands were tilled by the hands even of generals, the soil exulting beneath a ploughshare crowned with laurels, and guided by a husbandman graced with triumphs: "IPSORUM TUNC MANIBUS IMPERATORUM COLEBANTUR AGRI: UT FAS EST CREDERE, GAUDENTE TERRA VOMERE LAUREATO ET TRIUMPHALI ARATORE. " (1) It was only after slaves became extensively employed in all departments of industry that labour came to be regarded as dishonourable and servile. And so soon as indolence and luxury became the characteristics of the ruling classes of Rome, the downfall of the empire, sooner or later, was inevitable.

There is, perhaps, no tendency of our nature that has to be more carefully guarded against than indolence. When Mr. Gurney asked an intelligent foreigner who had travelled over the greater part of the world, whether he had observed any one quality which, more than another, could be regarded as a universal characteristic of our species, his answer was, in broken English, "Me tink dat all men LOVE LAZY. " It is characteristic of the savage as of the despot. It is natural to men to endeavour to enjoy the products of labour without its toils. Indeed, so universal is this desire, that James Mill has argued that it was to prevent its indulgence at the expense of society at large, that the expedient of Government was originally invented.(2)

Indolence is equally degrading to individuals as to nations. Sloth never made its mark in the world, and never will. Sloth never climbed a hill, nor overcame a difficulty that it could avoid. Indolence always failed in life, and always will. It is in the nature of things that it should not succeed in anything. It is a burden, an incumbrance, and a nuisance—always useless, complaining, melancholy, and miserable.

Burton, in his quaint and curious, book—the only one, Johnson says, that ever took him out of bed two hours sooner than he wished to rise—describes the causes of Melancholy as hingeing mainly on Idleness. "Idleness, " he says, "is the bane of body and mind, the nurse of naughtiness, the chief mother of all mischief, one of the seven deadly sins, the devil's cushion, his pillow and chief reposal.... An idle dog will be mangy; and how shall an idle person escape? Idleness of the mind is much worse than that of the body: wit, without employment, is a disease—the rust of the soul, a plague, a hell itself. As in a standing pool, worms and filthy creepers increase, so do evil and corrupt thoughts in an idle person; the soul is contaminated.... Thus much I dare boldly say: he or she that is idle, be they of what condition they will, never so rich, so well allied, fortunate, happy—let them have all things in abundance and felicity that heart can wish and desire, all contentment—so long as he, or she, or they, are idle, they shall never be pleased, never well in body or mind, but weary still, sickly still, vexed still, loathing still, weeping, sighing, grieving, suspecting, offended with the world, with every object, wishing themselves gone or dead, or else carried away with some foolish phantasie or other. " (3)

Burton says a great deal more to the same effect; the burden and lesson of his book being embodied in the pregnant sentence with which it winds up: - "Only take this for a corollary and conclusion, as thou tenderest thine own welfare in this, and all other melancholy, thy good health of body and mind, observe this short precept, Give not way to solitariness and idleness. BE NOT SOLITARY—BE NOT IDLE. " (4)

The indolent, however, are not wholly indolent. Though the body may shirk labour, the brain is not idle. If it do not grow corn, it will grow thistles, which will be found springing up all along the idle man's course in life. The ghosts of indolence rise up in the dark, ever staring the recreant in the face, and tormenting him:

> "The gods are just, and of our pleasant vices,
> Make instrument to scourge us."

True happiness is never found in torpor of the faculties, (5) but in their action and useful employment. It is indolence that exhausts, not action, in which there is life, health, and pleasure. The spirits may be exhausted and wearied by employment, but they are utterly wasted by idleness. Hense a wise physician was accustomed to regard occupation as one of his most valuable remedial measures. "Nothing is so injurious, " said Dr. Marshall Hall, "as unoccupied time. " An archbishop of Mayence used to say that "the human heart is like a millstone: if you put wheat under it, it grinds the wheat into flour; if you put no wheat, it grinds on, but then 'tis itself it wears away. "

Indolence is usually full of excuses; and the sluggard, though unwilling to work, is often an active sophist. "There is a lion in the path; " or "The hill is hard to climb; " or "There is no use trying—I have tried, and failed, and cannot do it. " To the sophistries of such an excuser, Sir Samuel Romilly once wrote to a young man: - "My attack upon your indolence, loss of time, &c., was most serious, and I really think that it can be to nothing but your habitual want of exertion that can be ascribed your using such curious arguments as you do in your defence. Your theory is this: Every man does all the good that he can. If a particular individual does no good, it is a proof that he is incapable of doing it. That you don't write proves that you can't; and your want of inclination demonstrates your want of talents. What an admirable system! —and what beneficial effects would it be attended with, if it were but universally received! "

It has been truly said, that to desire to possess, without being burdened with the trouble of acquiring, is as much a sign of weakness, as to recognise that everything worth having is only to be got by paying its price, is the prime secret of practical strength. Even leisure cannot be enjoyed unless it is won by effort. If it have not been earned by work, the price has not been paid for it. (6)

There must be work before and work behind, with leisure to fall back upon; but the leisure, without the work, can no more be enjoyed than a surfeit. Life must needs be disgusting alike to the idle rich man as to the idle poor man, who has no work to do, or, having work, will not do it. The words found tattooed on the right arm of a sentimental beggar of forty, undergoing his eighth imprisonment in the gaol of Bourges in France, might be adopted as the motto of all idlers: "LE PASSE M'A TROMPE; LE PRESENT ME TOURMENTE; L'AVENIR M'EPOUVANTE; "—(The past has deceived me; the present torments me; the future terrifies me)

The duty of industry applies to all classes and conditions of society. All have their work to do in the irrespective conditions of life—the rich as well as the poor. (7) The gentleman by birth and education, however richly he may be endowed with worldly possessions, cannot but feel that he is in duty bound to contribute his quota of endeavour towards the general wellbeing in which he shares. He cannot be satisfied with being fed, clad, and maintained by the labour of others, without making some suitable return to the society that upholds him. An honest highminded man would revolt at the idea of sitting down to and enjoying a feast, and then going away without paying his share of the reckoning. To be idle and useless is neither an honour nor a privilege; and though persons of small natures may be content merely to consume— FRUGES CONSUMERE NATI—men of average endowment, of manly aspirations, and of honest purpose, will feel such a condition to be incompatible with real honour and true dignity.

"I don't believe, " said Lord Stanley (now Earl of Derby) at Glasgow, "that an unemployed man, however amiable and otherwise respectable, ever was, or ever can be, really happy. As work is our life, show me what you can do, and I will show you what you are. I have spoken of love of one's work as the best preventive of merely low and vicious tastes. I will go further, and say that it is the best preservative against petty anxieties, and the annoyances that arise out of indulged self-love. Men have thought before now that they could take refuge from trouble and vexation by sheltering themselves as it were in a world of their own. The experiment has, often been tried, and always with one result. You cannot escape from anxiety and labour—it is the destiny of humanity.... Those who shirk from facing trouble, find that trouble comes to them. The indolent may contrive that he shall have less than his share of the world's work to do, but Nature proportioning the instinct to the work, contrives that the little shall be much and hard to him. The man who has only himself to please finds, sooner or later, and probably sooner than later, that he has got a very hard master; and the excessive weakness which shrinks from responsibility has its own punishment too, for where great interests are excluded little matters become great, and the same wear and tear of mind that might have been at least usefully and healthfully expended on the real business of life is often wasted in petty and imaginary vexations, such as breed and multiply in the unoccupied brain. " (8)

Even on the lowest ground—that of personal enjoyment—constant useful occupation is necessary. He who labours not, cannot enjoy the reward of labour. "We sleep sound, " said Sir Walter Scott, "and our waking hours are happy, when they are employed; and a little sense of toil is necessary to the enjoyment of leisure, even when earned by study and sanctioned by the discharge of duty. "

It is true, there are men who die of overwork; but many more die of selfishness, indulgence, and idleness. Where men break down by overwork, it is most commonly from want of duly ordering their lives, and neglect of the ordinary conditions of physical health. Lord Stanley was probably right when he said, in his address to the Glasgow students above mentioned, that he doubted whether "hard work, steadily and regularly carried on, ever yet hurt anybody. "

Then, again, length of YEARS is no proper test of length of LIFE. A man's life is to be measured by what he does in it, and what he feels in it. The more useful work the man does, and the more he thinks and feels, the more he really lives. The idle useless man, no matter to what extent his life may be prolonged, merely vegetates.

The early teachers of Christianity ennobled the lot of toil by their example. "He that will not work, " said Saint Paul, "neither shall he eat; " and he glorified himself in that he had laboured with his hands, and had not been chargeable to any man. When St. Boniface landed in Britain, he came with a gospel in one hand and a carpenter's rule in the other; and from England he afterwards passed over into Germany, carrying thither the art of building. Luther also, in the midst of a multitude of other employments, worked diligently for a living, earning his bread by gardening, building, turning, and even clockmaking. (9)

It was characteristic of Napoleon, when visiting a work of mechanical excellence, to pay great respect to the inventor, and on taking his leave, to salute him with a low bow. Once at St. Helena, when walking with Mrs. Balcombe, some servants came along carrying a load. The lady, in an angry tone, ordered them out of the way, on which Napoleon interposed, saying, "Respect the burden, madam. " Even the drudgery of the humblest labourer contributes towards the general wellbeing of society; and it was a wise saying of a Chinese Emperor, that "if there was a man who did not work, or a woman that was idle, somebody must suffer cold or hunger in the empire. "

The habit of constant useful occupation is as essential for the happiness and wellbeing of woman as of man. Without it, women are apt to sink into a state of listless ENNUI and uselessness, accompanied by sick headache and attacks of "nerves. " Caroline Perthes carefully warned her married daughter Louisa to beware of giving way to such listlessness. "I myself, " she said, "when the children are gone out for a half-holiday, sometimes feel as stupid and dull as an owl by daylight; but one must not yield to this, which happens more or less to all young wives. The best relief is WORK, engaged in with interest and diligence. Work, then, constantly and diligently, at something or other; for idleness is the devil's snare for small and great, as your grandfather says, and he says true. " (10)

Constant useful occupation is thus wholesome, not only for the body, but for the mind. While the slothful man drags himself indolently through life, and the better part of his nature sleeps a deep sleep, if not morally and spiritually dead, the energetic man is a source of activity and enjoyment to all who come within reach of his influence. Even any ordinary drudgery is better than idleness. Fuller says of Sir Francis Drake, who was early sent to sea, and kept close to his work by his master, that such "pains and patience in his youth knit the joints of his soul, and made them more solid and compact. " Schiller used to say that he considered it a great advantage to be employed in the discharge of some daily mechanical duty—some regular routine of work, that rendered steady application necessary.

Thousands can bear testimony to the truth of the saying of Greuze, the French painter, that work—employment, useful occupation—is one of the great secrets of happiness. Casaubon was once induced by the entreaties of his friends to take a few days entire rest, but he returned to his work with the remark, that it was easier to bear illness doing something, than doing nothing.

When Charles Lamb was released for life from his daily drudgery of desk-work at the India Office, he felt himself the happiest of men. "I would not go back to my prison, " he said to a friend, "ten years longer, for ten thousand pounds. " He also wrote in the same ecstatic mood to Bernard Barton: "I have scarce steadiness of head to compose a letter, " he said; "I am free! free as air! I will live another fifty years.... Would I could sell you some of my leisure! Positively the best thing a man can do is—Nothing; and next to that, perhaps, Good Works. " Two years—two long and tedious years passed; and Charles Lamb's feelings had undergone an entire change. He now discovered that official, even humdrum work —"the appointed round, the daily task"—had been good for him, though he knew it not. Time had formerly been his friend; it had now become his enemy. To Bernard Barton he again wrote: "I assure you, NO work is worse than overwork; the mind preys on itself— the most unwholesome of food. I have ceased to care for almost anything.... Never did the waters of heaven pour down upon a forlorner head. What I can do, and overdo, is to walk. I am a sanguinary murderer of time. But the oracle is silent. "

No man could be more sensible of the practical importance of industry than Sir Walter Scott, who was himself one of the most laborious and indefatigable of men. Indeed, Lockhart says of him that, taking all ages and countries together, the rare example of indefatigable energy, in union with serene self-possession of mind and manner, such as Scott's, must be sought for in the roll of great sovereigns or great captains, rather than in that of literary genius. Scott himself was most anxious to impress upon the minds of his own children the importance of industry as a means of usefulness and happiness in the world. To his son Charles, when at school, he wrote: - "I cannot too much impress upon your mind that LABOUR is the condition which God has imposed on us in every station of life; there is nothing worth having that can be had without it, from the bread which the peasant wins with the sweat of his brow, to the sports by which the rich man must get rid of his ENNUI.... As for knowledge, it can no more be planted in the human mind without labour than a field of wheat can be produced without the previous use of the plough. There is, indeed, this great difference, that chance or circumstances may so cause it that another shall reap what the farmer sows; but no man can be deprived, whether by accident or misfortune, of the fruits of his own studies; and the liberal and extended acquisitions of knowledge which he makes are all for his own use. Labour, therefore, my dear boy, and improve the time. In youth our steps are light, and our minds are ductile, and knowledge is easily laid up; but if we neglect our spring, our summers will be useless and contemptible, our harvest will be chaff, and the winter of our old age unrespected and desolate. " (11)

Southey was as laborious a worker as Scott. Indeed, work might almost be said to form part of his religion. He was only nineteen when he wrote these words: - "Nineteen years! certainly a fourth part of my life; perhaps how great a part! and yet I have been of no service to society. The clown who scares crows for twopence a day is a more useful man; he preserves the bread which I eat in idleness. " And yet Southey had not been idle as a boy—on the contrary, he had been a most diligent student. He had not only read largely in English literature, but was well acquainted, through translations, with Tasso, Ariosto, Homer, and Ovid. He felt, however, as if his life had been purposeless, and he determined to do something. He began, and from that time forward he pursued an unremitting career of literary labour down to the close of his life—"daily progressing in learning, " to use his own words—"not so learned as he is poor, not so poor as proud, not so proud as happy. "

The maxims of men often reveal their character. (12) That of Sir Walter Scott was, "Never to be doing nothing. " Robertson the historian, as early as his fifteenth year, adopted the maxim of "VITA SINE LITERIS MORS EST" (Life without learning is death). Voltaire's motto was, "TOUJOURS AU TRAVAIL" (Always at work). The favourite maxim of Lacepede, the naturalist, was, "VIVRE C'EST VEILLER" (To live is to observe): it was also the maxim of Pliny. When Bossuet was at college, he was so distinguished by his ardour in study, that his fellow students, playing upon his name, designated him as "BOS-SUETUS ARATRO" (The ox used to the plough). The name of VITA-LIS (Life a struggle), which the Swedish poet Sjoberg assumed, as Frederik von Hardenberg assumed that of NOVA- LIS, described the aspirations and the labours of both these men of genius.

We have spoken of work as a discipline: it is also an educator of character. Even work that produces no results, because it IS work, is better than torpor, —inasmuch as it educates faculty, and is thus preparatory to successful work. The habit of working teaches method. It compels economy of time, and the disposition of it with judicious forethought. And when the art of packing life with useful occupations is once acquired by practice, every minute will be turned to account; and leisure, when it comes, will be enjoyed with all the greater zest.

Coleridge has truly observed, that "if the idle are described as killing time, the methodical man may be justly said to call it into life and moral being, while he makes it the distinct object not only of the consciousness, but of the conscience. He organizes the hours and gives them a soul; and by that, the very essence of which is to fleet and to have been, he communicates an imperishable and spiritual nature. Of the good and faithful servant, whose energies thus directed are thus methodized, it is less truly affirmed that he lives in time than that time lives in him. His days and months and years, as the stops and punctual marks in the record of duties performed, will survive the wreck of worlds, and remain extant when time itself shall be no more. " (13)

It is because application to business teaches method most effectually, that it is so useful as an educator of character. The highest working qualities are best trained by active and sympathetic contact with others in the affairs of daily life. It does not matter whether the business relate to the management of a household or of a nation. Indeed, as we have endeavoured to show in a preceding chapter, the able housewife must necessarily be an efficient woman of business. She must regulate and control the details of her home, keep her expenditure within her means, arrange everything according to plan and system, and wisely manage and govern those subject to her rule. Efficient domestic management implies industry, application, method, moral discipline, forethought, prudence, practical ability, insight into character, and power of organization—all of which are required in the efficient management of business of whatever sort.

Business qualities have, indeed, a very large field of action. They mean aptitude for affairs, competency to deal successfully with the practical work of life—whether the spur of action lie in domestic management, in the conduct of a profession, in trade or commerce, in social organization, or in political government. And the training which gives efficiency in dealing with these various affairs is of all others the most useful in practical life. (14) Moreover, it is the best discipline of character; for it involves the exercise of diligence, attention, self-denial, judgment, tact, knowledge of and sympathy with others.

Such a discipline is far more productive of happiness5 as well as useful efficiency in life, than any amount of literary culture or meditative seclusion; for in the long run it will usually be found that practical ability carries it over intellect, and temper and habits over talent. It must, however, he added that this is a kind of culture that can only be acquired by diligent observation and carefully improved experience. "To be a good blacksmith, " said General Trochu in a recent publication, "one must have forged all his life: to be a good administrator one should have passed his whole life in the study and practice of business. "

It was characteristic of Sir Walter Scott to entertain the highest respect for able men of business; and he professed that he did not consider any amount of literary distinction as entitled to be spoken of in the same breath with a mastery in the higher departments of practical life—least of all with a first-rate captain.

The great commander leaves nothing to chance, but provides for every contingency. He condescends to apparently trivial details. Thus, when Wellington was at the head of his army in Spain, he directed the precise manner in which the soldiers were to cook their provisions. When in India, he specified the exact speed at which the bullocks were to be driven; every detail in equipment was carefully arranged beforehand. And thus not only was efficiency secured, but the devotion of his men, and their boundless confidence in his command. (15)

Like other great captains, Wellington had an almost boundless capacity for work. He drew up the heads of a Dublin Police Bill (being still the Secretary for Ireland), when tossing off the mouth of the Mondego, with Junot and the French army waiting for him on the shore. So Caesar, another of the greatest commanders, is said to have written an essay on Latin Rhetoric while crossing the Alps at the head of his army. And Wallenstein when at the head of 60,000 men, and in the midst of a campaign with the enemy before him, dictated from headquarters the medical treatment of his poultry-yard.

Washington, also, was an indefatigable man of business. From his boyhood he diligently trained himself in habits of application, of study, and of methodical work. His manuscript school-books, which are still preserved, show that, as early as the age of thirteen, he occupied himself voluntarily in copying out such things as forms of receipts, notes of hand, bills of exchange, bonds, indentures, leases, land-warrants, and other dry documents, all written out with great care. And the habits which he thus early acquired were, in a great measure, the foundation of those admirable business qualities which he afterwards so successfully brought to bear in the affairs of government.

The man or woman who achieves success in the management of any great affair of business is entitled to honour, —it may be, to as much as the artist who paints a picture, or the author who writes a book, or the soldier who wins a battle. Their success may have been gained in the face of as great difficulties, and after as great struggles; and where they have won their battle, it is at least a peaceful one, and there is no blood on their hands.

The idea has been entertained by some, that business habits are incompatible with genius. In the Life of Richard Lovell Edgeworth, (16) it is observed of a Mr. Bicknell—a respectable but ordinary man, of whom little is known but that he married Sabrina Sidney, the ELEVE of Thomas Day, author of 'Sandford and Merton'—that "he had some of the too usual faults of a man of genius: he detested the drudgery of business. " But there cannot be a greater mistake. The greatest geniuses have, without exception, been the greatest workers, even to the extent of drudgery. They have not only worked harder than ordinary men, but brought to their work higher faculties and a more ardent spirit. Nothing great and durable was ever improvised. It is only by noble patience and noble labour that the masterpieces of genius have been achieved.

Power belongs only to the workers; the idlers are always powerless. It is the laborious and painstaking men who are the rulers of the world. There has not been a statesman of eminence but was a man of industry. "It is by toil, " said even Louis XIV., "that kings govern. " When Clarendon described Hampden, he spoke of him as "of an industry and vigilance not to be tired out or wearied by the most laborious, and of parts not to be imposed on by the most subtle and sharp, and of a personal courage equal to his best parts. " While in the midst of his laborious though self- imposed duties, Hampden, on one occasion, wrote to his mother: "My lyfe is nothing but toyle, and hath been for many yeares, nowe to the Commonwealth, nowe to the Kinge.... Not so much tyme left as to doe my dutye to my deare parents, nor to sende to them. " Indeed, all the statesmen of the Commonwealth were great toilers; and Clarendon himself, whether in office or out of it, was a man of indefatigable application and industry.

The same energetic vitality, as displayed in the power of working, has distinguished all the eminent men in our own as well as in past times. During the Anti-Corn Law movement, Cobden, writing to a friend, described himself as "working like a horse, with not a moment to spare. " Lord Brougham was a remarkable instance of the indefatigably active and laborious man; and it might be said of Lord Palmerston, that he worked harder for success in his extreme old age than he had ever done in the prime of his manhood — preserving his working faculty, his good-humour and BONHOMMIE, unimpaired to the end. (17) He himself was accustomed to say, that being in office, and consequently full of work, was good for his health. It rescued him from ENNUI. Helvetius even held, that it is man's sense of ENNUI that is the chief cause of his superiority over the brute, — that it is the necessity which he feels for escaping from its intolerable suffering that forces him to employ himself actively, and is hence the great stimulus to human progress.

Indeed, this living principle of constant work, of abundant occupation, of practical contact with men in the affairs of life, has in all times been the best ripener of the energetic vitality of strong natures. Business habits, cultivated and disciplined, are found alike useful in every pursuit—whether in politics, literature, science, or art. Thus, a great deal of the best literary work has been done by men systematically trained in business pursuits. The same industry, application, economy of time and labour, which have rendered them useful in the one sphere of employment, have been found equally available in the other.

Most of the early English writers were men of affairs, trained to business; for no literary class as yet existed, excepting it might be the priesthood. Chaucer, the father of English poetry, was first a soldier, and afterwards a comptroller of petty customs. The office was no sinecure either, for he had to write up all the records with his own hand; and when he had done his "reckonings" at the custom-house, he returned with delight to his favourite studies at home—poring over his books until his eyes were "dazed" and dull.

The great writers in the reign of Elizabeth, during which there was such a development of robust life in England, were not literary men according to the modern acceptation of the word, but men of action trained in business. Spenser acted as secretary to the Lord Deputy of Ireland; Raleigh was, by turns, a courtier, soldier, sailor, and discoverer; Sydney was a politician, diplomatist, and soldier; Bacon was a laborious lawyer before he became Lord Keeper and Lord Chancellor; Sir Thomas Browne was a physician in country practice at Norwich; Hooker was the hardworking pastor of a country parish; Shakspeare was the manager of a theatre, in which he was himself but an indifferent actor, and he seems to have been even more careful of his money investments than he was of his intellectual offspring. Yet these, all men of active business habits, are among the greatest writers of any age: the period of Elizabeth and James I. standing out in the history of England as the era of its greatest literary activity and splendour.

In the reign of Charles I., Cowley held various offices of trust and confidence. He acted as private secretary to several of the royalist leaders, and was afterwards engaged as private secretary to the Queen, in ciphering and deciphering the correspondence which passed between her and Charles I. ; the work occupying all his days, and often his nights, during several years. And while Cowley was thus employed in the royal cause, Milton was employed by the Commonwealth, of which he was the Latin secretary, and afterwards secretary to the Lord Protector. Yet, in the earlier part of his life, Milton was occupied in the humble vocation of a teacher. Dr. Johnson says, "that in his school, as in everything else which he undertook, he laboured with great diligence, there is no reason for doubting" It was after the Restoration, when his official employment ceased, that Milton entered upon the principal literary work of his life; but before he undertook the writing of his great epic, he deemed it indispensable that to "industrious and select reading" he should add "steady observation" and "insight into all seemly and generous arts and affairs. " (18)

Locke held office in different reigns: first under Charles II. as Secretary to the Board of Trade and afterwards under William III. as Commissioner of Appeals and of Trade and Plantations. Many literary men of eminence held office in Queen Anne's reign. Thus Addison was Secretary of State; Steele, Commissioner of Stamps; Prior, Under-Secretary of State, and afterwards Ambassador to France; Tickell, Under-Secretary of State, and Secretary to the Lords Justices of Ireland; Congreve, Secretary of Jamaica;, and Gay, Secretary of Legation at Hanover.

Indeed, habits of business, instead of unfitting a cultivated mind for scientific or literary pursuits, are often the best training for them. Voltaire insisted with truth that the real spirit of business and literature are the same; the perfection of each being the union of energy and thoughtfulness, of cultivated intelligence and practical wisdom, of the active and contemplative essence—a union commended by Lord Bacon as the concentrated excellence of man's nature. It has been said that even the man of genius can write nothing worth reading in relation to human affairs, unless he has been in some way or other connected with the serious everyday business of life.

Hence it has happened that many of the best books, extant have been written by men of business, with whom literature was a pastime rather than a profession. Gifford, the editor of the 'Quarterly, ' who knew the drudgery of writing for a living, once observed that "a single hour of composition, won from the business of the day, is worth more than the whole day's toil of him who works at the trade of literature: in the one case, the spirit comes joyfully to refresh itself, like a hart to the waterbrooks; in the other, it pursues its miserable way, panting and jaded, with the dogs and hunger of necessity behind. " (19)

The first great men of letters in Italy were not mere men of letters; they were men of business — merchants, statesmen, diplomatists, judges, and soldiers. Villani, the author of the best History of Florence, was a merchant; Dante, Petrarch, and Boccacio, were all engaged in more or less important embassies; and Dante, before becoming a diplomatist, was for some time occupied as a chemist and druggist. Galileo, Galvani, and Farini were physicians, and Goldoni a lawyer. Ariosto's talent for affairs was as great as his genius for poetry. At the death of his father, he was called upon to manage the family estate for the benefit of his younger brothers and sisters, which he did with ability and integrity. His genius for business having been recognised, he was employed by the Duke of Ferrara on important missions to Rome and elsewhere. Having afterwards been appointed governor of a turbulent mountain district, he succeeded, by firm and just governments in reducing it to a condition of comparative good order and security. Even the bandits of the country respected him. Being arrested one day in the mountains by a body of outlaws, he mentioned his name, when they at once offered to escort him in safety wherever he chose.

It has been the same in other countries. Vattel, the author of the 'Rights of Nations, ' was a practical diplomatist, and a first- rate man of business. Rabelais was a physician, and a successful practitioner; Schiller was a surgeon; Cervantes, Lope de Vega, Calderon, Camoens, Descartes, Maupertius, La Rochefoucauld, Lacepede, Lamark, were soldiers in the early part of their respective lives.

In our own country, many men now known by their writings, earned their living by their trade. Lillo spent the greater part of his life as a working jeweller in the Poultry; occupying the intervals of his leisure in the production of dramatic works, some of them of acknowledged power and merit. Izaak Walton was a linendraper in Fleet Street, reading much in his leisure hours, and storing his mind with facts for future use in his capacity of biographer. De Foe was by turns horse-factor, brick and tile maker, shopkeeper, author, and political agent.

Samuel Richardson successfully combined literature, with business; writing his novels in his back-shop in Salisbury Court, Fleet Street, and selling them over the counter in his front-shop. William Hutton, of Birmingham, also successfully combined the occupations of bookselling and authorship. He says, in his Autobiography, that a man may live half a century and not be acquainted with his own character. He did not know that he was an antiquary until the world informed him of it, from having read his 'History of Birmingham, ' and then, he said, he could see it himself. Benjamin Franklin was alike eminent as a printer and bookseller—an author, a philosopher and a statesman.

Coming down to our own time, we find Ebenezer Elliott successfully carrying on the business of a bar-iron merchant in Sheffield, during which time he wrote and published the greater number of his poems; and his success in business was such as to enable him to retire into the country and build a house of his own, in which he spent the remainder of his days. Isaac Taylor, the author of the 'Natural History of Enthusiasm, ' was an engraver of patterns for Manchester calico-printers; and other members of this gifted family were followers of the same branch of art.

The principal early works of John Stuart Mill were written in the intervals of official work, while he held the office of principal examiner in the East India House, —in which Charles Lamb, Peacock the author of 'Headlong Hall, ' and Edwin Norris the philologist, were also clerks. Macaulay wrote his 'Lays of Ancient Rome' in the War Office, while holding the post of Secretary of War. It is well known that the thoughtful writings of Mr. Helps are literally "Essays written in the Intervals of Business. " Many of our best living authors are men holding important public offices—such as Sir Henry Taylor, Sir John Kaye, Anthony Trollope, Tom Taylor, Matthew Arnold, and Samuel Warren.

Mr. Proctor the poet, better known as "Barry Cornwall, " was a barrister and commissioner in lunacy. Most probably he assumed the pseudonym for the same reason that Dr. Paris published his 'Philosophy in Sport made Science in Earnest' anonymously— because he apprehended that, if known, it might compromise his professional position. For it is by no means an uncommon prejudice, still prevalent amongst City men, that a person who has written a book, and still more one who has written a poem, is good for nothing in the way of business. Yet Sharon Turner, though an excellent historian, was no worse a solicitor on that account; while the brothers Horace and James Smith, authors of 'The Rejected Addresses, ' were men of such eminence in their profession, that they were selected to fill the important and lucrative post of solicitors to the Admiralty, and they filled it admirably.

It was while the late Mr. Broderip, the barrister, was acting as a London police magistrate, that he was attracted to the study of natural history, in which he occupied the greater part of his leisure. He wrote the principal articles on the subject for the 'Penny Cyclopaedia, ' besides several separate works of great merit, more particularly the 'Zoological Recreations, ' and 'Leaves from the Notebook of a Naturalist. ' It is recorded of him that, though he devoted so much of his time to the production of his works, as well as to the Zoological Society and their admirable establishment in Regent's Park, of which he was one of the founders, his studies never interfered with the real business of his life, nor is it known that a single question was ever raised upon his conduct or his decisions. And while Mr. Broderip devoted himself to natural history, the late Lord Chief Baron Pollock devoted his leisure to natural science, recreating himself in the practice of photography and the study of mathematics, in both of which he was thoroughly proficient.

Among literary bankers we find the names of Rogers, the poet; Roscoe, of Liverpool, the biographer of Lorenzo de Medici; Ricardo, the author of 'Political Economy and Taxation; (20) Grote, the author of the 'History of Greece; ' Sir John Lubbock, the scientific antiquarian; (21) and Samuel Bailey, of Sheffield, the author of 'Essays on the Formation and Publication of Opinions, ' besides various important works on ethics, political economy, and philosophy.

Nor, on the other hand, have thoroughly-trained men of science and learning proved themselves inefficient as first-rate men of business. Culture of the best sort trains the habit of application and industry, disciplines the mind, supplies it with resources, and gives it freedom and vigour of action—all of which are equally requisite in the successful conduct of business. Thus, in young men, education and scholarship usually indicate steadiness of character, for they imply continuous attention, diligence, and the ability and energy necessary to master knowledge; and such persons will also usually be found possessed of more than average promptitude, address, resource, and dexterity.

Montaigne has said of true philosophers, that "if they were great in science, they were yet much greater in action;... and whenever they have been put upon the proof, they have been seen to fly to so high a pitch, as made it very well appear their souls were strangely elevated and enriched with the knowledge of things. " (22)

At the same time, it must be acknowledged that too exclusive a devotion to imaginative and philosophical literature, especially if prolonged in life until the habits become formed, does to a great extent incapacitate a man for the business of practical life. Speculative ability is one thing, and practical ability another; and the man who, in his study, or with his pen in hand, shows himself capable of forming large views of life and policy, may, in the outer world, be found altogether unfitted for carrying them into practical effect.

Speculative ability depends on vigorous thinking—practical ability on vigorous acting; and the two qualities are usually found combined in very unequal proportions. The speculative man is prone to indecision: he sees all the sides of a question, and his action becomes suspended in nicely weighing the pros and cons, which are often found pretty nearly to balance each other; whereas the practical man overleaps logical preliminaries, arrives at certain definite convictions, and proceeds forthwith to carry his policy into action.(23)

Yet there have been many great men of science who have proved efficient men of business. We do not learn that Sir Isaac Newton made a worse Master of the Mint because he was the greatest of philosophers. Nor were there any complaints as to the efficiency of Sir John Herschel, who held the same office. The brothers Humboldt were alike capable men in all that they undertook— whether it was literature, philosophy, mining, philology, diplomacy, or statesmanship.

Niebuhr, the historian, was distinguished for his energy and success as a man of business. He proved so efficient as secretary and accountant to the African consulate, to which he had been appointed by the Danish Government, that he was afterwards selected as one of the commissioners to manage the national finances; and he quitted that office to undertake the joint directorship of a bank at Berlin. It was in the midst of his business occupations that he found time to study Roman history, to master the Arabic, Russian, and other Sclavonic languages, and to build up the great reputation as an author by which he is now chiefly remembered.

Having regard to the views professed by the First Napoleon as to men of science, it was to have been expected that he would endeavour to strengthen his administration by calling them to his aid. Some of his appointments proved failures, while others were completely successful. Thus Laplace was made Minister of the Interior; but he had no sooner been appointed than it was seen that a mistake had been made. Napoleon afterwards said of him, that "Laplace looked at no question in its true point of view. He was always searching after subtleties; all his ideas were problems, and he carried the spirit of the infinitesimal calculus into the management of business. " But Laplace's habits had been formed in the study, and he was too old to adapt them to the purposes of practical life.

With Darn it was different. But Darn had the advantage of some practical training in business, having served as an intendant of the army in Switzerland under Massena, during which he also distinguished himself as an author. When Napoleon proposed to appoint him a councillor of state and intendant of the Imperial Household, Darn hesitated to accept the office. "I have passed the greater part of my life, " he said, "among books, and have not had time to learn the functions of a courtier. " "Of courtiers, " replied Napoleon, "I have plenty about me; they will never fail. But I want a minister, at once enlightened, firm, and vigilant; and it is for these qualities that I have selected you. " Darn complied with the Emperor's wishes, and eventually became his Prime Minister, proving thoroughly efficient in that capacity, and remaining the same modest, honourable, and disinterested man that he had ever been through life.

Men of trained working faculty so contract the habit of labour that idleness becomes intolerable to them; and when driven by circumstances from their own special line of occupation, they find refuge in other pursuits. The diligent man is quick to find employment for his leisure; and he is able to make leisure when the idle man finds none. "He hath no leisure, " says George Herbert, "who useth it not. " "The most active or busy man that hath been or can be, " says Bacon, "hath, no question, many vacant times of leisure, while he expecteth the tides and returns of business, except he be either tedious and of no despatch, or lightly and unworthily ambitious to meddle with things that may be better done by others. " Thus many great things have been done during such "vacant times of leisure, " by men to whom industry had become a second nature, and who found it easier to work than to be idle.

Even hobbies are useful as educators of the working faculty. Hobbies evoke industry of a certain kind, and at least provide agreeable occupation. Not such hobbies as that of Domitian, who occupied himself in catching flies. The hobbies of the King of Macedon who made lanthorns, and of the King of France who made locks, were of a more respectable order. Even a routine mechanical employment is felt to be a relief by minds acting under high-pressure: it is an intermission of labour—a rest—a relaxation, the pleasure consisting in the work itself rather than in the result.

But the best of hobbies are intellectual ones. Thus men of active mind retire from their daily business to find recreation in other pursuits— some in science, some in art, and the greater number in literature. Such recreations are among the best preservatives against selfishness and vulgar worldliness. We believe it was Lord Brougham who said, "Blessed is the man that hath a hobby! " and in the abundant versatility of his nature, he himself had many, ranging from literature to optics, from history and biography to social science. Lord Brougham is even said to have written a novel; and the remarkable story of the 'Man in the Bell, ' which appeared many years ago in 'Blackwood, ' is reputed to have been from his pen. Intellectual hobbies, however, must not be ridden too hard—else, instead of recreating, refreshing, and invigorating a man's nature, they may only have the effect of sending him back to his business exhausted, enervated, and depressed.

Many laborious statesmen besides Lord Brougham have occupied their leisure, or consoled themselves in retirement from office, by the composition of works which have become part of the standard literature of the world. Thus 'Caesar's Commentaries' still survive as a classic; the perspicuous and forcible style in which they are written placing him in the same rank with Xenophon, who also successfully combined the pursuit of letters with the business of active life.

When the great Sully was disgraced as a minister, and driven into retirement, he occupied his leisure in writing out his 'Memoirs, ' in anticipation of the judgment of posterity upon his career as a statesman. Besides these, he also composed part of a romance after the manner of the Scuderi school, the manuscript of which was found amongst his papers at his death.

Turgot found a solace for the loss of office, from which he had been driven by the intrigues of his enemies, in the study of physical science. He also reverted to his early taste for classical literature. During his long journeys, and at nights when tortured by the gout, he amused himself by making Latin verses; though the only line of his that has been preserved was that intended to designate the portrait of Benjamin Franklin:

"Eripuit caelo fulmen, sceptrumque tyrannis."

Among more recent French statesmen—with whom, however, literature has been their profession as much as politics—may be mentioned De Tocqueville, Thiers, Guizot, and Lamartine, while Napoleon III. challenged a place in the Academy by his 'Life of Caesar. '

Literature has also been the chief solace of our greatest English statesmen. When Pitt retired from office, like his great contemporary Fox, he reverted with delight to the study of the Greek and Roman classics. Indeed, Grenville considered Pitt the best Greek scholar he had ever known. Canning and Wellesley, when in retirement, occupied themselves in translating the odes and satires of Horace. Canning's passion for literature entered into all his pursuits, and gave a colour to his whole life. His biographer says of him, that after a dinner at Pitt's, while the rest of the company were dispersed in conversation, he and Pitt would be observed poring over some old Grecian in a corner of the drawing-room. Fox also was a diligent student of the Greek authors, and, like Pitt, read Lycophron. He was also the author of a History of James II., though the book is only a fragment, and, it must be confessed, is rather a disappointing work.

One of the most able and laborious of our recent statesmen—with whom literature was a hobby as well as a pursuit—was the late Sir George Cornewall Lewis. He was an excellent man of business— diligent, exact, and painstaking. He filled by turns the offices of President of the Poor Law Board—the machinery of which he created, —Chancellor of the Exchequer, Home Secretary, and Secretary at War; and in each he achieved the reputation of a thoroughly successful administrator. In the intervals of his official labours, he occupied himself with inquiries into a wide range of subjects—history, politics, philology, anthropology, and antiquarianism. His works on 'The Astronomy of the Ancients, ' and 'Essays on the Formation of the Romanic Languages, ' might have been written by the profoundest of German SAVANS. He took especial delight in pursuing the abstruser branches of learning, and found in them his chief pleasure and recreation. Lord Palmerston sometimes remonstrated with him, telling him he was "taking too much out of himself" by laying aside official papers after office-hours in order to study books; Palmerston himself declaring that he had no time to read books—that the reading of manuscript was quite enough for him.

Doubtless Sir George Lewis rode his hobby too hard, and but for his devotion to study, his useful life would probably have been prolonged. Whether in or out of office, he read, wrote, and studied. He relinquished the editorship of the 'Edinburgh Review' to become Chancellor of the Exchequer; and when no longer occupied in preparing budgets, he proceeded to copy out a mass of Greek manuscripts at the British Museum. He took particular delight in pursuing any difficult inquiry in classical antiquity. One of the odd subjects with which he occupied himself was an examination into the truth of reported cases of longevity, which, according to his custom, he doubted or disbelieved. This subject was uppermost in his mind while pursuing his canvass of Herefordshire in 1852. On applying to a voter one day for his support, he was met by a decided refusal. "I am sorry, " was the candidate's reply, "that you can't give me your vote; but perhaps you can tell me whether anybody in your parish has died at an extraordinary age! "

The contemporaries of Sir George Lewis also furnish many striking instances of the consolations afforded by literature to statesmen wearied with the toils of public life. Though the door of office may be closed, that of literature stands always open, and men who are at daggers-drawn in politics, join hands over the poetry of Homer and Horace. The late Earl of Derby, on retiring from power, produced his noble version of 'The Iliad, ' which will probably continue to be read when his speeches have been forgotten. Mr. Gladstone similarly occupied his leisure in preparing for the press his 'Studies on Homer, ' (24) and in editing a translation of 'Farini's Roman State; '

while Mr. Disraeli signalised his retirement from office by the production of his 'Lothair. ' Among statesmen who have figured as novelists, besides Mr. Disraeli, are Lord Russell, who has also contributed largely to history and biography; the Marquis of Normanby, and the veteran novelist, Lord Lytton, with whom, indeed, politics may be said to have been his recreation, and literature the chief employment of his life.

To conclude: a fair measure of work is good for mind as well as body. Man is an intelligence sustained and preserved by bodily organs, and their active exercise is necessary to the enjoyment of health. It is not work, but overwork, that is hurtful; and it is not hard work that is injurious so much as monotonous work, fagging work, hopeless work. All hopeful work is healthful; and to be usefully and hopefully employed is one of the great secrets of happiness. Brain-work, in moderation, is no more wearing than any other kind of work. Duly regulated, it is as promotive of health as bodily exercise; and, where due attention is paid to the physical system, it seems difficult to put more upon a man than he can bear. Merely to eat and drink and sleep one's way idly through life is vastly more injurious. The wear-and-tear of rust is even faster than the tear-and-wear of work.

But overwork is always bad economy. It is, in fact, great waste, especially if conjoined with worry. Indeed, worry kills far more than work does. It frets, it excites, it consumes the body — as sand and grit, which occasion excessive friction, wear out the wheels of a machine. Overwork and worry have both to be guarded against. For over-brain-work is strain-work; and it is exhausting and destructive according as it is in excess of nature. And the brain-worker may exhaust and overbalance his mind by excess, just as the athlete may overstrain his muscles and break his back by attempting feats beyond the strength of his physical system.

NOTES

(1)In the third chapter of his Natural History, Pliny relates in what high honour agriculture was held in the earlier days of Rome; how the divisions of land were measured by the quantity which could be ploughed by a yoke of oxen in a certain time (JUGERUM, in one day; ACTUS, at one spell); how the greatest recompence to a general or valiant citizen was a JUGERUM; how the earliest surnames were derived from agriculture (Pilumnus, from PILUM, the pestle for pounding corn; Piso, from PISO, to grind coin; Fabius, from FABA, a bean; Lentulus, from LENS, a lentil; Cicero, from CICER, a chickpea; Babulcus, from BOS, &c.); how the highest compliment was to call a man a good agriculturist, or a good husbandman (LOCUPLES, rich, LOCI PLENUS, PECUNIA, from PECUS, &c.); how the pasturing of cattle secretly by night upon unripe crops was a capital offence, punishable by hanging; how the rural tribes held the foremost rank, while those of the city had discredit thrown upon them as being an indolent race; and how "GLORIAM DENIQUE IPSAM, A FARRIS HONORE, 'ADOREAM' APPELLABANT; " ADOREA, or Glory, the reward of valour, being derived from Ador, or spelt, a kind of grain.

(2) 'Essay on Government, ' in 'Encyclopaedia Britannica. '

(3) Burton's 'Anatomy of Melancholy, ' Part i., Mem. 2, Sub. 6.

(4) Ibid. End of concluding chapter.

(5) It is characteristic of the Hindoos to regard entire inaction as the most perfect state, and to describe the Supreme Being as "The Unmoveable. "

(6) Lessing was so impressed with the conviction that stagnant satisfaction was fatal to man, that he went so far as to say: "If the All-powerful Being, holding in one hand Truth, and in the other the search for Truth, said to me, 'Choose, ' I would answer Him, 'O All-powerful, keep for Thyself the Truth; but leave to me the search for it, which is the better for me. '" On the other hand, Bossuet said: "Si je concevais une nature purement intelligente, il me semble que je n'y mettrais qu'entendre et aimer la verite, et que cela seul la rendrait heureux. "

(7) The late Sir John Patteson, when in his seventieth year, attended an annual ploughing-match dinner at Feniton, Devon, at which he thought it worth his while to combat the notion, still too prevalent, that because a man does not work merely with his bones and muscles, he is therefore not entitled to the appellation of a workingman. "In recollecting similar meetings to the present, " he said, "I remember my friend, John Pyle, rather throwing it in my teeth that I had not worked for nothing; but I told him, 'Mr. Pyle, you do not know what you are talking about. We are all workers. The man who ploughs the field and who digs the hedge is a worker; but there are other workers in other stations of life as well. For

myself, I can say that I have been a worker ever since I have been a boy. '... Then I told him that the office of judge was by no means a sinecure, for that a judge worked as hard as any man in the country. He has to work at very difficult questions of law, which are brought before him continually, giving him great anxiety; and sometimes the lives of his fellow-creatures are placed in his hands, and are dependent very much upon the manner in which he places the facts before the jury. That is a matter of no little anxiety, I can assure you. Let any man think as he will, there is no man who has been through the ordeal for the length of time that I have, but must feel conscious of the importance and gravity of the duty which is cast upon a judge."

(8) Lord Stanley's Address to the Students of Glasgow University, on his installation as Lord Rector, 1869.

(9) Writing to an abbot at Nuremberg, who had sent him a store of turning-tools, Luther said: "I have made considerable progress in clockmaking, and I am very much delighted at it, for these drunken Saxons need to be constantly reminded of what the real time is; not that they themselves care much about it, for as long as their glasses are kept filled, they trouble themselves very little as to whether clocks, or clockmakers, or the time itself, go right. "— Michelet's LUTHER (Bogue Ed.), p. 200.

(10) 'Life of Perthes, " ii. 20.

(11) Lockhart's 'Life of Scott' (8vo. Ed.), p. 442.

(12) Southey expresses the opinion in 'The Doctor', that the character of a person may be better known by the letters which other persons write to him than by what he himself writes.

(13) 'Dissertation on the Science of Method. '

(14) The following passage, from a recent article in the PALL MALL GAZETTE, will commend itself to general aproval: - "There can be no question nowadays, that application to work, absorption in affairs, contact with men, and all the stress which business imposes on us, gives a noble training to the intellect, and splendid opportunity for discipline of character. It is an utterly low view of business which regards it as only a means of getting a living. A man's business is his part of the world's work, his share of the great

activities which render society possible. He may like it or dislike it, but it is work, and as such requires application, self-denial, discipline. It is his drill, and he cannot be thorough in his occupation without putting himself into it, checking his fancies, restraining his impulses, and holding himself to the perpetual round of small details— without, in fact, submitting to his drill. But the perpetual call on a man's readiness, sell-control, and vigour which business makes, the constant appeal to the intellect, the stress upon the will, the necessity for rapid and responsible exercise of judgment —all these things constitute a high culture, though not the highest. It is a culture which strengthens and invigorates if it does not refine, which gives force if not polish—the FORTITER IN RE, if not the SUAVITER IN MODO. It makes strong men and ready men, and men of vast capacity for affairs, though it does not necessarily make refined men or gentlemen. "

(15) On the first publication of his 'Despatches, ' one of his friends said to him, on reading the records of his Indian campaigns: "It seems to me, Duke, that your chief business in India was to procure rice and bullocks. " "And so it was, " replied Wellington: "for if I had rice and bullocks, I had men; and if I had men, I knew I could beat the enemy. "

(16) Maria Edgeworth, 'Memoirs of R. L. Edgeworth, ' ii. 94.

(17) A friend of Lord Palmerston has communicated to us the following anecdote. Asking him one day when he considered a man to be in the prime of life, his immediate reply was, "Seventy-nine! " "But, " he added, with a twinkle in his eye, "as I have just entered my eightieth year, perhaps I am myself a little past it. "

(18) 'Reasons of Church Government, ' Book II.

(19) Coleridge's advice to his young friends was much to the same effect. "With the exception of one extraordinary man, " he says, "I have never known an individual, least of all an individual of genius, healthy or happy without a profession: i.e., some regular employment which does not depend on the will of the moment, and which can be carried on so far mechanically, that an average quantum only of health, spirits, and intellectual exertion are requisite to its faithful discharge. Three hours of leisure, unalloyed by any alien anxiety, and looked forward to with delight as a change and recreation, will suffice to realise in literature a larger product of what

is truly genial, than weeks of compulsion.... If facts are required to prove the possibility of combining weighty performances in literature with full and independent employment, the works of Cicero and Xenophon, among the ancients—of Sir Thomas More, Bacon, Baxter, or (to refer at once to later and contemporary instances) Darwin and Roscoe, are at once decisive of the question. "
—BIOGRAPHIA LITERARIA, Chap. xi.

(20) Mr. Ricardo published his celebrated 'Theory of Rent, ' at the urgent recommendation of James Mill (like his son, a chief clerk in the India House), author of the 'History of British India. ' When the 'Theory of Rent' was written, Ricardo was so dissatisfied with it that he wished to burn it; but Mr. Mill urged him to publish it, and the book was a great success.

(21) The late Sir John Lubbock, his father, was also eminent as a mathematician and astronomer.

(22) Thales, once inveighing in discourse against the pains and care men put themselves to, to become rich, was answered by one in the company that he did like the fox, who found fault with what he could not obtain. Thereupon Thales had a mind, for the jest's sake, to show them the contrary; and having upon this occasion for once made a muster of all his wits, wholly to employ them in the service of profit, he set a traffic on foot, which in one year brought him in so great riches, that the most experienced in that trade could hardly in their whole lives, with all their industry, have raked so much together. —Montaignes ESSAYS, Book I., chap. 24.

(23) "The understanding, " says Mr. Bailey, "that is accustomed to pursue a regular and connected train of ideas, becomes in some measure incapacitated for those quick and versatile movements which are learnt in the commerce of the world, and are indispensable to those who act a part in it. Deep thinking and practical talents require indeed habits of mind so essentially dissimilar, that while a man is striving after the one, he will be unavoidably in danger of losing the other. " "Thence, " he adds, "do we so often find men, who are 'giants in the closet, ' prove but 'children in the world. '"—
'Essays on the Formation and Publication of Opinions, ' pp. 251-3.

(24) Mr. Gladstone is as great an enthusiast in literature as Canning was. It is related of him that, while he was waiting in his committee-room at Liverpool for the returns coming in on the day of the South

Lancashire polling, he occupied himself in proceeding with the translation of a work which he was then preparing for the press.

CHAPTER V. —COURAGE.

"It is not but the tempest that doth show
The seaman's cunning; but the field that tries
The captain's courage; and we come to know
Best what men are, in their worst jeopardies." —DANIEL.

"If thou canst plan a noble deed,
And never flag till it succeed,
Though in the strife thy heart should bleed,
Whatever obstacles control,
Thine hour will come—go on, true soul!
Thou'lt win the prize, thou'lt reach the goal." —C. MACKAY.

"The heroic example of other days is in great part the source of the courage of each generation; and men walk up composedly to the most perilous enterprises, beckoned onwards by the shades of the brave that were. "—HELPS.

"That which we are, we are,
One equal temper of heroic hearts,
Made weak by time and fate, but strong in will
To strive, to seek, to find, and not to yield." —TENNYSON.

THE world owes much to its men and women of courage. We do not mean physical courage, in which man is at least equalled by the bulldog; nor is the bulldog considered the wisest of his species.

The courage that displays itself in silent effort and endeavour— that dares to endure all and suffer all for truth and duty—is more truly heroic than the achievements of physical valour, which are rewarded by honours and titles, or by laurels sometimes steeped in blood.

It is moral courage that characterises the highest order of manhood and womanhood—the courage to seek and to speak the truth; the courage to be just; the courage to be honest; the courage to resist temptation; the courage to do one's duty. If men and women do not possess this virtue, they have no security whatever for the preservation of any other.

Every step of progress in the history of our race has been made in the face of opposition and difficulty, and been achieved and secured by men of intrepidity and valour—by leaders in the van of thought—by great discoverers, great patriots, and great workers in all walks of life. There is scarcely a great truth or doctrine but has had to fight its way to public recognition in the face of detraction, calumny, and persecution. "Everywhere, " says Heine, "that a great soul gives utterance to its thoughts, there also is a Golgotha. "

"Many loved Truth and lavished life's best oil,
  Amid the dust of books to find her,
Content at last, for guerdon of their toil,
  With the cast mantle she had left behind her.
Many in sad faith sought for her,
Many with crossed hands sighed for her,
But these, our brothers, fought for her,
At life's dear peril wrought for her,
So loved her that they died for her,
Tasting the raptured fleetness
Of her divine completeness." (1)

Socrates was condemned to drink the hemlock at Athens in his seventy-second year, because his lofty teaching ran counter to the prejudices and party-spirit of his age. He was charged by his accusers with corrupting the youth of Athens by inciting them to despise the tutelary deities of the state. He had the moral courage to brave not only the tyranny of the judges who condemned him, but of the mob who could not understand him. He died discoursing of the doctrine of the immortality of the soul; his last words to his judges being, "It is now time that we depart—I to die, you to live; but which has the better destiny is unknown to all, except to the God. "

How many great men and thinkers have been persecuted in the name of religion! Bruno was burnt alive at Rome, because of his exposure of the fashionable but false philosophy of his time. When the judges of the Inquisition condemned him, to die, Bruno said proudly: "You are more afraid to pronounce my sentence than I am to receive it. "

To him succeeded Galileo, whose character as a man of science is almost eclipsed by that of the martyr. Denounced by the priests from the pulpit, because of the views he taught as to the motion of the earth, he was summoned to Rome, in his seventieth year, to answer for his heterodoxy. And he was imprisoned in the Inquisition, if he was not actually put to the torture there. He was pursued by persecution even when dead, the Pope refusing a tomb for his body.

Roger Bacon, the Franciscan monk, was persecuted on account of his studies in natural philosophy, and he was charged with, dealing in magic, because of his investigations in chemistry. His writings were condemned, and he was thrown into prison, where he lay for ten years, during the lives of four successive Popes. It is even averred that he died in prison.

Ockham, the early English speculative philosopher, was excommunicated by the Pope, and died in exile at Munich, where he was protected by the friendship of the then Emperor of Germany.

The Inquisition branded Vesalius as a heretic for revealing man to man, as it had before branded Bruno and Galileo for revealing the heavens to man. Vesalius had the boldness to study the structure of the human body by actual dissection, a practice until then almost entirely forbidden. He laid the foundations of a science, but he paid for it with his life. Condemned by the Inquisition, his penalty was commuted, by the intercession of the Spanish king, into a pilgrimage to the Holy Land; and when on his way back, while still in the prime of life, he died miserably at Zante, of fever and want—a martyr to his love of science.

When the 'Novum Organon' appeared, a hue-and-cry was raised against it, because of its alleged tendency to produce "dangerous revolutions, " to "subvert governments, " and to "overturn the authority of religion; " (2) and one Dr. Henry Stubbe (whose name would otherwise have been forgotten) wrote a book against the new philosophy, denouncing the whole tribe of experimentalists as "a Bacon-faced generation. " Even the establishment of the Royal Society was opposed, on the ground that "experimental philosophy is subversive of the Christian faith. "

While the followers of Copernicus were persecuted as infidels, Kepler was branded with the stigma of heresy, "because, " said he, "I take that side which seems to me to be consonant with the Word of God. " Even the pure and simpleminded Newton, of whom Bishop Burnet said that he had the WHITEST SOUL he ever knew—who was a very infant in the purity of his mind—even Newton was accused of "dethroning the Deity" by his sublime discovery of the law of gravitation; and a similar charge was made against Franklin for explaining the nature of the thunderbolt.

Spinoza was excommunicated by the Jews, to whom he belonged, because of his views of philosophy, which were supposed to be adverse to religion; and his life was afterwards attempted by an assassin for the same reason. Spinoza remained courageous and self-reliant to the last, dying in obscurity and poverty.

The philosophy of Descartes was denounced as leading to irreligion; the doctrines of Locke were said to produce materialism; and in our own day, Dr. Buckland, Mr. Sedgwick, and other leading geologists, have been accused of overturning revelation with regard to the constitution and history of the earth. Indeed, there has scarcely been a discovery in astronomy, in natural history, or in physical science, that has not been attacked by the bigoted and narrow-minded as leading to infidelity.

Other great discoverers, though they may not have been charged with irreligion, have had not less obloquy of a professional and public nature to encounter. When Dr. Harvey published his theory of the circulation of the blood, his practice fell off, (3) and the medical profession stigmatised him as a fool. "The few good things I have been able to do, " said John Hunter, "have been accomplished with the greatest difficulty, and encountered the greatest opposition. " Sir Charles Bell, while employed in his important investigations as to the nervous system, which issued in one of the greatest of physiological discoveries, wrote to a friend: "If I were not so poor, and had not so many vexations to encounter, how happy would I be!" But he himself observed that his practice sensibly fell off after the publication of each successive stage of his discovery.

Thus, nearly every enlargement of the domain of knowledge, which has made us better acquainted with the heavens, with the earth, and with ourselves, has been established by the energy, the devotion, the self-sacrifice, and the courage of the great spirits of past times, who, however much they have been opposed or reviled by their contemporaries, now rank amongst those whom the enlightened of the human race most delight to honour.

Nor is the unjust intolerance displayed towards men of science in the past, without its lesson for the present. It teaches us to be forbearant towards those who differ from us, provided they observe patiently, think honestly, and utter their convictions freely and truthfully. It was a remark of Plato, that "the world is God's epistle to mankind; " and to read and study that epistle, so as to elicit its true meaning, can have no other effect on a well- ordered mind than to lead to a deeper impression of His power, a clearer perception of His wisdom, and a more grateful sense of His goodness.

While such has been the courage of the martyrs of science, not less glorious has been the courage of the martyrs of faith. The passive endurance of the man or woman who, for conscience sake, is found ready to suffer and to endure in solitude, without so much as the encouragement of even a single sympathising voice, is an exhibition of courage of a far higher kind than that displayed in the roar of battle, where even the weakest feels encouraged and inspired by the enthusiasm of sympathy and the power of numbers. Time would fail to tell of the deathless names of those who through faith in principles, and in the face of difficulty, danger, and suffering, "have wrought righteousness and waxed valiant" in the moral warfare of the world, and been content to lay down their lives rather than prove false to their conscientious convictions of the truth.

Men of this stamp, inspired by a high sense of duty, have in past times exhibited character in its most heroic aspects, and continue to present to us some of the noblest spectacles to be seen in history. Even women, full of tenderness and gentleness, not less than men, have in this cause been found capable of exhibiting the most unflinching courage. Such, for instance, as that of Anne Askew, who, when racked until her bones were dislocated, uttered no cry, moved no muscle, but looked her tormentors calmly in the face, and refused either to confess or to recant; or such as that of Latimer and Ridley, who, instead of bewailing their hard fate and beating their breasts, went as cheerfully to their death as a bridegroom to the altar—the one bidding the other to "be of good comfort, " for that "we shall this day light such a candle in England, by God's grace, as shall never be put out; " or such, again, as that of Mary Dyer, the Quakeress, hanged by the Puritans of New England for preaching to the people, who ascended the scaffold with a willing step, and, after calmly addressing those who stood about, resigned herself into the hands of her persecutors, and died in peace and joy.

Not less courageous was the behaviour of the good Sir Thomas More, who marched willingly to the scaffold, and died cheerfully there, rather than prove false to his conscience. When More had made his final decision to stand upon his principles, he felt as if he had won a victory, and said to his son-in-law Roper: "Son Roper, I thank Our Lord, the field is won! " The Duke of Norfolk told him of his danger, saying: "By the mass, Master More, it is perilous striving with princes; the anger of a prince brings death! ". "Is that all, my lord? " said More; "then the difference between you and me is this — that I shall die to-day, and you to-morrow. "

While it has been the lot of many great men, in times of difficulty and danger, to be cheered and supported by their wives, More had no such consolation. His helpmate did anything but console him during his imprisonment in the Tower. (4) She could not conceive that there was any sufficient reason for his continuing to lie there, when by merely doing what the King required of him, he might at once enjoy his liberty, together with his fine house at Chelsea, his library, his orchard, his gallery, and the society of his wife and children. "I marvel, " said she to him one day, "that you, who have been alway hitherto taken for wise, should now so play the fool as to lie here in this close filthy prison, and be content to be shut up amongst mice and rats, when you might be abroad at your liberty, if you would but do as the bishops have done? " But More saw his duty from a different point of view: it was not a mere matter of personal comfort with him; and the expostulations of his wife were of no avail. He gently put her aside, saying cheerfully, "Is not this house as nigh heaven as my own? " — to which she contemptuously rejoined: "Tilly vally — tilly vally! "

More's daughter, Margaret Roper, on the contrary, encouraged her father to stand firm in his principles, and dutifully consoled and cheered him during his long confinement. Deprived of pen-and-ink, he wrote his letters to her with a piece of coal, saying in one of them: "If I were to declare in writing how much pleasure your daughterly loving letters gave me, a PECK OF COALS would not suffice to make the pens. " More was a martyr to veracity: he would not swear a false oath; and he perished because he was sincere. When his head had been struck off, it was placed on London Bridge, in accordance with the barbarous practice of the times. Margaret Roper had the courage to ask for the head to be taken down and given to her, and, carrying her affection for her father beyond the grave, she desired that it might be buried with her when she died; and long after, when Margaret Roper's tomb was opened, the precious relic was observed lying on the dust of what had been her bosom.

Martin Luther was not called upon to lay down his life for his faith; but, from the day that he declared himself against the Pope, he daily ran the risk of losing it. At the beginning of his great struggle, he stood almost entirely alone. The odds against him were tremendous. "On one side, " said he himself, "are learning, genius, numbers, grandeur, rank, power, sanctity, miracles; on the other Wycliffe, Lorenzo Valla, Augustine, and Luther—a poor creature, a man of yesterday, standing wellnigh alone with a few friends. " Summoned by the Emperor to appear at Worms; to answer the charge made against him of heresy, he determined to answer in person. Those about him told him that he would lose his life if he went, and they urged him to fly. "No, " said he, "I will repair thither, though I should find there thrice as many devils as there are tiles upon the housetops! " Warned against the bitter enmity of a certain Duke George, he said—"I will go there, though for nine whole days running it rained Duke Georges. "

Luther was as good as his word; and he set forth upon his perilous journey. When he came in sight of the old bell-towers of Worms, he stood up in his chariot and sang, "EIN FESTE BURG IST UNSER GOTT. "—the 'Marseillaise' of the Reformation—the words and music of which he is said to have improvised only two days before. Shortly before the meeting of the Diet, an old soldier, George Freundesberg, put his hand upon Luther's shoulder, and said to him: "Good monk, good monk, take heed what thou doest; thou art going into a harder fight than any of us have ever yet been in. But Luther's only answer to the veteran was, that he had "determined to stand upon the Bible and his conscience. "

Luther's courageous defence before the Diet is on record, and forms one of the most glorious pages in history. When finally urged by the Emperor to retract, he said firmly: "Sire, unless I am convinced of my error by the testimony of Scripture, or by manifest evidence, I cannot and will not retract, for we must never act contrary to our conscience. Such is my profession of faith, and you must expect none other from me. HIER STEHE ICH: ICH KANN NICHT ANDERS: GOTT HELFE MIR! " (Here stand I: I cannot do otherwise: God help me!). He had to do his duty—to obey the orders of a Power higher than that of kings; and he did it at all hazards.

Afterwards, when hard pressed by his enemies at Augsburg, Luther said that "if he had five hundred heads, he would lose them all rather than recant his article concerning faith. " Like all courageous men, his strength only seemed to grow in proportion to the difficulties he had to encounter and overcome. "There is no man in Germany, " said Hutten, "who more utterly despises death than does Luther. " And to his moral courage, perhaps more than to that of any other single man, do we owe the liberation of modern thought, and the vindication of the great rights of the human understanding.

The honourable and brave man does not fear death compared with ignominy. It is said of the Royalist Earl of Strafford that, as he walked to the scaffold on Tower Hill, his step and manner were those of a general marching at the head of an army to secure victory, rather than of a condemned man to undergo sentence of death. So the Commonwealth's man, Sir John Eliot, went alike bravely to his death on the same spot, saying: "Ten thousand deaths rather than defile my conscience, the chastity and purity of which I value beyond all this world. " Eliot's greatest tribulation was on account of his wife, whom he had to leave behind. When he saw her looking down upon him from the Tower window, he stood up in the cart, waved his hat, and cried: "To heaven, my love! —to heaven! —and leave you in the storm! " As he went on his way, one in the crowd called out, "That is the most glorious seat you ever sat on; " to which he replied: "It is so, indeed! " and rejoiced exceedingly. (5)

Although success is the guerdon for which all men toil, they have nevertheless often to labour on perseveringly, without any glimmer of success in sight. They have to live, meanwhile, upon their courage—sowing their seed, it may be, in the dark, in the hope that it will yet take root and spring up in achieved result. The best of causes have had to fight their way to triumph through a long succession of failures, and many of the assailants have died in the breach before the fortress has been won. The heroism they have displayed is to be measured, not so much by their immediate success, as by the opposition they have encountered, and the courage with which they have maintained the struggle.

The patriot who fights an always-losing battle—the martyr who goes to death amidst the triumphant shouts of his enemies—the discoverer, like Columbus, whose heart remains undaunted through the bitter years of his "long wandering woe"—are examples of the moral sublime which excite a profounder interest in the hearts of men than even the most complete and conspicuous success. By the side of such instances as these, how small by comparison seem the greatest deeds of valour, inciting men to rush upon death and die amidst the frenzied excitement of physical warfare!

But the greater part of the courage that is needed in the world is not of a heroic kind. Courage may be displayed in everyday life as well as in historic fields of action. There needs, for example, the common courage to be honest—the courage to resist temptation—the courage to speak the truth—the courage to be what we really are, and not to pretend to be what we are not—the courage to live honestly within our own means, and not dishonestly upon the means of others.

A great deal of the unhappiness, and much of the vice, of the world is owing to weakness and indecision of purpose—in other words, to lack of courage. Men may know what is right, and yet fail to exercise the courage to do it; they may understand the duty they have to do, but will not summon up the requisite resolution to perform it. The weak and undisciplined man is at the mercy of every temptation; he cannot say "No, " but falls before it. And if his companionship be bad, he will be all the easier led away by bad example into wrongdoing.

Nothing can be more certain than that the character can only be sustained and strengthened by its own energetic action. The will, which is the central force of character, must be trained to habits of decision—otherwise it will neither be able to resist evil nor to follow good. Decision gives the power of standing firmly, when to yield, however slightly, might be only the first step in a downhill course to ruin.

Calling upon others for help in forming a decision is worse than useless. A man must so train his habits as to rely upon his own powers and depend upon his own courage in moments of emergency. Plutarch tells of a King of Macedon who, in the midst of an action, withdrew into the adjoining town under pretence of sacrificing to Hercules; whilst his opponent Emilius, at the same time that he implored the Divine aid, sought for victory sword in hand, and won the battle. And so it ever is in the actions of daily life.

Many are the valiant purposes formed, that end merely in words; deeds intended, that are never done; designs projected, that are never begun; and all for want of a little courageous decision. Better far the silent tongue but the eloquent deed. For in life and in business, despatch is better than discourse; and the shortest answer of all is, DOING. "In matters of great concern, and which must be done, " says Tillotson, "there is no surer argument of a weak mind than irresolution—to be undetermined when the case is so plain and the necessity so urgent. To be always intending to live a new life, but never to find time to set about it, —this is as if a man should put off eating and drinking and sleeping from one day to another, until he is starved and destroyed. "

There needs also the exercise of no small degree of moral courage to resist the corrupting influences of what is called "Society. " Although "Mrs. Grundy" may be a very vulgar and commonplace personage, her influence is nevertheless prodigious. Most men, but especially women, are the moral slaves of the class or caste to which they belong. There is a sort of unconscious conspiracy existing amongst them against each other's individuality. Each circle and section, each rank and class, has its respective customs and observances, to which conformity is required at the risk of being tabooed. Some are immured within a bastile of fashion, others of custom, others of opinion; and few there are who have the courage to think outside their sect, to act outside their party, and to step out into the free air of individual thought and action. We dress, and eat, and follow fashion, though it may be at the risk of debt, ruin, and misery; living not so much according to our means, as according to the superstitious observances of our class. Though we may speak contemptuously of the Indians who flatten their heads, and of the Chinese who cramp their toes, we have only to look at the deformities of fashion amongst ourselves, to see that the reign of "Mrs. Grundy" is universal.

But moral cowardice is exhibited quite as much in public as in private life. Snobbism is not confined to the toadying of the rich, but is quite as often displayed in the toadying of the poor. Formerly, sycophancy showed itself in not daring to speak the truth to those in high places; but in these days it rather shows itself in not daring to speak the truth to those in low places. Now that "the masses" (6) exercise political power, there is a growing tendency to fawn upon them, to flatter them, and to speak nothing but smooth words to them. They are credited with virtues which they themselves know they do not possess. The public enunciation of wholesome because disagreeable truths is avoided; and, to win their favour, sympathy is often pretended for views, the carrying out of which in practice is known to be hopeless.

It is not the man of the noblest character—the highest-cultured and best-conditioned man—whose favour is now sought, so much as that of the lowest man, the least-cultured and worst-conditioned man, because his vote is usually that of the majority. Even men of rank, wealth, and education, are seen prostrating themselves before the ignorant, whose votes are thus to be got. They are ready to be unprincipled and unjust rather than unpopular. It is so much easier for some men to stoop, to bow, and to flatter, than to be manly, resolute, and magnanimous; and to yield to prejudices than run counter to them. It requires strength and courage to swim against the stream, while any dead fish can float with it.

This servile pandering to popularity has been rapidly on the increase of late years, and its tendency has been to lower and degrade the character of public men. Consciences have become more elastic. There is now one opinion for the chamber, and another for the platform. Prejudices are pandered to in public, which in private are despised. Pretended conversions—which invariably jump with party interests are more sudden; and even hypocrisy now appears to be scarcely thought discreditable.

The same moral cowardice extends downwards as well as upwards. The action and reaction are equal. Hypocrisy and timeserving above are accompanied by hypocrisy and timeserving below. Where men of high standing have not the courage of their opinions, what is to be expected from men of low standing? They will only follow such examples as are set before them. They too will skulk, and dodge, and prevaricate—be ready to speak one way and act another —just like their betters. Give them but a sealed box, or some hole-and-corner to hide their act in, and they will then enjoy their "liberty! "

Popularity, as won in these days, is by no means a presumption in a man's favour, but is quite as often a presumption against him. "No man, " says the Russian proverb, "can rise to honour who is cursed with a stiff backbone. " But the backbone of the popularity-hunter is of gristle; and he has no difficulty in stooping and bending himself in any direction to catch the breath of popular applause.

Where popularity is won by fawning upon the people, by withholding the truth from them, by writing and speaking down to the lowest tastes, and still worse by appeals to class-hatred, (7) such a popularity must be simply contemptible in the sight of all honest men. Jeremy Bentham, speaking of a well-known public character, said: "His creed of politics results less from love of the many than from hatred of the few; it is too much under the influence of selfish and dissocial affection. " To how many men in our own day might not the same description apply?

Men of sterling character have the courage to speak the truth, even when it is unpopular. It was said of Colonel Hutchinson by his wife, that he never sought after popular applause, or prided himself on it: "He more delighted to do well than to be praised, and never set vulgar commendations at such a rate as to act contrary to his own conscience or reason for the obtaining them; nor would he forbear a good action which he was bound to, though all the world disliked it; for he ever looked on things as they were in themselves, not through the dim spectacles of vulgar estimation. " (8)

"Popularity, in the lowest and most common sense, " said Sir John Pakington, on a recent occasion, (9) "is not worth the having. Do your duty to the best of your power, win the approbation of your own conscience, and popularity, in its best and highest sense, is sure to follow. "

When Richard Lovell Edgeworth, towards the close of his life, became very popular in his neighbourhood, he said one day to his daughter: "Maria, I am growing dreadfully popular; I shall be good for nothing soon; a man cannot be good for anything who is very popular. " Probably he had in his mind at the time the Gospel curse of the popular man, "Woe unto you, when all men shall speak well of you! for so did their fathers to the false prophets. "

Intellectual intrepidity is one of the vital conditions of independence and self-reliance of character. A man must have the courage to be himself, and not the shadow or the echo of another. He must exercise his own powers, think his own thoughts, and speak his own sentiments. He must elaborate his own opinions, and form his own convictions. It has been said that he who dare not form an opinion, must be a coward; he who will not, must be an idler; he who cannot, must be a fool.

But it is precisely in this element of intrepidity that so many persons of promise fall short, and disappoint the expectations of their friends. They march up to the scene of action, but at every step their courage oozes out. They want the requisite decision, courage, and perseverance. They calculate the risks, and weigh the chances, until the opportunity for effective effort has passed, it may be never to return.

Men are bound to speak the truth in the love of it. "I had rather suffer, " said John Pym, the Commonwealth man, "for speaking the truth, than that the truth should suffer for want of my speaking. " When a man's convictions are honestly formed, after fair and full consideration, he is justified in striving by all fair means to bring them into action. There are certain states of society and conditions of affairs in which a man is bound to speak out, and be antagonistic — when conformity is not only a weakness, but a sin. Great evils are in some cases only to be met by resistance; they cannot be wept down, but must be battled down.

The honest man is naturally antagonistic to fraud, the truthful man to lying, the justice-loving man to oppression, the pureminded man to vice and iniquity. They have to do battle with these conditions, and if possible overcome them. Such men have in all ages represented the moral force of the world. Inspired by benevolence and sustained by courage, they have been the mainstays of all social renovation and progress. But for their continuous antagonism to evil conditions, the world were for the most part given over to the dominion of selfishness and vice. All the great reformers and martyrs were antagonistic men — enemies to falsehood and evildoing. The Apostles themselves were an organised band of social antagonists, who contended with pride, selfishness, superstition, and irreligion. And in our own time the lives of such men as Clarkson and Granville Sharpe, Father Mathew and Richard Cobden, inspired by singleness of purpose, have shown what highminded social antagonism can effect.

It is the strong and courageous men who lead and guide and rule the world. The weak and timid leave no trace behind them; whilst the life of a single upright and energetic man is like a track of light. His example is remembered and appealed to; and his thoughts, his spirit, and his courage continue to be the inspiration of succeeding generations.

It is energy — the central element of which is will — that produces the miracles of enthusiasm in all ages. Everywhere it is the mainspring of what is called force of character, and the sustaining power of all great action. In a righteous cause the determined man stands upon his courage as upon a granite block; and, like David, he will go forth to meet Goliath, strong in heart though an host be encamped against him.

Men often conquer difficulties because they feel they can. Their confidence in themselves inspires the confidence of others. When Caesar was at sea, and a storm began to rage, the captain of the ship which carried him became unmanned by fear. "What art thou afraid of? " cried the great captain; "thy vessel carries Caesar! " The courage of the brave man is contagious, and carries others along with it. His stronger nature awes weaker natures into silence, or inspires them with his own will and purpose.

The persistent man will not be baffled or repulsed by opposition. Diogenes, desirous of becoming the disciple of Antisthenes, went and offered himself to the cynic. He was refused. Diogenes still persisting, the cynic raised his knotty staff, and threatened to strike him if he did not depart. "Strike! " said Diogenes; "you will not find a stick hard enough to conquer my perseverance. " Antisthenes, overcome, had not another word to say, but forthwith accepted him as his pupil.

Energy of temperament, with a moderate degree of wisdom, will carry a man further than any amount of intellect without it. Energy makes the man of practical ability. It gives him VIS, force, MOMENTUM. It is the active motive power of character; and if combined with sagacity and self-possession, will enable a man to employ his powers to the best advantage in all the affairs of life.

Hence it is that, inspired by energy of purpose, men of comparatively mediocre powers have often been enabled to accomplish such extraordinary results. For the men who have most powerfully influenced the world have not been so much men of genius as men of strong convictions and enduring capacity for work, impelled by irresistible energy and invincible determination: such men, for example, as were Mahomet, Luther, Knox, Calvin, Loyola, and Wesley.

Courage, combined with energy and perseverance, will overcome difficulties apparently insurmountable. It gives force and impulse to effort, and does not permit it to retreat. Tyndall said of Faraday, that "in his warm moments he formed a resolution, and in his cool ones he made that resolution good. " Perseverance, working in the right direction, grows with time, and when steadily practised, even by the most humble, will rarely fail of its reward. Trusting in the help of others is of comparatively little use. When one of Michael Angelo's principal patrons died, he said: "I begin to understand that the promises of the world are for the most part vain phantoms, and that to confide in one's self, and become something of worth and value, is the best and safest course. "

Courage is by no means incompatible with tenderness. On the contrary, gentleness and tenderness have been found to characterise the men, not less than the women, who have done the most courageous deeds. Sir Charles Napier gave up sporting, because he could not bear to hurt dumb creatures. The same gentleness and tenderness characterised his brother, Sir William, the historian of the Peninsular War. (10) Such also was the character of Sir James Outram, pronounced by Sir Charles Napier to be "the Bayard of India, SANS PEUR ET SANS REPROCHE"—one of the bravest and yet gentlest of men; respectful and reverent to women, tender to children, helpful of the weak, stern to the corrupt, but kindly as summer to the honest and deserving. Moreover, he was himself as honest as day, and as pure as virtue. Of him it might be said with truth, what Fulke Greville said of Sidney: "He was a true model of worth—a man fit for conquest, reformation, plantation, or what action soever is the greatest and hardest among men; his chief ends withal being above all things the good of his fellows, and the service of his sovereign and country. "

When Edward the Black Prince won the Battle of Poictiers, in which he took prisoner the French king and his son, he entertained them in the evening at a banquet, when he insisted on waiting upon and serving them at table. The gallant prince's knightly courtesy and demeanour won the hearts of his captives as completely as his valour had won their persons; for, notwithstanding his youth, Edward was a true knight, the first and bravest of his time—a noble pattern and example of chivalry; his two mottoes, 'Hochmuth' and 'Ich dien' (high spirit and reverent service) not inaptly expressing his prominent and pervading qualities.

It is the courageous man who can best afford to be generous; or rather, it is his nature to be so. When Fairfax, at the Battle of Naseby, seized the colours from an ensign whom he had struck down in the fight, he handed them to a common soldier to take care of. The soldier, unable to resist the temptation, boasted to his comrades that he had himself seized the colours, and the boast was repeated to

Fairfax. "Let him retain the honour, " said the commander; "I have enough beside. "

So when Douglas, at the Battle of Bannockburn, saw Randolph, his rival, outnumbered and apparently overpowered by the enemy, he prepared to hasten to his assistance; but, seeing that Randolph was already driving them back, he cried out, "Hold and halt! We are come too late to aid them; let us not lessen the victory they have won by affecting to claim a share in it. "

Quite as chivalrous, though in a very different field of action, was the conduct of Laplace to the young philosopher Biot, when the latter had read to the French Academy his paper, "SUR LES EQUATIONS AUX DIFFERENCE MELEES. " The assembled SAVANS, at its close, felicitated the reader of the paper on his originality. Monge was delighted at his success. Laplace also praised him for the clearness of his demonstrations, and invited Biot to accompany him home. Arrived there, Laplace took from a closet in his study a paper, yellow with age, and handed it to the young philosopher. To Biot's surprise, he found that it contained the solutions, all worked out, for which he had just gained so much applause. With rare magnanimity, Laplace withheld all knowledge of the circumstance from Biot until the latter had initiated his reputation before the Academy; moreover, he enjoined him to silence; and the incident would have remained a secret had not Biot himself published it, some fifty years afterwards.

An incident is related of a French artisan, exhibiting the same characteristic of self-sacrifice in another form. In front of a lofty house in course of erection at Paris was the usual scaffold, loaded with men and materials. The scaffold, being too weak, suddenly broke down, and the men upon it were precipitated to the ground — all except two, a young man and a middle-aged one, who hung on to a narrow ledge, which trembled under their weight, and was evidently on the point of giving way. "Pierre, " cried the elder of the two, "let go; I am the father of a family. " "C'EST JUSTE! " said Pierre; and, instantly letting go his hold, he fell and was killed on the spot. The father of the family was saved.

The brave man is magnanimous as well as gentle. He does not take even an enemy at a disadvantage, nor strike a man when he is down and unable to defend himself. Even in the midst of deadly strife such instances of generosity have not been uncommon. Thus, at the Battle of Dettingen, during the heat of the action, a squadron of French cavalry charged an English regiment; but when the young French officer who led them, and was about to attack the English leader, observed that he had only one arm, with which he held his bridle, the Frenchman saluted him courteously with his sword, and passed on. (11)

It is related of Charles V., that after the siege and capture of Wittenburg by the Imperialist army, the monarch went to see the tomb of Luther. While reading the inscription on it, one of the servile courtiers who accompanied him proposed to open the grave, and give the ashes of the "heretic" to the winds. The monarch's cheek flushed with honest indignation: "I war not with the dead, " said he; "let this place be respected. "

The portrait which the great heathen, Aristotle, drew of the Magnanimous Man, in other words the True Gentleman, more than two thousand years ago, is as faithful now as it was then. "The magnanimous man, " he said, "will behave with moderation under both good fortune and bad. He will know how to be exalted and how to be abased. He will neither be delighted with success nor grieved by failure. He will neither shun danger nor seek it, for there are few things which he cares for. He is reticent, and somewhat slow of speech, but speaks his mind openly and boldly when occasion calls for it. He is apt to admire, for nothing is great to him. He overlooks injuries. He is not given to talk about himself or about others; for he does not care that he himself should be praised, or that other people should be blamed. He does not cry out about trifles, and craves help from none. "

On the other hand, mean men admire meanly. They have neither modesty, generosity, nor magnanimity. They are ready to take advantage of the weakness or defencelessness of others, especially where they have themselves succeeded, by unscrupulous methods, in climbing to positions of authority. Snobs in high places are always much less tolerable than snobs of low degree, because they have more frequent opportunities of making their want of manliness felt. They assume greater airs, and are pretentious in all that they do; and the higher their elevation, the more conspicuous is the incongruity of their position. "The higher the monkey climbs, " says the proverb, "the more he shows his tail. "

Much depends on the way in which a thing is done. An act which might be taken as a kindness if done in a generous spirit, when done in a grudging spirit, may be felt as stingy, if not harsh and even cruel. When Ben Jonson lay sick and in poverty, the king sent him a paltry message, accompanied by a gratuity. The sturdy plainspoken poet's reply was: "I suppose he sends me this because I live in an alley; tell him his soul lives in an alley. "

From what we have said, it will be obvious that to be of an enduring and courageous spirit, is of great importance in the formation of character. It is a source not only of usefulness in life, but of happiness. On the other hand, to be of a timid and, still more, of a cowardly nature is one of the greatest misfortunes. A. wise man was accustomed to say that one of the principal objects he aimed at in the education of his sons and daughters was to train them in the habit of fearing nothing so much as fear. And the habit of avoiding fear is, doubtless, capable of being trained like any other habit, such as the habit of attention, of diligence, of study, or of cheerfulness.

Much of the fear that exists is the offspring of imagination, which creates the images of evils which MAY happen, but perhaps rarely do; and thus many persons who are capable of summoning up courage to grapple with and overcome real dangers, are paralysed or thrown into consternation by those which are imaginary. Hence, unless the imagination be held under strict discipline, we are prone to meet evils more than halfway—to suffer them by forestalment, and to assume the burdens which we ourselves create.

Education in courage is not usually included amongst the branches of female training, and yet it is really of greater importance than either music, French, or the use of the globes. Contrary to the view of Sir Richard Steele, that women should be characterised by a "tender fear, " and "an inferiority which makes her lovely, " we would have women educated in resolution and courage, as a means of rendering them more helpful, more self-reliant, and vastly more useful and happy.

There is, indeed, nothing attractive in timidity, nothing loveable in fear. All weakness, whether of mind or body, is equivalent to deformity, and the reverse of interesting. Courage is graceful and dignified, whilst fear, in any form, is mean and repulsive. Yet the utmost tenderness and gentleness are consistent with courage. Ary Scheffer, the artist, once wrote to his daughter: - "Dear daughter, strive to be of good courage, to be gentle- hearted; these are the true qualities for woman. 'Troubles' everybody must expect. There is but one way of looking at fate— whatever that be, whether blessings or afflictions—to behave with dignity under both. We must not lose heart, or it will be the worse both for ourselves and for those whom we love. To struggle, and again and again to renew the conflict — THIS is life's inheritance. " (12)

In sickness and sorrow, none are braver and less complaining sufferers than women. Their courage, where their hearts are concerned, is indeed proverbial:

"Oh! femmes c'est a tort qu'on vous nommes timides,
A la voix de vos coeurs vous etes intrepides."

Experience has proved that women can be as enduring as men, under the heaviest trials and calamities; but too little pains are taken to teach them to endure petty terrors and frivolous vexations with fortitude. Such little miseries, if petted and indulged, quickly run into sickly sensibility, and become the bane of their life, keeping themselves and those about them in a state of chronic discomfort.

The best corrective of this condition of mind is wholesome moral and mental discipline. Mental strength is as necessary for the development of woman's character as of man's. It gives her capacity to deal with the affairs of life, and presence of mind, which enable her to act with vigour and effect in moments of emergency. Character, in a woman, as in a man, will always be found the best safeguard of virtue, the best nurse of religion, the best corrective of Time. Personal beauty soon passes; but beauty of mind and character increases in attractiveness the older it grows.

Ben Jonson gives a striking portraiture of a noble woman in these lines: -

"I meant she should be courteous, facile, sweet,
  Free from that solemn vice of greatness, pride;
I meant each softed virtue there should meet,
  Fit in that softer bosom to abide.
Only a learned and a manly soul,
  I purposed her, that should with even powers,
The rock, the spindle, and the shears control
  Of destiny, and spin her own free hours.'

The courage of woman is not the less true because it is for the most part passive. It is not encouraged by the cheers of the world, for it is mostly exhibited in the recesses of private life. Yet there are cases of heroic patience and endurance on the part of women which occasionally come to the light of day. One of the most celebrated instances in history is that of Gertrude Von der Wart. Her husband, falsely accused of being an accomplice in the murder of the Emperor Albert, was condemned to the most frightful of all punishments — to be broken alive on the wheel. With most profound conviction of her husband's innocence the faithful woman stood by his side to the last, watching over him during two days and nights, braving the empress's anger and the inclemency of the weather, in the hope of contributing to soothe his dying agonies. (13)

But women have not only distinguished themselves for their passive courage: impelled by affection, or the sense of duty, they have occasionally become heroic. When the band of conspirators, who sought the life of James II. of Scotland, burst into his lodgings at Perth, the king called to the ladies, who were in the chamber outside his room, to keep the door as well as they could, and give him time to escape. The conspirators had previously destroyed the locks of the doors, so that the keys could not be turned; and when they reached the ladies' apartment, it was found that the bar also had been removed. But, on hearing them approach, the brave Catherine Douglas, with the hereditary courage of her family, boldly thrust her arm across the door instead of the bar; and held it there until, her arm being broken, the conspirators burst into the room with drawn swords and daggers, overthrowing the ladies, who, though unarmed, still endeavoured to resist them.

The defence of Lathom House by Charlotte de la Tremouille, the worthy descendant of William of Nassau and Admiral Coligny, was another striking instance of heroic bravery on the part of a noble woman. When summoned by the Parliamentary forces to surrender, she declared that she had been entrusted by her husband with the defence of the house, and that she could not give it up without her dear lord's orders, but trusted in God for protection and deliverance. In her arrangements for the defence, she is described as having "left nothing with her eye to be excused afterwards by fortune or negligence, and added to her former patience a most resolved fortitude. " The brave lady held her house and home good against the enemy for a whole year — during three months of which the place was strictly besieged and bombarded — until at length the siege was raised, after a most gallant defence, by the advance of the Royalist army.

Nor can we forget the courage of Lady Franklin, who persevered to the last, when the hopes of all others had died out, in prosecuting the search after the Franklin Expedition. On the occasion of the Royal Geographical Society determining to award the Founder's Medal to Lady Franklin, Sir Roderick Murchison observed, that in the course of a long friendship with her, he had abundant opportunities of observing and testing the sterling qualities of a woman who had proved herself worthy of the admiration of mankind. "Nothing daunted by failure after failure, through twelve long years of hope deferred, she had persevered, with a singleness of purpose and a sincere devotion which were truly unparalleled. And now that her one last expedition of the FOX, under the gallant M'Clintock, had realised the two great facts—that her husband had traversed wide seas unknown to former navigators, and died in discovering a north-west passage—then, surely, the adjudication of the medal would be hailed by the nation as one of the many recompences to which the widow of the illustrious Franklin was so eminently entitled. "

But that devotion to duty which marks the heroic character has more often been exhibited by women in deeds of charity and mercy. The greater part of these are never known, for they are done in private, out of the public sight, and for the mere love of doing good. Where fame has come to them, because of the success which has attended their labours in a more general sphere, it has come unsought and unexpected, and is often felt as a burden. Who has not heard of Mrs. Fry and Miss Carpenter as prison visitors and reformers; of Mrs. Chisholm and Miss Rye as promoters of emigration; and of Miss Nightingale and Miss Garrett as apostles of hospital nursing?

That these women should have emerged from the sphere of private and domestic life to become leaders in philanthropy, indicates no small, degree of moral courage on their part; for to women, above all others, quiet and ease and retirement are most natural and welcome. Very few women step beyond the boundaries of home in search of a larger field of usefulness. But when they have desired one, they have had no difficulty in finding it. The ways in which men and women can help their neighbours are innumerable. It needs but the willing heart and ready hand. Most of the philanthropic workers we have named, however, have scarcely been influenced by choice. The duty lay in their way—it seemed to be the nearest to them—and they set about doing it without desire for fame, or any other reward but the approval of their own conscience.

Among prison-visitors, the name of Sarah Martin is much less known than that of Mrs. Fry, although she preceded her in the work. How she was led to undertake it, furnishes at the same time an illustration of womanly trueheartedness and earnest womanly courage.

Sarah Martin was the daughter of poor parents, and was left an orphan at an early age. She was brought up by her grandmother, at Caistor, near Yarmouth, and earned her living by going out to families as assistant-dressmaker, at a shilling a day. In 1819, a woman was tried and sentenced to imprisonment in Yarmouth Gaol, for cruelly beating and illusing her child, and her crime became the talk of the town. The young dressmaker was much impressed by the report of the trial, and the desire entered her mind of visiting the woman in gaol, and trying to reclaim her. She had often before, on passing the walls of the borough gaol, felt impelled to seek admission, with the object of visiting the inmates, reading the Scriptures to them, and endeavouring to lead them back to the society whose laws they had violated.

At length she could not resist her impulse to visit the mother. She entered the gaol-porch, lifted the knocker, and asked the gaoler for admission. For some reason or other she was refused; but she returned, repeated her request, and this time she was admitted. The culprit mother shortly stood before her. When Sarah Martin told the motive of her visit, the criminal burst into tears, and thanked her. Those tears and thanks shaped the whole course of Sarah Martin's after-life; and the poor seamstress, while maintaining herself by her needle, continued to spend her leisure hours in visiting the prisoners, and endeavouring to alleviate their condition. She constituted herself their chaplain and schoolmistress, for at that time they had neither; she read to them from the Scriptures, and taught them to read and write. She gave up an entire day in the week for this purpose, besides Sundays, as well as other intervals of spare time, "feeling, " she says, "that the blessing of God was upon her. " She taught the women to knit, to sew, and to cut out; the sale of the articles enabling her to buy other materials, and to continue the industrial education thus begun. She also taught the men to make straw hats, men's and boys' caps, gray cotton shirts, and even patchwork—anything to keep them out of idleness, and from preying on their own thoughts. Out of the earnings of the prisoners in this way, she formed a fund, which she applied to furnishing them with work on their discharge; thus enabling them again to begin the world honestly, and at the same time affording her, as she herself says, "the advantage of observing their conduct. "

By attending too exclusively to this prison-work, however, Sarah Martin's dressmaking business fell off; and the question arose with her, whether in order to recover her business she was to suspend her prison-work. But her decision had already been made. "I had counted the cost, " she said, "and my mind, was made up. If, whilst imparting truth to others, I became exposed to temporal want, the privations so momentary to an individual would not admit of comparison with following the Lord, in thus administering to others." She now devoted six or seven hours every day to the prisoners, converting what would otherwise have been a scene of dissolute idleness into a hive of orderly industry. Newly- admitted prisoners were sometimes refractory, but her persistent gentleness eventually won their respect and co-operation. Men old in years and crime, pert London pickpockets, depraved boys and dissolute sailors, profligate women, smugglers, poachers, and the promiscuous horde of criminals which usually fill the gaol of a seaport and county town, all submitted to the benign influence of this good woman; and under her eyes they might be seen, for the first time in their lives, striving to hold a pen, or to master the characters in a penny primer. She entered into their confidences — watched, wept, prayed, and felt for all by turns. She strengthened their good resolutions, cheered the hopeless and despairing, and endeavoured to put all, and hold all, in the right road of amendment.

For more than twenty years this good and truehearted woman pursued her noble course, with little encouragement, and not much help; almost her only means of subsistence consisting in an annual income of ten or twelve pounds left by her grandmother, eked out by her little earnings at dressmaking. During the last two years of her ministrations, the borough magistrates of Yarmouth, knowing that her self-imposed labours saved them the expense of a schoolmaster and chaplain (which they had become bound by law to appoint), made a proposal to her of an annual salary of œ12 a year; but they did it in so indelicate a manner as greatly to wound her sensitive feelings. She shrank from becoming the salaried official of the corporation, and bartering for money those serviced which had throughout been labours of love. But the Gaol Committee coarsely informed her, "that if they permitted her to visit the prison she must submit to their terms, or be excluded. " For two years, therefore, she received the salary of œ12 a year—the acknowledgment of the Yarmouth corporation for her services as gaol chaplain and schoolmistress! She was now, however, becoming old and infirm, and the unhealthy atmosphere of the gaol did much towards finally disabling her. While she lay on her deathbed, she resumed the exercise of a talent she had occasionally practised before in her moments of leisure—the composition of sacred poetry. As works of art, they may not excite admiration; yet never were verses written truer in spirit, or fuller of Christian love. But her own life was a nobler poem than any she ever wrote—full of true courage, perseverance, charity, and wisdom. It was indeed a commentary upon her own words:

"The high desire that others may be blest
Savours of heaven."

NOTES

(1) James Russell Lowell.

(2) Yet Bacon himself had written, "I would rather believe all the faiths in the Legend, and the Talmud, and the Alcoran, than that this universal frame is without a mind. "

(3) Aubrey, in his 'Natural History of Wiltshire, ' alluding to Harvey, says: "He told me himself that upon publishing that book he fell in his practice extremely. "

(4) Sir Thomas More's first wife, Jane Colt, was originally a young country girl, whom he himself instructed in letters, and moulded to his own tastes and manners. She died young, leaving a son and three daughters, of whom the noble Margaret Roper most resembled More himself. His second wife was Alice Middleton, a widow, some seven years older than More, not beautiful—for he characterized her as "NEC BELLA, NEC PUELLA"—but a shrewd worldly woman, not by any means disposed to sacrifice comfort and good cheer for considerations such as those which so powerfully influenced the mind of her husband.

(5)Before being beheaded, Eliot said, "Death is but a little word; but "tis a great work to die. '" In his 'Prison Thoughts' before his execution, he wrote: "He that fears not to die, fears nothing.... There is a time to live, and a time to die. A good death is far better and more eligible than an ill life. A wise man lives but so long as his life is worth more than his death. The longer life is not always the better."

(6) Mr. J. S. Mill, in his book 'On Liberty, ' describes "the masses, " as "collective mediocrity. " "The initiation of all wise or noble things, " he says, "comes, and must come, from individuals— generally at first from some one individual. The honour and glory of the average man is that he is capable of following that imitation; that he can respond internally to wise and noble things, and be led to them with his eyes open.... In this age, the mere example of nonconformity, the mere refusal to bend the knee to custom, is itself a service. Precisely because the tyranny of opinion is such as to make eccentricity a reproach, it is desirable, in order to break through that tyranny, that people should be eccentric. Eccentricity has always abounded when and where strength of character has abounded; and the amount of eccentricity in a society has generally been proportional to the amount of genius, mental vigour, and moral courage which it contained. That so few now dare to be eccentric, marks the chief danger of the time. "—Pp. 120-1.

(7) Mr. Arthur Helps, in one of his thoughtful books, published in 1845, made some observations on this point, which are not less applicable now. He there said: "it is a grievous thing to see literature made a vehicle for encouraging the enmity of class to class. Yet this, unhappily, is not unfrequent now. Some great man summed up the nature of French novels by calling them the Literature of Despair; the kind of writing that I deprecate may be called the Literature of Envy.... Such writers like to throw their influence, as they might say, into the weaker scale. But that is not the proper way of looking at the matter. I think, if they saw the ungenerous nature of their proceedings, that alone would stop them. They should recollect that literature may fawn upon the masses as well as the aristocracy; and in these days the temptation is in the former direction. But what is most grievous in this kind of writing is the mischief it may do to the working- people themselves. If you have their true welfare at heart, you will not only care for their being fed and clothed, but you will be anxious not to encourage unreasonable expectations in them— not to make them ungrateful or greedy-minded. Above all, you will be solicitous to preserve some self-reliance in them. You will be careful not to let them think that their condition can be wholly changed

without exertion of their own. You would not desire to have it so changed. Once elevate your ideal of what you wish to happen amongst the labouring population, and you will not easily admit anything in your writings that may injure their moral or their mental character, even if you thought it might hasten some physical benefit for them. That is the way to make your genius most serviceable to mankind. Depend upon it, honest and bold things require to be said to the lower as well as the higher classes; and the former are in these times much less likely to have, such things addressed to them. "-Claims of Labour, pp. 253-4.

(8) 'Memoirs of Colonel Hutchinson' (Bohn's Ed.), p. 32.

(9) At a public meeting held at Worcester, in 1867, in recognition of Sir J. Pakington's services as Chairman of Quarter Sessions for a period of twenty-four years, the following remarks, made by Sir John on the occasion, are just and valuable as they are modest: - "I am indebted for whatever measure of success I have attained in my public life, to a combination of moderate abilities, with honesty of intention, firmness of purpose, and steadiness of conduct. If I were to offer advice to any young man anxious to make himself useful in public life, I would sum up the results of my experience in three short rules—rules so simple that any man may understand them, and so easy that any man may act upon them. My first rule would be—leave it to others to judge of what duties you are capable, and for what position you are fitted; but never refuse to give your services in whatever capacity it may be the opinion of others who are competent to judge that you may benefit your neighbours or your country. My second rule is—when you agree to undertake public duties, concentrate every energy and faculty in your possession with the determination to discharge those duties to the best of your ability. Lastly, I would counsel you that, in deciding on the line which you will take in public affairs, you should be guided in your decision by that which, after mature deliberation, you believe to be right, and not by that which, in the passing hour, may happen to be fashionable or popular. "

(10) The following illustration of one of his minute acts of kindness is given in his biography: - "He was one day taking a long country walk near Freshford, when he met a little girl, about five years old, sobbing over a broken bowl; she had dropped and broken it in bringing it back from the field to which she had taken her father's dinner in it, and she said she would be beaten on her return home

for having broken it; when, with a sudden gleam of hope, she innocently looked up into his face, and said, 'But yee can mend it, can't ee? '

"My father explained that he could not mend the bowl, but the trouble he could, by the gift of a sixpence to buy another. However, on opening his purse it was empty of silver, and he had to make amends by promising to meet his little friend in the same spot at the same hour next day, and to bring the sixpence with him, bidding her, meanwhile, tell her mother she had seen a gentleman who would bring her the money for the bowl next day. The child, entirely trusting him, went on her way comforted. On his return home he found an invitation awaiting him to dine in Bath the following evening, to meet some one whom he specially wished to see. He hesitated for some little time, trying to calculate the possibility of giving the meeting to his little friend of the broken bowl and of still being in time for the dinner-party in Bath; but finding this could not be, he wrote to decline accepting the invitation on the plea of 'a pre-engagement, ' saying to us, 'I cannot disappoint her, she trusted me so implicitly. '"

(11) Miss Florence Nightingale has related the following incident as having occurred before Sebastopol: - "I remember a sergeant who, on picket, the rest of the picket killed and himself battered about the head, stumbled back to camp, and on his way picked up a wounded man and brought him in on his shoulders to the lines, where he fell down insensible. When, after many hours, he recovered his senses, I believe after trepanning, his first words were to ask after his comrade, 'Is he alive? ' 'Comrade, indeed; yes, he's alive—it is the general. ' At that moment the general, though badly wounded, appeared at the bedside. 'Oh, general, it's you, is it, I brought in? I'm so glad; I didn't know your honour. But, —-, if I'd known it was you, I'd have saved you all the same. ' This is the true soldier's spirit. "

In the same letter, Miss Nightingale says: "England, from her grand mercantile and commercial successes, has been called sordid; God knows she is not. The simple courage, the enduring patience, the good sense, the strength to suffer in silence—what nation shows more of this in war than is shown by her commonest soldier? I have seen men dying of dysentery, but scorning to report themselves sick lest they should thereby throw more labour on their comrades, go down to the trenches and make the trenches their deathbed. There is nothing in history to compare with it....

Say what men will, there is something more truly Christian in the man who gives his time, his strength, his life, if need be, for something not himself—whether he call it his Queen, his country, or his colours—than in all the asceticism, the fasts, the humiliations, and confessions which have ever been made: and this spirit of giving one's life, without calling it a sacrifice, is found nowhere so truly as in England. "

(12) Mrs. Grote's 'Life of Ary Scheffer, ' pp. 154-5.

(13) The sufferings of this noble woman, together with those of her unfortunate husband, were touchingly described in a letter afterwards addressed by her to a female friend, which was published some years ago at Haarlem, entitled, 'Gertrude von der Wart; or, Fidelity unto Death. ' Mrs. Hemans wrote a poem of great pathos and beauty, commemorating the sad story in her 'Records of Woman. '

CHAPTER VI. —SELF-CONTROL.

"Honour and profit do not always lie in the same sack. "—GEORGE HERBERT.

"The government of one's self is the only true freedom for the Individual. "—FREDERICK PERTHES.

"It is in length of patience, and endurance, and forbearance, that so much of what is good in mankind and womankind is shown. "— ARTHUR HELPS.

> "Temperance, proof
> Against all trials; industry severe
> And constant as the motion of the day;
> Stern self-denial round him spread, with shade
> That might be deemed forbidding, did not there
> All generous feelings flourish and rejoice;
> Forbearance, charity indeed and thought,
> And resolution competent to take
> Out of the bosom of simplicity
> All that her holy customs recommend." —WORDSWORTH.

Self-control is only courage under another form. It may almost be regarded as the primary essence of character. It is in virtue of this quality that Shakspeare defines man as a being "looking before and after. " It forms the chief distinction between man and the mere animal; and, indeed, there can be no true manhood without it.

Self-control is at the root of all the virtues. Let a man give the reins to his impulses and passions, and from that moment he yields up his moral freedom. He is carried along the current of life, and becomes the slave of his strongest desire for the time being.

To be morally free—to be more than an animal—man must be able to resist instinctive impulse, and this can only be done by the exercise of self-control. Thus it is this power which constitutes the real distinction between a physical and a moral life, and that forms the primary basis of individual character.

In the Bible praise is given, not to the strong man who "taketh a city, " but to the stronger man who "ruleth his own spirit. " This stronger man is he who, by discipline, exercises a constant control over his thoughts, his speech, and his acts. Nine-tenths of the vicious desires that degrade society, and which, when indulged, swell into the crimes that disgrace it, would shrink into insignificance before the advance of valiant self-discipline, self-respect, and self-control. By the watchful exercise of these virtues, purity of heart and mind become habitual, and the character is built up in chastity, virtue, and temperance.

The best support of character will always be found in habit, which, according as the will is directed rightly or wrongly, as the case may be, will prove either a benignant ruler or a cruel despot. We may be its willing subject on the one hand, or its servile slave on the other. It may help us on the road to good, or it may hurry us on the road to ruin.

Habit is formed by careful training. And it is astonishing how much can be accomplished by systematic discipline and drill. See how, for instance, out of the most unpromising materials—such as roughs picked up in the streets, or raw unkempt country lads taken from the plough—steady discipline and drill will bring out the unsuspected qualities of courage, endurance, and self-sacrifice; and how, in the field of battle, or even on the more trying occasions of perils by sea— such as the burning of the SARAH SANDS or the wreck of the BIRKENHEAD—such men, carefully disciplined, will exhibit the unmistakable characteristics of true bravery and heroism!

Nor is moral discipline and drill less influential in the formation of character. Without it, there will be no proper system and order in the regulation of the life. Upon it depends the cultivation of the sense of self-respect, the education of the habit of obedience, the development of the idea of duty. The most self-reliant, self-governing man is always under discipline: and the more perfect the discipline, the higher will be his moral condition. He has to drill his desires, and keep them in subjection to the higher powers of his nature. They must obey the word of command of the internal monitor, the conscience— otherwise they will be but the mere slaves of their inclinations, the sport of feeling and impulse.

"In the supremacy of self-control, " says Herbert Spencer, "consists one of the perfections of the ideal man. Not to be impulsive—not to be spurred hither and thither by each desire that in turn comes uppermost—but to be self-restrained, self- balanced, governed by the joint decision of the feelings in council assembled, before whom every action shall have been fully debated and calmly determined — that it is which education, moral education at least, strives to produce. " (1)

The first seminary of moral discipline, and the best, as we have already shown, is the home; next comes the school, and after that the world, the great school of practical life. Each is preparatory to the other, and what the man or woman becomes, depends for the most part upon what has gone before. If they have enjoyed the advantage of neither the home nor the school, but have been allowed to grow up untrained, untaught, and undisciplined, then woe to themselves — woe to the society of which they form part!

The best-regulated home is always that in which the discipline is the most perfect, and yet where it is the least felt. Moral discipline acts with the force of a law of nature. Those subject to it yield themselves to it unconsciously; and though it shapes and forms the whole character, until the life becomes crystallized in habit, the influence thus exercised is for the most part unseen and almost unfelt.

The importance of strict domestic discipline is curiously illustrated by a fact mentioned in Mrs. Schimmelpenninck's Memoirs, to the following effect: that a lady who, with her husband, had inspected most of the lunatic asylums of England and the Continent, found the most numerous class of patients was almost always composed of those who had been only children, and whose wills had therefore rarely been thwarted or disciplined in early life; whilst those who were members of large families, and who had been trained in self-discipline, were far less frequent victims to the malady.

Although the moral character depends in a great degree on temperament and on physical health, as well as on domestic and early training and the example of companions, it is also in the power of each individual to regulate, to restrain, and to discipline it by watchful and persevering self-control. A competent teacher has said of the propensities and habits, that they are as teachable as Latin and Greek, while they are much more essential to happiness.

Dr. Johnson, though himself constitutionally prone to melancholy, and afflicted by it as few have been from his earliest years, said that "a man's being in a good or bad humour very much depends upon his will. " We may train ourselves in a habit of patience and contentment on the one hand, or of grumbling and discontent on the other. We may accustom ourselves to exaggerate small evils, and to underestimate great blessings. We may even become the victim of petty miseries by giving way to them. Thus, we may educate ourselves in a happy disposition, as well as in a morbid one. Indeed, the habit of viewing things cheerfully, and of thinking about life hopefully, may be made to grow up in us like any other habit. (2) It was not an exaggerated estimate of Dr. Johnson to say, that the habit of looking at the best side of any event is worth far more than a thousand pounds a year.

Th religious man's life is pervaded by rigid self-discipline and self-restraint. He is to be sober and vigilant, to eschew evil and do good, to walk in the spirit, to be obedient unto death, to withstand in the evil day, and having done all, to stand; to wrestle against spiritual wickedness, and against the rulers of the darkness of this world; to be rooted and built up in faith, and not to be weary of well-doing; for in due season he shall reap, if he faint not.

The man of business also must needs be subject to strict rule and system. Business, like life, is managed by moral leverage; success in both depending in no small degree upon that regulation of temper and careful self-discipline, which give a wise man not only a command over himself, but over others. Forbearance and self-control smooth the road of life, and open many ways which would otherwise remain closed. And so does self-respect: for as men respect themselves, so will they usually respect the personality of others.

It is the same in politics as in business. Success in that sphere of life is achieved less by talent than by temper, less by genius than by character. If a man have not self-control, he will lack patience, be wanting in tact, and have neither the power of governing himself nor of managing others. When the quality most needed in a Prime Minister was the subject of conversation in the presence of Mr. Pitt, one of the speakers said it was "Eloquence; " another said it was "Knowledge; " and a third said it was "Toil, " "No, " said Pitt, "it is Patience! " And patience means self- control, a quality in which he himself was superb. His friend George Rose has said of him that he never once saw Pitt out of temper. (3) Yet, although patience is usually regarded as a "slow" virtue, Pitt combined with it the most extraordinary readiness, vigour, and rapidity of thought as well as action.

It is by patience and self-control that the truly heroic character is perfected. These were among the most prominent characteristics of the great Hampden, whose noble qualities were generously acknowledged even by his political enemies. Thus Clarendon described him as a man of rare temper and modesty, naturally cheerful and vivacious, and above all, of a flowing courtesy. He was kind and intrepid, yet gentle, of unblameable conversation, and his heart glowed with love to all men. He was not a man of many words, but, being of unimpeachable character, every word he uttered carried weight. "No man had ever a greater power over himself.... He was very temperate in diet, and a supreme governor over all his passions and affections; and he had thereby great power over other men's. " Sir Philip Warwick, another of his political opponents, incidentally describes his great influence in a certain debate: "We had catched at each other's locks, and sheathed our swords in each other's bowels, had not the sagacity and great calmness of Mr. Hampden, by a short speech, prevented it, and led us to defer our angry debate until the next morning. "

A strong temper is not necessarily a bad temper. But the stronger the temper, the greater is the need of self-discipline and self- control. Dr. Johnson says men grow better as they grow older, and improve with experience; but this depends upon the width, and depth, and generousness of their nature. It is not men's faults that ruin them so much as the manner in which they conduct themselves after the faults have been committed. The wise will profit by the suffering they cause, and eschew them for the future; but there are those on whom experience exerts no ripening influence, and who only grow narrower and bitterer and more vicious with time.

What is called strong temper in a young man, often indicates a large amount of unripe energy, which will expend itself in useful work if the road be fairly opened to it. It is said of Stephen Gerard, a Frenchman, who pursued a remarkably successful career in the United States, that when he heard of a clerk with a strong temper, he would readily take him into his employment, and set him to work in a room by himself; Gerard being of opinion that such persons were the best workers, and that their energy would expend itself in work if removed from the temptation to quarrel.

Strong temper may only mean a strong and excitable will. Uncontrolled, it displays itself in fitful outbreaks of passion; but controlled and held in subjection—like steam pent-up within the organised mechanism of a steam-engine, the use of which is regulated and controlled by slide-valves and governors and levers — it may become a source of energetic power and usefulness. Hence, some of the greatest characters in history have been men of strong temper, but of equally strong determination to hold their motive power under strict regulation and control.

The famous Earl of Strafford was of an extremely choleric and passionate nature, and had great struggles with himself in his endeavours to control his temper. Referring to the advice of one of his friends, old Secretary Cooke, who was honest enough to tell him of his weakness, and to caution him against indulging it, he wrote: "You gave me a good lesson to be patient; and, indeed, my years and natural inclinations give me heat more than enough, which, however, I trust more experience shall cool, and a watch over myself in time altogether overcome; in the meantime, in this at least it will set forth itself more pardonable, because my earnestness shall ever be for the honour, justice, and profit of my master; and it is not always anger, but the misapplying of it, that is the vice so blameable, and of disadvantage to those that let themselves loose there-unto."(4)

Cromwell, also, is described as having been of a wayward and violent temper in his youth—cross, untractable, and masterless— with a vast quantity of youthful energy, which exploded in a variety of youthful mischiefs. He even obtained the reputation of a roysterer in his native town, and seemed to be rapidly going to the bad, when religion, in one of its most rigid forms, laid hold upon his strong nature, and subjected it to the iron discipline of Calvinism. An entirely new direction was thus given to his energy of temperament, which forced an outlet for itself into public life, and eventually became the dominating influence in England for a period of nearly twenty years.

The heroic princes of the House of Nassau were all distinguished for the same qualities of self-control, self-denial, and determination of purpose. William the Silent was so called, not because he was a taciturn man—for he was an eloquent and powerful speaker where eloquence was necessary—but because he was a man who could hold his tongue when it was wisdom not to speak, and because he carefully kept his own counsel when to have revealed it might have been dangerous to the liberties of his country. He was so gentle and conciliatory in his manner that his enemies even described him as timid and pusillanimous. Yet, when the time for action came, his courage was heroic, his determination unconquerable. "The rock in the ocean, " says Mr. Motley, the historian of the Netherlands, "tranquil amid raging billows, was the favourite emblem by which his friends expressed their sense of his firmness. "

Mr. Motley compares William the Silent to Washington, whom he in many respects resembled. The American, like the Dutch patriot, stands out in history as the very impersonation of dignity, bravery, purity, and personal excellence. His command over his feelings, even in moments of great difficulty and danger, was such as to convey the impression, to those who did not know him intimately, that he was a man of inborn calmness and almost impassiveness of disposition. Yet Washington was by nature ardent and impetuous; his mildness, gentleness, politeness, and consideration for others, were the result of rigid self-control and unwearied self-discipline, which he diligently practised even from his boyhood. His biographer says of him, that "his temperament was ardent, his passions strong, and amidst the multiplied scenes of temptation and excitement through which he passed, it was his constant effort, and ultimate triumph, to check the one and subdue the other. " And again: "His passions were strong, and sometimes they broke out with vehemence, but he had the power of checking them in an instant. Perhaps self-control was the most remarkable trait of his character. It was in part the effect of discipline; yet he seems by nature to have possessed this power in a degree which has been denied to other men. (*5)

The Duke of Wellington's natural temper, like that of Napoleon, was irritable in the extreme; and it was only by watchful self- control that he was enabled to restrain it. He studied calmness and coolness in the midst of danger, like any Indian chief. At Waterloo, and elsewhere, he gave his orders in the most critical moments, without the slightest excitement, and in a tone of voice almost more than usually subdued. (6)

Wordsworth the poet was, in his childhood, "of a stiff, moody, and violent temper, " and "perverse and obstinate in defying chastisement. " When experience of life had disciplined his temper, he learnt to exercise greater self-control; but, at the same time, the qualities which distinguished him as a child were afterwards useful in enabling him to defy the criticism of his enemies. Nothing was more marked than Wordsworth's self-respect and self-determination, as well as his self-consciousness of power, at all periods of his history.

Henry Martyn, the missionary, was another instance of a man in whom strength of temper was only so much pent-up, unripe energy. As a boy he was impatient, petulant, and perverse; but by constant wrestling against his tendency to wrongheadedness, he gradually gained the requisite strength, so as to entirely overcome it, and to acquire what he so greatly coveted—the gift of patience.

A man may be feeble in organization, but, blessed with a happy temperament, his soul may be great, active, noble, and sovereign. Professor Tyndall has given us a fine picture of the character of Faraday, and of his self-denying labours in the cause of science—exhibiting him as a man of strong, original, and even fiery nature, and yet of extreme tenderness and sensibility. "Underneath his sweetness and gentleness, " he says, "was the heat of a volcano. He was a man of excitable and fiery nature; but, through high self-discipline, he had converted the fire into a central glow and motive power of life, instead of permitting it to waste itself in useless passion. "

There was one fine feature in Faraday's character which is worthy of notice—one closely akin to self-control: it was his self- denial. By devoting himself to analytical chemistry, he might have speedily realised a large fortune; but he nobly resisted the temptation, and preferred to follow the path of pure science. "Taking the duration of his life into account, " says Mr. Tyndall, "this son of a blacksmith and apprentice to a bookbinder had to decide between a fortune of œ150,000 on the one side, and his undowered science on the other. He chose the latter, and died a poor man. But his was the glory of holding aloft among the nations the scientific name of England for a period of forty years. " (7)

Take a like instance of the self-denial of a Frenchman. The historian Anquetil was one of the small number of literary men in France who refused to bow to the Napoleonic yoke. He sank into great poverty, living on bread-and-milk, and limiting his expenditure to only three sous a day. "I have still two sous a day left, " said he, "for the conqueror of Marengo and Austerlitz. " "But if you fall sick, " said a friend to him, "you will need the help of a pension. Why not do as others do? Pay court to the Emperor—you have need of him to live. " "I do not need him to die, " was the historian's reply. But Anquetil did not die of poverty; he lived to the age of ninety-four, saying to a friend, on the eve of his death, "Come, see a man who dies still full of life! "

Sir James Outram exhibited the same characteristic of noble self-denial, though in an altogether different sphere of life. Like the great King Arthur, he was emphatically a man who "forbore his own advantage. " He was characterised throughout his whole career by his noble unselfishness. Though he might personally disapprove of the policy he was occasionally ordered to carry out, he never once faltered in the path of duty. Thus he did not approve of the policy of invading Scinde; yet his services throughout the campaign were acknowledged by General Sir C. Napier to have been of the most brilliant character. But when the war was over, and the rich spoils of Scinde lay at the conqueror's feet, Outram said: "I disapprove of the policy of this war—I will accept no share of the prize-money! "

Not less marked was his generous self-denial when despatched with a strong force to aid Havelock in fighting his way to Lucknow. As superior officer, he was entitled to take upon himself the chief command; but, recognising what Havelock had already done, with rare disinterestedness, he left to his junior officer the glory of completing the campaign, offering to serve under him as a volunteer. "With such reputation, " said Lord Clyde, "as Major- General Outram has won for himself, he can afford to share glory and honour with others. But that does not lessen the value of the sacrifice he has made with such disinterested generosity. "

If a man would get through life honourably and peaceably, he must necessarily learn to practise self-denial in small things as well as great. Men have to bear as well as forbear. The temper has to be held in subjection to the judgment; and the little demons of ill-humour, petulance, and sarcasm, kept resolutely at a distance. If once they find an entrance to the mind, they are very apt to return, and to establish for themselves a permanent occupation there.

It is necessary to one's personal happiness, to exercise control over one's words as well as acts: for there are words that strike even harder than blows; and men may "speak daggers, " though they use none. "UN COUP DE LANGUE, " says the French proverb, "EST PIRE QU'UN COUP DE LANCE. " The stinging repartee that rises to the lips, and which, if uttered, might cover an adversary with confusion, how difficult it sometimes is to resist saying it! "Heaven keep us, " says Miss Bremer in her 'Home, ' "from the destroying power of words! There are words which sever hearts more than sharp swords do; there are words the point of which sting the heart through the course of a whole life. "

Thus character exhibits itself in self-control of speech as much as in anything else. The wise and forbearant man will restrain his desire to say a smart or severe thing at the expense of another's feelings; while the fool blurts out what he thinks, and will sacrifice his friend rather than his joke. "The mouth of a wise man, " said Solomon, "is in his heart; the heart of a fool is in his mouth. "

There are, however, men who are no fools, that are headlong in their language as in their acts, because of their want of forbearance and self-restraining patience. The impulsive genius, gifted with quick thought and incisive speech—perhaps carried away by the cheers of the moment—lets fly a sarcastic sentence which may return upon him to his own infinite damage. Even statesmen might be named, who have failed through their inability to resist the temptation of saying clever and spiteful things at their adversary's expense. "The turn of a sentence, " says Bentham, "has decided the fate of many a friendship, and, for aught that we know, the fate of many a kingdom. " So, when one is tempted to write a clever but harsh thing, though it may be difficult to restrain it, it is always better to leave it in the inkstand. "A goose's quill, " says the Spanish proverb, "often hurts more than a lion's claw. "

Carlyle says, when speaking of Oliver Cromwell, "He that cannot withal keep his mind to himself, cannot practise any considerable thing whatsoever. " It was said of William the Silent, by one of his greatest enemies, that an arrogant or indiscreet word was never known to fall from his lips. Like him, Washington was discretion itself in the use of speech, never taking advantage of an opponent, or seeking a shortlived triumph in a debate. And it is said that in the long run, the world comes round to and supports the wise man who knows when and how to be silent.

We have heard men of great experience say that they have often regretted having spoken, but never once regretted holding their tongue. "Be silent, " says Pythagoras, "or say something better than silence. " "Speak fitly, " says George Herbert, "or be silent wisely. " St. Francis de Sales, whom Leigh Hunt styled "the Gentleman Saint," has said: "It is better to remain silent than to speak the truth ill-humouredly, and so spoil an excellent dish by covering it with bad sauce. " Another Frenchman, Lacordaire, characteristically puts speech first, and silence next. "After speech, " he says, "silence is the greatest power in the world. " Yet a word spoken in season, how powerful it may be! As the old Welsh proverb has it, "A golden tongue is in the mouth of the blessed. "

It is related, as a remarkable instance of self-control on the part of De Leon, a distinguished Spanish poet of the sixteenth century, who lay for years in the dungeons of the Inquisition without light or society, because of his having translated a part of the Scriptures into his native tongue, that on being liberated and restored to his professorship, an immense crowd attended his first lecture, expecting some account of his long imprisonment; but Do Leon was too wise and too gentle to indulge in recrimination. He merely resumed the lecture which, five years before, had been so sadly interrupted, with the accustomed formula "HERI DICEBAMUS, " and went directly into his subject.

There are, of course, times and occasions when the expression of indignation is not only justifiable but necessary. We are bound to be indignant at falsehood, selfishness, and cruelty. A man of true feeling fires up naturally at baseness or meanness of any sort, even in cases where he may be under no obligation to speak out. "I would have nothing to do, " said Perthes, "with the man who cannot be moved to indignation. There are more good people than bad in the world, and the bad get the upper hand merely because they are bolder. We cannot help being pleased with a man who uses his powers with decision; and we often take his side for no other reason than because he does so use them. No doubt, I have often repented speaking; but not less often have I repented keeping silence. " (8)

One who loves right cannot be indifferent to wrong, or wrongdoing. If he feels warmly, he will speak warmly, out of the fulness of his heart. As a noble lady (9) has written:

> "A noble heart doth teach a virtuous scorn —
> To scorn to owe a duty overlong,
> To scorn to be for benefits forborne,
> To scorn to lie, to scorn to do a wrong,
> To scorn to bear an injury in mind,
> To scorn a freeborn heart slave-like to bind."

We have, however, to be on our guard against impatient scorn. The best people are apt to have their impatient side; and often, the very temper which makes men earnest, makes them also intolerant. (10) "Of all mental gifts, " says Miss Julia Wedgwood, "the rarest is intellectual patience; and the last lesson of culture is to believe in difficulties which are invisible to ourselves. "

The best corrective of intolerance in disposition, is increase of wisdom and enlarged experience of life. Cultivated good sense will usually save men from the entanglements in which moral impatience is apt to involve them; good sense consisting chiefly in that temper of mind which enables its possessor to deal with the practical affairs of life with justice, judgment, discretion, and charity. Hence men of culture and experience are invariably, found the most forbearant and tolerant, as ignorant and narrowminded persons are found the most unforgiving and intolerant. Men of large and generous natures, in proportion to their practical wisdom, are disposed to make allowance for the defects and disadvantages of others—allowance for the controlling power of circumstances in the formation of character, and the limited power of resistance of weak and fallible natures to temptation and error. "I see no fault committed, " said Goethe, "which I also might not have committed. " So a wise and good man exclaimed, when he saw a criminal drawn on his hurdle to Tyburn: "There goes Jonathan Bradford—but for the grace of God! "

Life will always be, to a great extent, what we ourselves make it. The cheerful man makes a cheerful world, the gloomy man a gloomy one. We usually find but our own temperament reflected in the dispositions of those about us. If we are ourselves querulous, we will find them so; if we are unforgiving and uncharitable to them, they will be the same to us. A person returning from an evening party not long ago, complained to a policeman on his beat that an ill-looking fellow was following him: it turned out to be only his own shadow! And such usually is human life to each of us; it is, for the most part, but the reflection of ourselves.

If we would be at peace with others, and ensure their respect, we must have regard for their personality. Every man has his peculiarities of manner and character, as he has peculiarities of form and feature; and we must have forbearance in dealing with them, as we expect them to have forbearance in dealing with us. We may not be conscious of our own peculiarities, yet they exist nevertheless. There is a village in South America where gotos or goitres are so common that to be without one is regarded as a deformity. One day a party of Englishmen passed through the place, when quite a crowd collected to jeer them, shouting: "See, see these people—they have got NO GOTOS! "

Many persons give themselves a great deal of fidget concerning what other people think of them and their peculiarities. Some are too much disposed to take the illnatured side, and, judging by themselves, infer the worst. But it is very often the case that the uncharitableness of others, where it really exists, is but the reflection of our own want of charity and want of temper. It still oftener happens, that the worry we subject ourselves to, has its source in our own imagination. And even though those about us may think of us uncharitably, we shall not mend matters by exasperating ourselves against them. We may thereby only expose ourselves unnecessarily to their illnature or caprice. "The ill that comes out of our mouth, " says Herbert, "ofttimes falls into our bosom. "

The great and good philosopher Faraday communicated the following piece of admirable advice, full of practical wisdom, the result of a rich experience of life, in a letter to his friend Professor Tyndall: - "Let me, as an old man, who ought by this time to have profited by experience, say that when I was younger I found I often misrepresented the intentions of people, and that they did not mean what at the time I supposed they meant; and further, that, as a general rule, it was better to be a little dull of apprehension where phrases seemed to imply pique, and quick in perception when, on the contrary, they seemed to imply kindly feeling. The real truth never fails ultimately to appear; and opposing parties, if wrong, are sooner convinced when replied to forbearingly, than when overwhelmed. All I mean to say is, that it is better to be blind to the results of partisanship, and quick to see goodwill. One has more happiness in one's self in endeavouring to follow the things that make for peace. You can hardly imagine how often I have been heated in private when opposed, as I have thought unjustly and superciliously, and yet I have striven, and succeeded, I hope, in keeping down replies of the like kind. And I know I have never lost by it. " (11)

While the painter Barry was at Rome, he involved himself, as was his wont, in furious quarrels with the artists and dilettanti, about picture-painting and picture-dealing, upon which his friend and countryman, Edmund Burke—always the generous friend of struggling merit—wrote to him kindly and sensibly: "Believe me, dear Barry, that the arms with which the ill-dispositions of the world are to be combated, and the qualities by which it is to be reconciled to us, and we reconciled to it, are moderation, gentleness, a little indulgence to others, and a great deal of distrust of ourselves; which are not qualities of a mean spirit, as some may possibly think them, but virtues of a great and noble kind, and such as dignify our nature as much as they contribute to our repose and fortune; for nothing can be so unworthy of a well- composed soul as to pass away life in bickerings and litigations— in snarling and scuffling with every one about us. We must be at peace with our species, if not for their sakes, at least very much for our own. " (12)

No one knew the value of self-control better than the poet Burns, and no one could teach it more eloquently to others; but when it came to practice, Burns was as weak as the weakest. He could not deny himself the pleasure of uttering a harsh and clever sarcasm at another's expense. One of his biographers observes of him, that it was no extravagant arithmetic to say that for every ten jokes he made himself a hundred enemies. But this was not all. Poor Burns exercised no control over his appetites, but freely gave them rein:

> "Thus thoughtless follies laid him low
> And stained his name."

Nor had he the self-denial to resist giving publicity to compositions originally intended for the delight of the tap-room, but which continue secretly to sow pollution broadcast in the minds of youth. Indeed, notwithstanding the many exquisite poems of this writer, it is not saying too much to aver that his immoral writings have done far more harm than his purer writings have done good; and that it would be better that all his writings should be destroyed and forgotten provided his indecent songs could be destroyed with them.

The remark applies alike to Beranger, who has been styled "The Burns of France. " Beranger was of the same bright incisive genius; he had the same love of pleasure, the same love of popularity; and while he flattered French vanity to the top of its bent, he also painted the vices most loved by his countrymen with the pen of a master. Beranger's songs and Thiers' History probably did more than anything else to reestablish the Napoleonic dynasty in France. But that was a small evil compared with the moral mischief which many of Beranger's songs are calculated to produce; for, circulating freely as they do in French households, they exhibit pictures of nastiness and vice, which are enough to pollute and destroy a nation.

One of Burns's finest poems, written, in his twenty-eighth year, is entitled 'A Bard's Epitaph. ' It is a description, by anticipation, of his own life. Wordsworth has said of it: "Here is a sincere and solemn avowal; a public declaration from his own will; a confession at once devout, poetical and human; a history in the shape of a prophecy. " It concludes with these lines: -

"Reader, attend—whether thy soul
Soars fancy's flights beyond the pole,
Or darkling grubs this earthly hole
    In low pursuit;
Know—prudent, cautious self-control,
    Is Wisdom's root."

One of the vices before which Burns fell—and it may be said to be a master-vice, because it is productive of so many other vices —was drinking. Not that he was a drunkard, but because he yielded to the temptations of drink, with its degrading associations, and thereby lowered and depraved his whole nature. (13) But poor Burns did not stand alone; for, alas! of all vices, the unrestrained appetite for drink was in his time, as it continues to be now, the most prevalent, popular, degrading, and destructive.

Were it possible to conceive the existence of a tyrant who should compel his people to give up to him one-third or more of their earnings, and require them at the same time to consume a commodity that should brutalise and degrade them, destroy the peace and comfort of their families, and sow in themselves the seeds of disease and premature death—what indignation meetings, what monster processions there would be! 'What eloquent speeches and apostrophes to the spirit of liberty! —what appeals against a despotism so monstrous and so unnatural! And yet such a tyrant really exists amongst us—the tyrant of unrestrained appetite, whom no force of arms, or voices, or votes can resist, while men are willing to be his slaves.

The power of this tyrant can only be overcome by moral means—by self-discipline, self-respect, and self-control. There is no other way of withstanding the despotism of appetite in any of its forms. No reform of institutions, no extended power of voting, no improved form of government, no amount of scholastic instruction, can possibly elevate the character of a people who voluntarily abandon themselves to sensual indulgence. The pursuit of ignoble pleasure is the degradation of true happiness; it saps the morals, destroys the energies, and degrades the manliness and robustness of individuals as of nations.

The courage of self-control exhibits itself in many ways, but in none more clearly than in honest living. Men without the virtue of self-denial are not only subject to their own selfish desires, but they are usually in bondage to others who are likeminded with themselves. What others do, they do. They must live according to the artificial standard of their class, spending like their neighbours, regardless of the consequences, at the same time that all are, perhaps, aspiring after a style of living higher than their means. Each carries the others along with him, and they have not the moral courage to stop. They cannot resist the temptation of living high, though it may be at the expense of others; and they gradually become reckless of debt, until it enthrals them. In all this there is great moral cowardice, pusillanimity, and want of manly independence of character.

A rightminded man will shrink from seeming to be what he is not, or pretending to be richer than he really is, or assuming a style of living that his circumstances will not justify. He will have the courage to live honestly within his own means, rather than dishonestly upon the means of other people; for he who incurs debts in striving to maintain a style of living beyond his income, is in spirit as dishonest as the man who openly picks your pocket.

To many, this may seem an extreme view, but it will bear the strictest test. Living at the cost of others is not only dishonesty, but it is untruthfulness in deed, as lying is in word. The proverb of George Herbert, that "debtors are liars, " is justified by experience. Shaftesbury somewhere says that a restlessness to have something which we have not, and to be something which we are not, is the root of all immorality. (14) No reliance is to be placed on the saying—a very dangerous one—of Mirabeau, that "LA PETITE MORALE ETAIT L'ENNEMIE DE LA GRANDE. " On the contrary, strict adherence to even the smallest details of morality is the foundation of all manly and noble character.

The honourable man is frugal of his means, and pays his way honestly. He does not seek to pass himself off as richer than he is, or, by running into debt, open an account with ruin. As that man is not poor whose means are small, but whose desires are uncontrolled, so that man is rich whose means are more than sufficient for his wants. When Socrates saw a great quantity of riches, jewels, and furniture of great value, carried in pomp through Athens, he said, "Now do I see how many things I do NOT desire. " "I can forgive everything but selfishness, " said Perthes. "Even the narrowest circumstances admit of greatness with reference to 'mine and thine'; and none but the very poorest need fill their daily life with thoughts of money, if they have but prudence to arrange their housekeeping within the limits of their income. "

A man may be indifferent to money because of higher considerations, as Faraday was, who sacrificed wealth to pursue science; but if he would have the enjoyments that money can purchase, he must honestly earn it, and not live upon the earnings of others, as those do who habitually incur debts which they have no means of paying. When Maginn, always drowned in debt, was asked what he paid for his wine, he replied that he did not know, but he believed they "put something down in a book. " (15)

This "putting-down in a book" has proved the ruin of a great many weakminded people, who cannot resist the temptation of taking things upon credit which they have not the present means of paying for; and it would probably prove of great social benefit if the law which enables creditors to recover debts contracted under certain circumstances were altogether abolished. But, in the competition for trade, every encouragement is given to the incurring of debt, the creditor relying upon the law to aid him in the last extremity. When Sydney Smith once went into a new neighbourhood, it was given out in the local papers that he was a man of high connections, and he was besought on all sides for his "custom. " But he speedily undeceived his new neighbours. "We are not great people at all, " he said: "we are only common honest people—people that pay our debts. "

Hazlitt, who was a thoroughly honest though rather thriftless man, speaks of two classes of persons, not unlike each other—those who cannot keep their own money in their hands, and those who cannot keep their hands from other people's. The former are always in want of money, for they throw it away on any object that first presents itself, as if to get rid of it; the latter make away with what they have of their own, and are perpetual borrowers from all who will lend to them; and their genius for borrowing, in the long run, usually proves their ruin.

Sheridan was one of such eminent unfortunates. He was impulsive and careless in his expenditure, borrowing money, and running into debt with everybody who would trust him. When he stood for Westminster, his unpopularity arose chiefly from his general indebtedness. "Numbers of poor people, " says Lord Palmerston in one of his letters, "crowded round the hustings, demanding payment for the bills he owed them. " In the midst of all his difficulties, Sheridan was as lighthearted as ever, and cracked many a good joke at his creditors' expense. Lord Palmerston was actually present at the dinner given by him, at which the sheriff's in possession were dressed up and officiated as waiters

Yet however loose Sheridan's morality may have been as regarded his private creditors, he was honest(so far as the public money was concerned. Once, at dinner, at which Lord Byron happened to be present, an observation happened to be made as to the sturdiness of the Whigs in resisting office, and keeping to their principles—on which Sheridan turned sharply and said: "Sir, it is easy for my Lord this, or Earl that, or the Marquis of t'other, with thousands upon thousands a year, some of it either presently derived or inherited in sinecure or acquisitions from the public money, to boast of their patriotism, and keep aloof from temptation; but they do not know from what temptation those have kept aloof who had equal pride, at least equal talents, and not unequal passions, and nevertheless knew not, in the course of their lives, what it was to have a shilling of their own. " And Lord Byron adds, that, in saying this, Sheridan wept.(16)

The tone of public morality in money-matters was very low in those days. Political peculation was not thought discreditable; and heads of parties did not hesitate to secure the adhesion of their followers by a free use of the public money. They were generous, but at the expense of others—like that great local magnate, who,

> "Out of his great bounty,
> Built a bridge at the expense of the county."

When Lord Cornwallis was appointed Lord-Lieutenant of Ireland, he pressed upon Colonel Napier, the father of THE Napiers, the comptrollership of army accounts. "I want, " said his Lordship, "AN HONEST MAN, and this is the only thing I have been able to wrest from the harpies around me. "

It is said that Lord Chatham was the first to set the example of disdaining to govern by petty larceny; and his great son was alike honest in his administration. While millions of money were passing through Pitt's hands, he himself was never otherwise than poor; and he died poor. Of all his rancorous libellers, not one ever ventured to call in question his honesty.

In former times, the profits of office were sometimes enormous. When Audley, the famous annuity-monger of the sixteenth century, was asked the value of an office which he had purchased in the Court of Wards, he replied: - "Some thousands to any one who wishes to get to heaven immediately; twice as much to him who does not mind being in purgatory; and nobody knows what to him who is not afraid of the devil. "

Sir Walter Scott was a man who was honest to the core of his nature and his strenuous and determined efforts to pay his debts, or rather the debts of the firm with which he had become involved, has always appeared to us one of the grandest things in biography. When his publisher and printer broke down, ruin seemed to stare him in the face. There was no want of sympathy for him in his great misfortune, and friends came forward who offered to raise money enough to enable him to arrange with his creditors. "No! "said he, proudly; "this right hand shall work it all off! " "If we lose everything else, " he wrote to a friend, "we will at least keep our honour unblemished. " (17) While his health was already becoming undermined by overwork, he went on "writing like a tiger, " as he himself expressed it, until no longer able to wield a pen; and though he paid the penalty of his supreme efforts with his life, he nevertheless saved his honour and his self-respect.

Everybody knows bow Scott threw off 'Woodstock, ' the 'Life of Napoleon' (which he thought would be his death (18)), articles for the 'Quarterly, ' 'Chronicles of the Canongate, ' 'Prose Miscellanies, ' and 'Tales of a Grandfather'—all written in the midst of pain, sorrow, and ruin. The proceeds of those various works went to his creditors. "I could not have slept sound, " he wrote, "as I now can, under the comfortable impression of receiving the thanks of my creditors, and the conscious feeling of discharging my duty as a man of honour and honesty. I see before me a long, tedious, and dark path, but it leads to stainless reputation. If I die in the harrows, as is very likely, I shall die with honour. If I achieve my task, I shall have the thanks of all concerned, and the approbation of my own conscience. " (19)

And then followed more articles, memoirs, and even sermons —'The Fair Maid of Perth, ' a completely revised edition of his novels, 'Anne of Geierstein, ' and more 'Tales of a Grandfather' —until he was suddenly struck down by paralysis. But he had no sooner recovered sufficient strength to be able to hold a pen, than we find him again at his desk writing the 'Letters on Demonology and Witchcraft, ' a volume of Scottish History for 'Lardner's Cyclopaedia, ' and a fourth series of 'Tales of a Grandfather' in his French History. In vain his doctors told him to give up work; he would not be dissuaded. "As for bidding me not work, " he said to Dr. Abercrombie, "Molly might just as well put the kettle on the fire and say, 'Now, kettle, don't boil; '" to which he added, "If I were to be idle I should go mad! "

By means of the profits realised by these tremendous efforts, Scott saw his debts in course of rapid diminution, and he trusted that, after a few more years' work, he would again be a free man. But it was not to be. He went on turning out such works as his 'Count Robert of Paris' with greatly impaired skill, until he was prostrated by another and severer attack of palsy. He now felt that the plough was nearing the end of the furrow; his physical strength was gone; he was "not quite himself in all things, " and yet his courage and perseverance never failed. "I have suffered terribly, " he wrote in his Diary, "though rather in body than in mind, and I often wish I could lie down and sleep without waking. But I WILL FIGHT IT OUT IF I CAN. " He again recovered sufficiently to be able to write 'Castle Dangerous, ' though the cunning of the workman's hand had departed. And then there was his last tour to Italy in search of rest and health, during which, while at Naples, in spite of all remonstrances, he gave several hours every morning to the composition of a new novel, which, however, has not seen the light.

Scott returned to Abbotsford to die. "I have seen much, " he said on his return, "but nothing like my own house —give me one turn more. " One of the last things he uttered, in one of his lucid intervals, was worthy of him. "I have been, " he said, "perhaps the most voluminous author of my day, and it IS a comfort to me to think that I have tried to unsettle no man's faith, to corrupt no man's principles, and that I have written nothing which on my deathbed I should wish blotted out. " His last injunction to his son-in-law was:

"Lockhart, I may have but a minute to speak to you. My dear, be virtuous—be religious—be a good man. Nothing else will give you any comfort when you come to lie here. "

The devoted conduct of Lockhart himself was worthy of his great relative. The 'Life of Scott, ' which he afterwards wrote, occupied him several years, and was a remarkably successful work. Yet he himself derived no pecuniary advantage from it; handing over the profits of the whole undertaking to Sir Walter's creditors in payment of debts which he was in no way responsible, but influenced entirely by a spirit of honour, of regard for the memory of the illustrious dead.

NOTES

(1) 'Social Statics, ' p. 185.

(2) "In all cases, " says Jeremy Bentham, "when the power of the will can be exercised over the thoughts, let those thoughts be directed towards happiness. Look out for the bright, for the brightest side of things, and keep your face constantly turned to it.... A large part of existence is necessarily passed in inaction. By day (to take an instance from the thousand in constant recurrence), when in attendance on others, and time is lost by being kept waiting; by night when sleep is unwilling to close the eyelids, the economy of happiness recommends the occupation of pleasurable thought. In walking abroad, or in resting at home, the mind cannot be vacant; its thoughts may be useful, useless, or pernicious to happiness. Direct them aright; the habit of happy thought will spring up like any other habit. " DEONTOLOGY, ii. 105-6.

(3) The following extract from a letter of M. Boyd, Esq., is given by Earl Stanhope in his 'Miscellanies': - "There was a circumstance told me by the late Mr. Christmas, who for many years held an important official situation in the Bank of England. He was, I believe, in early life a clerk in the Treasury, or one of the government offices, and for some time acted for Mr. Pitt as his confidential clerk, or temporary private secretary. Christmas was one of the most obliging men I ever knew; and, from the, position he occupied, was constantly exposed to interruptions, yet I never saw his temper in the least ruffled. One day I found him more than usually engaged, having a mass of accounts to prepare for one of the law-courts—still the same equanimity, and I could not resist the opportunity of asking the old

gentleman the secret. 'Well, Mr. Boyd, you shall know it. Mr. Pitt gave it to me: — NOT TO LOSE MY TEMPER, IF POSSIBLE, AT ANY TIME, AND NEVER DURING THE HOURS OF BUSINESS. My labours here (Bank of England) commence at nine and end at three; and, acting on the advice of the illustrious statesman, I NEVER LOSE MY TEMPER DURING THOSE HOURS. '"

(4) 'Strafford Papers, ' i. 87.

(5) Jared Sparks' 'Life of Washington, ' pp. 7, 534.

(6) Brialmont's 'Life of Wellington. '

(7) Professor Tyndall, on 'Faraday as a Discoverer, ' p. 156.

(8) 'Life of Perthes, ' ii. 216.

(9) Lady Elizabeth Carew.

(10) Francis Horner, in one of his letters, says: "It is among the very sincere and zealous friends of liberty that you will find the most perfect specimens of wrongheadedness; men of a dissenting, provincial cast of virtue—who (according to one of Sharpe's favourite phrases) WILL drive a wedge the broad end foremost — utter strangers to all moderation in political business. " —Francis Horner's LIFE AND CORRESPONDENCE (1843), ii. 133.

(11) Professor Tyndall on 'Faraday as a Discoverer, ' pp. 40-1.

(12) Yet Burke himself; though capable of giving Barry such excellent advice, was by no means immaculate as regarded his own temper. When he lay ill at Beaconsfield, Fox, from whom he had become separated by political differences arising out of the French Revolution, went down to see his old friend. But Burke would not grant him an interview; he positively refused to see him. On his return to town, Fox told his friend Coke the result of his journey; and when Coke lamented Burke's obstinacy, Fox only replied, goodnaturedly: "Ah! never mind, Tom; I always find every Irishman has got a piece of potato in his head. " Yet Fox, with his usual generosity, when he heard of Burke's impending death, wrote a most kind and cordial letter to Mrs. Burke, expressive of his grief and sympathy; and when Burke was no more, Fox was the first to propose that he should be interred with public honours in

Westminster Abbey—which only Burke's own express wish, that he should be buried at Beaconsfield, prevented being carried out.

(13) When Curran, the Irish barrister, visited Burns's cabin in 1810, he found it converted into a public house, and the landlord who showed it was drunk. "There, " said he, pointing to a corner on one side of the fire, with a most MALAPROPOS laugh-"there is the very spot where Robert Burns was born. " "The genius and the fate of the man, " says Curran, "were already heavy on my heart; but the drunken laugh of the landlord gave me such a view of the rock on which he had foundered, that I could not stand it, but burst into tears. "

(14) The chaplain of Horsemongerlane Gaol, in his annual report to the Surrey justices, thus states the result of his careful study of the causes of dishonesty: "From my experience of predatory crime, founded upon careful study of the character of a great variety of prisoners, I conclude that habitual dishonesty is to be referred neither to ignorance, nor to drunkenness, nor to poverty, nor to overcrowding in towns, nor to temptation from surrounding wealth— nor, indeed, to any one of the many indirect causes to which it is sometimes referred—but mainly TO A DISPOSITION TO ACQUIRE PROPERTY WITH A LESS DEGREE OF LABOUR THAN ORDINARY INDUSTRY. " The italics are the author's.

(15) S. C. Hall's 'Memories. '

(16) Moore's 'Life of Byron, ' 8vo. Ed., p. 182.

(17) Captain Basil Hall records the following conversation with Scott:- "It occurs to me, " I observed, "that people are apt to make too much fuss about the loss of fortune, which is one of the smallest of the great evils of life, and ought to be among the most tolerable. "—"Do you call it a small misfortune to be ruined in money-matters? " he asked. "It is not so painful, at all events, as the loss of friends. "—"I grant that, " he said. "As the loss of character? "—"True again. " "As the loss of health? "—"Ay, there you have me, " he muttered to himself, in a tone so melancholy that I wished I had not spoken. "What is the loss of fortune to the loss of peace of mind? " I continued. "In short, " said he, playfully, "you will make it out that there is no harm in a man's being plunged over-head-and-ears in a debt he cannot remove. " "Much depends, I think, on how it was incurred, and what efforts are made to redeem it—at least, if the

sufferer be a rightminded man. " "I hope it does, " he said, cheerfully and firmly. —FRAGMENTS OF VOYAGES AND TRAVELS, 3rd series, pp. 308-9.

(18) "These battles, " he wrote in his Diary, "have been the death of many a man, I think they will be mine. "

(19) Scott's Diary, December 17th, 1827.

CHAPTER VII. —DUTY—TRUTHFULNESS.

"I slept, and dreamt that life was Beauty; I woke, and found that life was Duty. "

"Duty! wondrous thought, that workest neither by fond insinuation, flattery, nor by any threat, but merely by holding up thy naked law in the soul, and so extorting for thyself always reverence, if not always obedience; before whom all appetites are dumb, however secretly they rebel" —KANT.

"How happy is he born and taught,
    That serveth not another's will!
Whose armour is his honest thought,
    And simple truth his utmost skill!

"Whose passions not his masters are,
    Whose soul is still prepared for death;
Unti'd unto the world by care
    Of public fame, or private breath.

"This man is freed from servile bands,
    Of hope to rise, or fear to fall:
Lord of himself, though not of land;
    And having nothing, yet hath all." —WOTTON.

"His nay was nay without recall;
    His yea was yea, and powerful all;
He gave his yea with careful heed,
    His thoughts and words were well agreed;
His word, his bond and seal."
    INSCRIPTION ON BARON STEIN'S TOMB.

DUTY is a thing that is due, and must be paid by every man who would avoid present discredit and eventual moral insolvency. It is an obligation—a debt—which can only be discharged by voluntary effort and resolute action in the affairs of life.

Duty embraces man's whole existence. It begins in the home, where there is the duty which children owe to their parents on the one hand, and the duty which parents owe to their children on the other. There are, in like manner, the respective duties of husbands and wives, of masters and servants; while outside the home there are the duties which men and women owe to each other as friends and neighbours, as employers and employed, as governors and governed.

"Render, therefore, " says St. Paul, "to all their dues: tribute to whom tribute is due; custom to whom custom; fear to whom fear; honour to whom honour. Owe no man anything, but to love one another; for he that loveth another hath fulfilled the law, "

Thus duty rounds the whole of life, from our entrance into it until our exit from it—duty to superiors, duty to inferiors, and duty to equals—duty to man, and duty to God. Wherever there is power to use or to direct, there is duty. For we are but as stewards, appointed to employ the means entrusted to us for our own and for others' good.

The abiding sense of duty is the very crown of character. It is the upholding law of man in his highest attitudes. Without it, the individual totters and falls before the first puff of adversity or temptation; whereas, inspired by it, the weakest becomes strong and full of courage. "Duty, " says Mrs. Jameson, "is the cement which binds the whole moral edifice together; without which, all power, goodness, intellect, truth, happiness, love itself, can have no permanence; but all the fabric of existence crumbles away from under us, and leaves us at last sitting in the midst of a ruin, astonished at our own desolation. "

Duty is based upon a sense of justice—justice inspired by love, which is the most perfect form of goodness. Duty is not a sentiment, but a principle pervading the life: and it exhibits itself in conduct and in acts, which are mainly determined by man's conscience and freewill.

The voice of conscience speaks in duty done; and without its regulating and controlling influence, the brightest and greatest intellect may be merely as a light that leads astray. Conscience sets a man upon his feet, while his will holds him upright. Conscience is the moral governor of the heart—the governor of right action, of right thought, of right faith, of right life— and only through its dominating influence can the noble and upright character be fully developed.

The conscience, however, may speak never so loudly, but without energetic will it may speak in vain. The will is free to choose between the right course and the wrong one, but the choice is nothing unless followed by immediate and decisive action. If the sense of duty be strong, and the course of action clear, the courageous will, upheld by the conscience, enables a man to proceed on his course bravely, and to accomplish his purposes in the face of all opposition and difficulty. And should failure be the issue, there will remain at least this satisfaction, that it has been in the cause of duty.

"Be and continue poor, young man, " said Heinzelmann, " while others around you grow rich by fraud and disloyalty; be without place or power while others beg their way upwards; bear the pain of disappointed hopes, while others gain the accomplishment of theirs by flattery; forego the gracious pressure of the hand, for which others cringe and crawl. Wrap yourself in your own virtue, and seek a friend and your daily bread. If you have in your own cause grown gray with unbleached honour, bless God and die! "

Men inspired by high principles are often required to sacrifice all that they esteem and love rather than fail in their duty. The old English idea of this sublime devotion to duty was expressed by the loyalist poet to his sweetheart, on taking up arms for his sovereign: -

> "I could love thee, dear, so much,
> Loved I not honour more.' (1)

And Sertorius has said: "The man who has any dignity of character, should conquer with honour, and not use any base means even to save his life. " So St. Paul, inspired by duty and faith, declared himself as not only "ready to be bound, but to die at Jerusalem. "

When the Marquis of Pescara was entreated by the princes of Italy to desert the Spanish cause, to which he was in honour bound, his noble wife, Vittoria Colonna, reminded him of his duty. She wrote to him: "Remember your honour, which raises you above fortune and above kings; by that alone, and not by the splendour of titles, is glory acquired—that glory which it will be your happiness and pride to transmit unspotted to your posterity. " Such was the dignified view which she took of her husband's honour; and when he fell at Pavia, though young and beautiful, and besought by many admirers, she betook herself to solitude, that she might lament over her husband's loss and celebrate his exploits. (2)

To live really, is to act energetically. Life is a battle to be fought valiantly. Inspired by high and honourable resolve, a man must stand to his post, and die there, if need be. Like the old Danish hero, his determination should be, "to dare nobly, to will strongly, and never to falter in the path of duty. " The power of will, be it great or small, which God has given us, is a Divine gift; and we ought neither to let it perish for want of using on the one hand, nor profane it by employing it for ignoble purposes on the other. Robertson, of Brighton, has truly said, that man's real greatness consists not in seeking his own pleasure, or fame, or advancement—"not that every one shall save his own life, not that every man shall seek his own glory—but that every man shall do his own duty. "

What most stands in the way of the performance of duty, is irresolution, weakness of purpose, and indecision. On the one side are conscience and the knowledge of good and evil; on the other are indolence, selfishness, love of pleasure, or passion. The weak and ill-disciplined will may remain suspended for a time between these influences; but at length the balance inclines one way or the other, according as the will is called into action or otherwise. If it be allowed to remain passive, the lower influence of selfishness or passion will prevail; and thus manhood suffers abdication, individuality is renounced, character is degraded, and the man permits himself to become the mere passive slave of his senses.

Thus, the power of exercising the will promptly, in obedience to the dictates of conscience, and thereby resisting the impulses of the lower nature, is of essential importance in moral discipline, and absolutely necessary for the development of character in its best forms. To acquire the habit of well-doing, to resist evil propensities, to fight against sensual desires, to overcome inborn selfishness, may require a long and persevering discipline; but when once the practice of duty is learnt, it becomes consolidated in habit, and thenceforward is comparatively easy.

The valiant good man is he who, by the resolute exercise of his freewill, has so disciplined himself as to have acquired the habit of virtue; as the bad man is he who, by allowing his freewill to remain inactive, and giving the bridle to his desires and passions, has acquired the habit of vice, by which he becomes, at last, bound as by chains of iron.

A man can only achieve strength of purpose by the action of his own freewill. If he is to stand erect, it must be by his own efforts; for he cannot be kept propped up by the help of others. He is master of himself and of his actions. He can avoid falsehood, and be truthful; he can shun sensualism, and be continent; he can turn aside from doing a cruel thing, and be benevolent and forgiving. All these lie within the sphere of individual efforts, and come within the range of self-discipline. And it depends upon men themselves whether in these respects they will be free, pure, and good on the one hand; or enslaved, impure, and miserable on the other.

Among the wise sayings of Epictetus we find the following: "We do not choose our own parts in life, and have nothing to do with those parts: our simple duty is confined to playing them well. The slave may be as free as the consul; and freedom is the chief of blessings; it dwarfs all others; beside it all others are insignificant; with it all others are needless; without it no others are possible.... You must teach men that happiness is not where, in their blindness and misery, they seek it. It is not in strength, for Myro and Ofellius were not happy; not in wealth, for Croesus was not happy; not in power, for the Consuls were not happy; not in all these together, for Nero and Sardanapulus and Agamemnon sighed and wept and tore their hair, and were the slaves of circumstances and the dupes of semblances. It lies in yourselves; in true freedom, in the absence or conquest of every ignoble fear; in perfect self-government; and in a power of contentment and peace, and the even flow of life amid poverty, exile, disease, and the very valley of the shadow of death. " (3)

The sense of duty is a sustaining power even to a courageous man. It holds him upright, and makes him strong. It was a noble saying of Pompey, when his friends tried to dissuade him from embarking for Rome in a storm, telling him that he did so at the great peril of his life: "It is necessary for me to go, " he said; "it is not necessary for me to live. " What it was right that he should do, he would do, in the face of danger and in defiance of storms.

As might be expected of the great Washington, the chief motive power in his life was the spirit of duty. It was the regal and commanding element in his character which gave it unity, compactness, and vigour. When he clearly saw his duty before him, he did it at all hazards, and with inflexible integrity. He did not do it for effect; nor did he think of glory, or of fame and its rewards; but of the right thing to be done, and the best way of doing it.

Yet Washington had a most modest opinion of himself; and when offered the chief command of the American patriot army, he hesitated to accept it until it was pressed upon him. When acknowledging in Congress the honour which had been done him in selecting him to so important a trust, on the execution of which the future of his country in a great measure depended, Washington said: "I beg it may be remembered, lest some unlucky event should happen unfavourable to my reputation, that I this day declare, with the utmost sincerity, I do not think myself equal to the command I am honoured with. "

And in his letter to his wife, communicating to her his appointment as Commander-in-Chief, he said: "I have used every endeavour in my power to avoid it, not only from my unwillingness to part with you and the family, but from a consciousness of its being a trust too great for my capacity; and that I should enjoy more real happiness in one month with you at home, than I have the most distant prospect of finding abroad, if my stay were to be seven times seven years. But, as it has been a kind of destiny that has thrown me upon this service, I shall hope that my undertaking it is designed for some good purpose. It was utterly out of my power to refuse the appointment, without exposing my character to such censures as would have reflected dishonour upon myself, and given pain to my friends. This, I am sure, could not, and ought not, to be pleasing to you, and must have lessened me considerably in my own esteem. " (4)

Washington pursued his upright course through life, first as Commander-in-Chief, and afterwards as President, never faltering in the path of duty. He had no regard for popularity, but held to his purpose, through good and through evil report, often at the risk of his power and influence. Thus, on one occasion, when the ratification of a treaty, arranged by Mr. Jay with Great Britain, was in question, Washington was urged to reject it. But his honour, and the honour of his country, was committed, and he refused to do so. A great outcry was raised against the treaty, and for a time Washington was so unpopular that he is said to have been actually stoned by the mob. But he, nevertheless, held it to be his duty to ratify the treaty; and it was carried out, in despite of petitions and remonstrances from all quarters. "While I feel, " he said, in answer to the remonstrants, "the most lively gratitude for the many instances of approbation from my country, I can no otherwise deserve it than by obeying the dictates of my conscience. " Wellington's watchword, like Washington's, was duty; and no man could be more loyal to it than he was. (5) "There is little or nothing, " he once said, "in this life worth living for; but we can all of us go straight forward and do our duty. " None recognised more cheerfully than he did the duty of obedience and willing service; for unless men can serve faithfully, they will not rule others wisely. There is no motto that becomes the wise man better than ICH DIEN, "I serve; " and "They also serve who only stand and wait. "

When the mortification of an officer, because of his being appointed to a command inferior to what he considered to be his merits, was communicated to the Duke, he said: "In the course of my military career, I have gone from the command of a brigade to that of my regiment, and from the command of an army to that of a brigade or a division, as I was ordered, and without any feeling of mortification. "

Whilst commanding the allied army in Portugal, the conduct of the native population did not seem to Wellington to be either becoming or dutiful. "We have enthusiasm in plenty, " he said, "and plenty of cries of 'VIVA! ' We have illuminations, patriotic songs, and FETES everywhere. But what we want is, that each in his own station should do his duty faithfully, and pay implicit obedience to legal authority. "

This abiding ideal of duty seemed to be the governing principle of Wellington's character. It was always uppermost in his mind, and directed all the public actions of his life. Nor did it fail to communicate itself to those under him, who served him in the like spirit. When he rode into one of his infantry squares at Waterloo, as its diminished numbers closed up to receive a charge of French cavalry, he said to the men, "Stand steady, lads; think of what they will say of us in England; " to which the men replied, "Never fear, sir—we know our duty. "

Duty was also the dominant idea in Nelson's mind. The spirit in which he served his country was expressed in the famous watchword, "England expects every man to do his duty, " signalled by him to the fleet before going into action at Trafalgar, as well as in the last words that passed his lips, —"I have done my duty; I praise God for it! "

And Nelson's companion and friend—the brave, sensible, homely-minded Collingwood—he who, as his ship bore down into the great sea-fight, said to his flag-captain, "Just about this time our wives are going to church in England, "—Collingwood too was, like his commander, an ardent devotee of duty. "Do your duty to the best of your ability, " was the maxim which he urged upon many young men starting on the voyage of life. To a midshipman he once gave the following manly and sensible advice: - "You may depend upon it, that it is more in your own power than in anybody else's to promote both your comfort and advancement. A strict and unwearied attention to your duty, and a complacent and respectful behaviour, not only to your superiors but to everybody, will ensure you their regard, and the reward will surely come; but if it should not, I am convinced you have too much good sense to let disappointment sour you. Guard carefully against letting discontent appear in you. It will be sorrow to your friends, a triumph to your competitors, and cannot be productive of any good. Conduct yourself so as to deserve the best that can come to you, and the consciousness of your own proper behaviour will keep you in spirits if it should not come. Let it be your ambition to be foremost in all duty. Do not be a nice observer of turns, but ever present yourself ready for everything, and, unless your officers are very inattentive men, they will not allow others to impose more duty on you than they should. "

This devotion to duty is said to be peculiar to the English nation; and it has certainly more or less characterised our greatest public men. Probably no commander of any other nation ever went into action with such a signal flying as Nelson at Trafalgar—not "Glory, " or "Victory, " or "Honour, " or "Country"— but simply "Duty! " How few are the nations willing to rally to such a battle-cry!

Shortly after the wreck of the BIRKENHEAD off the coast of Africa, in which the officers and men went down firing a FEU-DE-JOIE after seeing the women and children safely embarked in the boats, — Robertson of Brighton, referring to the circumstance in one of his letters, said: "Yes! Goodness, Duty, Sacrifice, —these are the qualities that England honours. She gapes and wonders every now and then, like an awkward peasant, at some other things—railway kings, electro-biology, and other trumperies; but nothing stirs her grand old heart down to its central deeps universally and long, except the Right. She puts on her shawl very badly, and she is awkward enough in a concert-room, scarce knowing a Swedish nightingale from a jackdaw; but—blessings large and long upon her! —she knows how to teach her sons to sink like men amidst sharks and billows, without parade, without display, as if Duty were the most natural thing in the world; and she never mistakes long an actor for a hero, or a hero for an actor. " (6)

It is a grand thing, after all, this pervading spirit of Duty in a nation; and so long as it survives, no one need despair of its future. But when it has departed, or become deadened, and been supplanted by thirst for pleasure, or selfish aggrandisement, or "glory" — then woe to that nation, for its dissolution is near at hand!

If there be one point on which intelligent observers are agreed more than another as to the cause of the late deplorable collapse of France as a nation, it was the utter absence of this feeling of duty, as well as of truthfulness, from the mind, not only of the men, but of the leaders of the French people. The unprejudiced testimony of Baron Stoffel, French military attache at Berlin, before the war, is conclusive on this point. In his private report to the Emperor, found at the Tuileries, which was written in August, 1869, about a year before the outbreak of the war, Baron Stoffel pointed out that the highly-educated and disciplined German people were pervaded by an ardent sense of duty, and did not think it beneath them to reverence sincerely what was noble and lofty; whereas, in all respects, France presented a melancholy contrast. There the people, having sneered at everything, had lost the faculty of respecting anything, and virtue, family life, patriotism, honour, and religion, were represented to a frivolous generation as only fitting subjects for ridicule. (7) Alas! how terribly has France been punished for her sins against truth and duty!

Yet the time was, when France possessed many great men inspired by duty; but they were all men of a comparatively remote past. The race of Bayard, Duguesclin, Coligny, Duquesne, Turenne, Colbert, and Sully, seems to have died out and left no lineage. There has been an occasional great Frenchman of modern times who has raised the cry of Duty; but his voice has been as that of one crying in the wilderness. De Tocqueville was one of such; but, like all men of his stamp, he was proscribed, imprisoned, and driven from public life. Writing on one occasion to his friend Kergorlay, he said: "Like you, I become more and more alive to the happiness which consists in the fulfilment of Duty. I believe there is no other so deep and so real. There is only one great object in the world which deserves our efforts, and that is the good of mankind. " (8)

Although France has been the unquiet spirit among the nations of Europe since the reign of Louis XIV., there have from time to time been honest and faithful men who have lifted up their voices against the turbulent warlike tendencies of the people, and not only preached, but endeavoured to carry into practice, a gospel of peace. Of these, the Abbe de St. -Pierre was one of the most courageous. He had even the boldness to denounce the wars of Louis XIV., and to deny that monarch's right to the epithet of 'Great, ' for which he was punished by expulsion from the Academy. The Abbe was as enthusiastic an agitator for a system of international peace as any member of the modern Society of Friends. As Joseph Sturge went to St. Petersburg to convert the Emperor of Russia to his views, so the Abbe went to Utrecht to convert the Conference sitting there, to his project for a Diet; to secure perpetual peace. Of course he was regarded as an enthusiast, Cardinal Dubois characterising his scheme as "the dream of an honest man. " Yet the Abbe had found his dream in the Gospel; and in what better way could he exemplify the spirit of the Master he served than by endeavouring to abate the horrors and abominations of war? The Conference was an assemblage of men representing Christian States: and the Abbe merely called upon them to put in practice the doctrines they professed to believe. It was of no use: the potentates and their representatives turned to him a deaf ear.

The Abbe de St. -Pierre lived several hundred years too soon. But he determined that his idea should not be lost, and in 1713 he published his 'Project of Perpetual Peace. ' He there proposed the formation of a European Diet, or Senate, to be composed of representatives of all nations, before which princes should be bound, before resorting to arms, to state their grievances and require redress. Writing about eighty years after the publication of this project, Volney asked: "What is a people? —an individual of the society at large. What a war? —a duel between two individual people. In what manner ought a society to act when two of its members fight? —Interfere, and reconcile or repress them. In the days of the Abbe de St. -Pierre, this was treated as a dream; but, happily for the human race, it begins to be realised. " Alas for the prediction of Volney! The twenty-five years that followed the date at which this passage was written, were distinguished by more devastating and furious wars on the part of France than had ever been known in the world before.

The Abbe was not, however, a mere dreamer. He was an active practical philanthropist and anticipated many social improvements which have since become generally adopted. He was the original founder of industrial schools for poor children, where they not only received a good education, but learned some useful trade, by which they might earn an honest living when they grew up to manhood. He advocated the revision and simplification of the whole code of laws—an idea afterwards carried out by the First Napoleon. He wrote against duelling, against luxury, against gambling, against monasticism, quoting the remark of Segrais, that "the mania for a monastic life is the smallpox of the mind. " He spent his whole income in acts of charity—not in almsgiving, but in helping poor children, and poor men and women, to help themselves. His object always was to benefit permanently those whom he assisted. He continued his love of truth and his freedom of speech to the last. At the age of eighty he said: "If life is a lottery for happiness, my lot has been one of the best. " When on his deathbed, Voltaire asked him how he felt, to which he answered, "As about to make a journey into the country. " And in this peaceful frame of mind he died. But so outspoken had St. - Pierre been against corruption in high places, that Maupertius, his Successor at the Academy, was not permitted to pronounce his ELOGE; nor was it until thirty-two years after his death that this honour was done to his memory by D'Alembert. The true and emphatic epitaph of the good, truth-loving, truth-speaking Abbe was this—"HE LOVED MUCH! "

Duty is closely allied to truthfulness of character; and the dutiful man is, above all things, truthful in his words as in his actions. He says and he does the right thing, in the right way, and at the right time.

There is probably no saying of Lord Chesterfield that commends itself more strongly to the approval of manly-minded men, than that it is truth that makes the success of the gentleman. Clarendon, speaking of one of the noblest and purest gentlemen of his age, says of Falkland, that he "was so severe an adorer of truth that he could as easily have given himself leave to steal as to dissemble. "

It was one of the finest things that Mrs. Hutchinson could say of her husband, that he was a thoroughly truthful and reliable man: "He never professed the thing he intended not, nor promised what he believed out of his power, nor failed in the performance of anything that was in his power to fulfil. "

Wellington was a severe admirer of truth. An illustration may be given. When afflicted by deafness he consulted a celebrated aurist, who, after trying all remedies in vain, determined, as a last resource, to inject into the ear a strong solution of caustic. It caused the most intense pain, but the patient bore it with his usual equanimity. The family physician accidentally calling one day, found the Duke with flushed cheeks and bloodshot eyes, and when he rose he staggered about like a drunken man. The doctor asked to be permitted to look at his ear, and then he found that a furious inflammation was going on, which, if not immediately checked, must shortly reach the brain and kill him. Vigorous remedies were at once applied, and the inflammation was checked. But the hearing of that ear was completely destroyed. When the aurist heard of the danger his patient had run, through the violence of the remedy he had employed, he hastened to Apsley House to express his grief and mortification; but the Duke merely said: "Do not say a word more about it—you did all for the best. " The aurist said it would be his ruin when it became known that he had been the cause of so much suffering and danger to his Grace. "But nobody need know anything about it: keep your own counsel, and, depend upon it, I won't say a word to any one. " "Then your Grace will allow me to attend you as usual, which will show the public that you have not withdrawn your confidence from me? " "No, " replied the Duke, kindly but firmly; "I can't do that, for that would be a lie. " He would not act a falsehood any more than he would speak one. (9)

Another illustration of duty and truthfulness, as exhibited in the fulfilment of a promise, may be added from the life of Blucher. When he was hastening with his army over bad roads to the help of Wellington, on the 18th of June, 1815, he encouraged his troops by words and gestures. "Forwards, children—forwards! " "It is impossible; it can't be done, " was the answer. Again and again he urged them. "Children, we must get on; you may say it can't be done, but it MUST be done! I have promised my brother Wellington —PROMISED, do you hear? You wouldn't have me BREAK MY WORD! " And it was done.

Truth is the very bond of society, without which it must cease to exist, and dissolve into anarchy and chaos. A household cannot be governed by lying; nor can a nation. Sir Thomas Browne once asked, "Do the devils lie? " "No, " was his answer; "for then even hell could not subsist. " No considerations can justify the sacrifice of truth, which ought to be sovereign in all the relations of life.

Of all mean vices, perhaps lying is the meanest. It is in some cases the offspring of perversity and vice, and in many others of sheer moral cowardice. Yet many persons think so lightly of it that they will order their servants to lie for them; nor can they feel surprised if, after such ignoble instruction, they find their servants lying for themselves.

Sir Harry Wotton's description of an ambassador as "an honest man sent to lie abroad for the benefit of his country, " though meant as a satire, brought him into disfavour with James I. when it became published; for an adversary quoted it as a principle of the king's religion. That it was not Wotton's real view of the duty of an honest man, is obvious from the lines quoted at the head of this chapter, on 'The Character of a Happy Life, ' in which he eulogises the man

> "Whose armour is his honest thought,
> And simple truth his utmost skill."

But lying assumes many forms — such as diplomacy, expediency, and moral reservation; and, under one guise or another, it is found more or less pervading all classes of society. Sometimes it assumes the form of equivocation or moral dodging — twisting and so stating the things said as to convey a false impression — a kind of lying which a Frenchman once described as "walking round about the truth. "

There are even men of narrow minds and dishonest natures, who pride themselves upon their jesuitical cleverness in equivocation, in their serpent-wise shirking of the truth and getting out of moral back-doors, in order to hide their real opinions and evade the consequences of holding and openly professing them. Institutions or systems based upon any such expedients must necessarily prove false and hollow. "Though a lie be ever so well dressed, " says George Herbert, "it is ever overcome. " Downright lying, though bolder and more vicious, is even less contemptible than such kind of shuffling and equivocation.

Untruthfulness exhibits itself in many other forms: in reticency on the one hand, or exaggeration on the other; in disguise or concealment; in pretended concurrence in others opinions; in assuming an attitude of conformity which is deceptive; in making promises, or allowing them to be implied, which are never intended to be performed; or even in refraining from speaking the truth when to do so is a duty. There are also those who are all things to all men, who say one thing and do another, like Bunyan's Mr. Facing-both-ways; only deceiving themselves when they think they are deceiving others—and who, being essentially insincere, fail to evoke confidence, and invariably in the end turn out failures, if not impostors.

Others are untruthful in their pretentiousness, and in assuming merits which they do not really possess. The truthful man is, on the contrary, modest, and makes no parade of himself and his deeds. When Pitt was in his last illness, the news reached England of the great deeds of Wellington in India. "The more I hear of his exploits, " said Pitt, "the more I admire the modesty with which he receives the praises he merits for them. He is the only man I ever knew that was not vain of what he had done, and yet had so much reason to be so. "

So it is said of Faraday by Professor Tyndall, that "pretence of all kinds, whether in life or in philosophy, was hateful to him. " Dr. Marshall Hall was a man of like spirit—courageously truthful, dutiful, and manly. One of his most intimate friends has said of him that, wherever he met with untruthfulness or sinister motive, he would expose it, saying—"I neither will, nor can, give my consent to a lie. " The question, "right or wrong, " once decided in his own mind, the right was followed, no matter what the sacrifice or the difficulty—neither expediency nor inclination weighing one jot in the balance.

There was no virtue that Dr. Arnold laboured more sedulously to instil into young men than the virtue of truthfulness, as being the manliest of virtues, as indeed the very basis of all true manliness. He designated truthfulness as "moral transparency, " and he valued it more highly than any other quality. When lying was detected, he treated it as a great moral offence; but when a pupil made an assertion, he accepted it with confidence. "If you say so, that is quite enough; OF COURSE I believe your word. " By thus trusting and believing them, he educated the young in truthfulness; the boys at length coming to say to one another: "It's a shame to tell Arnold a lie—he always believes one. " (10)

One of the most striking instances that could be given of the character of the dutiful, truthful, laborious man, is presented in the life of the late George Wilson, Professor of Technology in the University of Edinburgh. (11) Though we bring this illustration under the head of Duty, it might equally have stood under that of

Courage, Cheerfulness, or Industry, for it is alike illustrative of these several qualities.

Wilson's life was, indeed, a marvel of cheerful laboriousness; exhibiting the power of the soul to triumph over the body, and almost to set it at defiance. It might be taken as an illustration of the saying of the whaling-captain to Dr. Kane, as to the power of moral force over physical: "Bless you, sir, the soul will any day lift the body out of its boots! "

A fragile but bright and lively boy, he had scarcely entered manhood ere his constitution began to exhibit signs of disease. As early, indeed, as his seventeenth year, he began to complain of melancholy and sleeplessness, supposed to be the effects of bile. "I don't think I shall live long, " he then said to a friend; "my mind will—must work itself out, and the body will soon follow it. " A strange confession for a boy to make! But he gave his physical health no fair chance. His life was all brain-work, study, and competition. When he took exercise it was in sudden bursts, which did him more harm than good. Long walks in the Highlands jaded and exhausted him; and he returned to his brain- work unrested and unrefreshed.

It was during one of his forced walks of some twenty-four miles in the neighbourhood of Stirling, that he injured one of his feet, and he returned home seriously ill. The result was an abscess, disease of the ankle-joint, and long agony, which ended in the amputation of the right foot. But he never relaxed in his labours. He was now writing, lecturing, and teaching chemistry. Rheumatism and acute inflammation of the eye next attacked him; and were treated by cupping, blisetring, and colchicum. Unable himself to write, he went on preparing his lectures, which he dictated to his sister. Pain haunted him day and night, and sleep was only forced by morphia. While in this state of general prostration, symptoms of pulmonary disease began to show themselves. Yet he continued to give the weekly lectures to which he stood committed to the Edinburgh School of Arts. Not one was shirked, though their delivery, before a large audience, was a most exhausting duty. "Well, there's another nail put into my coffin, " was the remark made on throwing off his top-coat on returning home; and a sleepless night almost invariably followed.

At twenty-seven, Wilson was lecturing ten, eleven, or more hours weekly, usually with setons or open blister-wounds upon him—his "bosom friends, " he used to call them. He felt the shadow of death upon him; and he worked as if his days were numbered. "Don't be surprised, " he wrote to a friend, "if any morning at breakfast you hear that I am gone. " But while he said so, he did not in the least degree indulge in the feeling of sickly sentimentality. He worked on as cheerfully and hopefully as if in the very fulness of his strength. "To none, " said he, "is life so sweet as to those who have lost all fear to die. "

Sometimes he was compelled to desist from his labours by sheer debility, occasioned by loss of blood from the lungs; but after a few weeks' rest and change of air, he would return to his work, saying, "The water is rising in the well again! " Though disease had fastened on his lungs, and was spreading there, and though suffering from a distressing cough, he went on lecturing as usual. To add to his troubles, when one day endeavouring to recover himself from a stumble occasioned by his lameness, he overstrained his arm, and broke the bone near the shoulder. But he recovered from his successive accidents and illnesses in the most extraordinary way. The reed bent, but did not break: the storm passed, and it stood erect as before.

There was no worry, nor fever, nor fret about him; but instead, cheerfulness, patience, and unfailing perseverance. His mind, amidst all his sufferings, remained perfectly calm and serene. He went about his daily work with an apparently charmed life, as if he had the strength of many men in him. Yet all the while he knew he was dying, his chief anxiety being to conceal his state from those about him at home, to whom the knowledge of his actual condition would have been inexpressibly distressing. "I am cheerful among strangers," he said, "and try to live day by day as a dying man. " (12)

He went on teaching as before—lecturing to the Architectural Institute and to the School of Arts. One day, after a lecture before the latter institute, he lay down to rest, and was shortly awakened by the rupture of a bloodvessel, which occasioned him the loss of a considerable quantity of blood. He did not experience the despair and agony that Keats did on a like occasion; (13) though he equally knew that the messenger of death had come, and was waiting for him. He appeared at the family meals as usual, and next day he lectured twice, punctually fulfilling his engagements; but the exertion of speaking was followed by a second attack of haemorrhage. He now became seriously ill, and it was doubted whether he would survive the night. But he did survive; and during his convalescence he was appointed to an important public office — that of Director of the Scottish Industrial Museum, which involved a great amount of labour, as well as lecturing, in his capacity of Professor of Technology, which he held in connection with the office.

From this time forward, his "dear museum, " as he called it, absorbed all his surplus energies. While busily occupied in collecting models and specimens for the museum, he filled up his odds-and-ends of time in lecturing to Ragged Schools, Ragged Kirks, and Medical Missionary Societies. He gave himself no rest, either of mind or body; and "to die working" was the fate he envied. His mind would not give in, but his poor body was forced to yield, and a severe attack of haemorrhage—bleeding from both lungs and stomach (14)—compelled him to relax in his labours. "For a month, or some forty days, " he wrote—"a dreadful Lent —the mind has blown geographically from 'Araby the blest, ' but thermometrically from Iceland the accursed. I have been made a prisoner of war, hit by an icicle in the lungs, and have shivered and burned alternately for a large portion of the last month, and spat blood till I grew pale with coughing. Now I am better, and to-morrow I give my concluding lecture (on Technology), thankful that I have contrived, notwithstanding all my troubles, to carry on without missing a lecture to the last day of the Faculty of Arts, to which I belong. " (15)

How long was it to last? He himself began to wonder, for he had long felt his life as if ebbing away. At length he became languid, weary, and unfit for work; even the writing of a letter cost him a painful effort, and. he felt "as if to lie down and sleep were the only things worth doing. " Yet shortly after, to help a Sunday-school, he wrote his 'Five Gateways of Knowledge, ' as a lecture, and afterwards expanded it into a book. He also recovered strength sufficient to enable him to proceed with his lectures to the institutions to which he belonged, besides on various occasions undertaking to do other people's work. "I am looked upon as good as mad, " he wrote to his brother, "because, on a hasty notice, I took a defaulting lecturer's place at the Philosophical Institution, and discoursed on the Polarization of Light.... But I like work: it is a family weakness. "

Then followed chronic malaise—sleepless nights, days of pain, and more spitting of blood. "My only painless moments, " he says, "were when lecturing. " In this state of prostration and disease, the indefatigable man undertook to write the 'Life of Edward Forbes'; and he did it, like everything he undertook, with admirable ability. He proceeded with his lectures as usual. To an association of teachers he delivered a discourse on the educational value of industrial science. After he had spoken to his audience for an hour, he left them to say whether he should go on or not, and they cheered him on to another half-hour's address. "It is curious, " he wrote, "the feeling of having an audience, like clay in your hands, to mould for a season as you please. It is a terribly responsible power.... I do not mean for a moment to imply that I am indifferent to the good opinion of others—far otherwise; but to gain this is much less a concern with me than to deserve it. It was not so once. I had no wish for unmerited praise, but I was too ready to settle that I did merit it. Now, the word DUTY seems to me the biggest word in the world, and is uppermost in all my serious doings. "

This was written only about four months before his death. A little later he wrote, "I spin my thread of life from week to week, rather than from year to year. " Constant attacks of bleeding from the lungs sapped his little remaining strength, but did not altogether disable him from lecturing. He was amused by one of his friends proposing to put him under trustees for the purpose of looking after his health. But he would not be restrained from working, so long as a vestige of strength remained.

One day, in the autumn of 1859, he returned from his customary lecture in the University of Edinburgh with a severe pain in his side. He was scarcely able to crawl upstairs. Medical aid was sent for, and he was pronounced to be suffering from pleurisy and inflammation of the lungs. His enfeebled frame was ill able to resist so severe a disease, and he sank peacefully to the rest he so longed for, after a few days' illness:

> "Wrong not the dead with tears!
> A glorious bright to-morrow
> Endeth a weary life of pain and sorrow."

The life of George Wilson—so admirably and affectionately related by his sister—is probably one of the most marvellous records of pain and longsuffering, and yet of persistent, noble, and useful work, that is to be found in the whole history of literature. His entire career was indeed but a prolonged illustration of the lines which he himself addressed to his deceased friend, Dr. John Reid, a likeminded man, whose memoir he wrote: -

"Thou wert a daily lesson
  Of courage, hope, and faith;
We wondered at thee living,
  We envy thee thy death.

Thou wert so meek and reverent,
  So resolute of will,
So bold to bear the uttermost,
  And yet so calm and still."

NOTES

(1) From Lovelace's lines to Lucusta (Lucy Sacheverell), 'Going to the Wars. '

(2) Amongst other great men of genius, Ariosto and Michael Angelo devoted to her their service and their muse.

(3) See the Rev. F. W. Farrar's admirable book, entitled 'Seekers after God' (Sunday Library). The author there says: "Epictetus was not a Christian. He has only once alluded to the Christians in his works, and then it is under the opprobrious title of 'Galileans, ' who practised a kind of insensibility in painful circumstances, and an indifference to worldly interests, which Epictetus unjustly sets down to 'mere habit. ' Unhappily, it was not granted to these heathen philosophers in any true sense to know what Christianity was. They thought that it was an attempt to imitate the results of philosophy, without having passed through the necessary discipline. They viewed it with suspicion, they treated it with injustice. And yet in Christianity, and in Christianity alone, they would have found an ideal which would have surpassed their loftiest anticipations. "

(4) Sparks' 'Life of Washington, ' pp. 141-2.

(5) Wellington, like Washington, had to pay the penalty of his adherence to the cause he thought right, in his loss of "popularity. " He was mobbed in the streets of London, and had his windows smashed by the mob, while his wife lay dead in the house. Sir Walter Scott also was hooted and pelted at Hawick by "the people, " amidst cries of "Burke Sir Walter! "

(6) Robertson's 'Life and Letters, ' ii. 157.

(7) We select the following passages from this remarkable report of Baron Stoffel, as being of more than merely temporary interest: -

Who that has lived here (Berlin) will deny that the Prussians are energetic, patriotic, and teeming with youthful vigour; that they are not corrupted by sensual pleasures, but are manly, have earnest convictions, do not think it beneath them to reverence sincerely what is noble and lofty? What a melancholy contrast does France offer in all this? Having sneered at everything, she has lost the faculty of respecting anything. Virtue, family life, patriotism, honour, religion, are represented to a frivolous generation as fitting subjects of ridicule. The theatres have become schools of shamelessness and obscenity. Drop by drop, poison is instilled into the very core of an ignorant and enervated society, which has neither the insight nor the energy left to amend its institutions, nor—which would be the most necessary step to take—become better informed or more moral. One after the other the fine qualities of the nation are dying out. Where is the generosity, the loyalty, the charm of our ESPRIT, and our former elevation of soul? If this goes on, the time will come when this noble race of France will be known only by its faults. And France has no idea that while she is sinking, more earnest nations are stealing the march upon her, are distancing her on the road to progress, and are preparing for her a secondary position in the world.

"I am afraid that these opinions will not be relished in France. However correct, they differ too much from what is usually said and asserted at home. I should wish some enlightened and unprejudiced Frenchmen to come to Prussia and make this country their study. They would soon discover that they were living in the midst of a strong, earnest, and intelligent nation, entirely destitute, it is true, of noble and delicate feelings, of all fascinating charms, but endowed with every solid virtue, and alike distinguished for untiring industry, order, and economy, as well as for patriotism, a strong sense of duty, and that consciousness of personal dignity which in their case is so happily blended with respect for authority and obedience to the law. They would see a country with firm, sound, and moral institutions, whose upper classes are worthy of their rank, and, by possessing the highest degree of culture, devoting themselves to the service of the State, setting an example of patriotism, and knowing how to preserve the influence legitimately their own. They would find a State with an excellent administration where everything is in its right place, and where the most admirable order prevails in every branch of the social and political system. Prussia may be well compared to a massive structure of lofty proportions and astounding solidity, which, though it has nothing to delight the eye or speak to the heart, cannot but impress us with its grand symmetry, equally observable in its broad foundations as in its strong and sheltering roof.

"And what is France? What is French society in these latter days? A hurly-burly of disorderly elements, all mixed and jumbled together; a country in which everybody claims the right to occupy the highest posts, yet few remember that a man to be employed in a responsible position ought to have a well-balanced mind, ought to be strictly moral, to know something of the world, and possess certain intellectual powers; a country in which the highest offices are frequently held by ignorant and uneducated persons, who either boast some special talent, or whose only claim is social position and some versatility and address. What a baneful and degrading state of things! And how natural that, while it lasts, France should be full of a people without a position, without a calling, who do not know what to do with themselves, but are none the less eager to envy and malign every one who does....

"The French do not possess in any very marked degree the qualities required to render general conscription acceptable, or to turn it to account. Conceited and egotistic as they are, the people would object to an innovation whose invigorating force they are unable to comprehend, and which cannot be carried out without virtues which they do not possess—self-abnegation, conscientious recognition of duty, and a willingness to sacrifice personal interests to the loftier demands of the country. As the character of individuals is only improved by experience, most nations require a chastisement before they set about reorganising their political institutions. So Prussia wanted a Jena to make her the strong and healthy country she is. "

(8) Yet even in De Tocqueville's benevolent nature, there was a pervading element of impatience. In the very letter in which the above passage occurs, he says: "Some persons try to be of use to men while they despise them, and others because they love them. In the services rendered by the first, there is always something incomplete, rough, and contemptuous, that inspires neither confidence nor gratitude. I should like to belong to the second class, but often I cannot. I love mankind in general, but I constantly meet with

individuals whose baseness revolts me. I struggle daily against a universal contempt for my fellow, creatures. "—MEMOIRS AND REMAINS OF DE TOCQUEVILLE, vol. i. p. 813. (Letter to Kergorlay, Nov. 13th, 1833).

(9) Gleig's 'Life of Wellington, ' pp. 314, 315.

(10) 'Life of Arnold, ' i. 94.

(11) See the 'Memoir of George Wilson, M.D., F.R. S.E. ' By his sister (Edinburgh, 1860).

(12) Such cases are not unusual. We personally knew a young lady, a countrywoman of Professor Wilson, afflicted by cancer in the breast, who concealed the disease from her parents lest it should occasion them distress. An operation became necessary; and when the surgeons called for the purpose of performing it, she herself answered the door, received them with a cheerful countenance, led them upstairs to her room, and submitted to the knife; and her parents knew nothing of the operation until it was all over. But the disease had become too deeply seated for recovery, and the noble self-denying girl died, cheerful and uncomplaining to the end.

(13) "One night, about eleven o'clock, Keats returned home in a state of strange physical excitement—it might have appeared, to those who did not know him, one of fierce intoxication. He told his friend he had been outside the stage-coach, had received a severe chill, was a little fevered, but added, 'I don't feel it now. ' He was easily persuaded to go to bed, and as he leapt into the cold sheets, before his head was on the pillow, he slightly coughed and said, 'That is blood from my mouth; bring me the candle; let me see this blood' He gazed steadfastly for some moments at the ruddy stain, and then, looking in his friend's face with an expression of sudden calmness never to be forgotten, said, 'I know the colour of that blood—it is arterial blood. I cannot be deceived in that colour; that drop is my death-warrant. I must die! '" —Houghton's LIFE OF KEATS, Ed. 1867, p. 289.

In the case of George Wilson, the bleeding was in the first instance from the stomach, though he afterwards suffered from lung haemorrhage like Keats. Wilson afterwards, speaking of the Lives of Lamb and Keats, which had just appeared, said he had been reading them with great sadness. "There is, " said he, "something in the noble brotherly love of Charles to brighten, and hallow, and relieve that sadness; but Keats's deathbed is the blackness of midnight, unmitigated by one ray of light! "

(14) On the doctors, who attended him in his first attack, mistaking the haemorrhage from the stomach for haemorrhage from the lungs, he wrote: "It would have been but poor consolation to have had as an epitaph: -

"Here lies George Wilson,
  Overtaken by Nemesis;
He died not of Haemoptysis,
  But of Haematemesis."

(15) 'Memoir, ' p. 427.

CHAPTER VIII. —TEMPER.

"Temper is nine-tenths of Christianity."—BISHOP WILSON.

"Heaven is a temper, not a place."—DR. CHALMERS.

"And should my youth, as youth is apt I know,
        Some harshness show;
All vain asperities I day by day
        Would wear away,
Till the smooth temper of my age should be
Like the high leaves upon the Holly Tree"—SOUTHEY.

Even Power itself hath not one-half the might of Gentleness"
        —LEIGH HUNT.

It has been said that men succeed in life quite as much by their temper as by their talents. However this may be, it is certain that their happiness in life depends mainly upon their equanimity of disposition, their patience and forbearance, and their kindness and thoughtfulness for those about them. It is really true what Plato says, that in seeking the good of others we find our own.

There are some natures so happily constituted that they can find good in everything. There is no calamity so great but they can educe comfort or consolation from it—no sky so black but they can discover a gleam of sunshine issuing through it from some quarter or another; and if the sun be not visible to their eyes, they at least comfort themselves with the thought that it IS there, though veiled from them for some good and wise purpose.

Such happy natures are to be envied. They have a beam in the eye — a beam of pleasure, gladness, religious cheerfulness, philosophy, call it what you will. Sunshine is about their hearts, and their mind gilds with its own hues all that it looks upon. When they have burdens to bear, they bear them cheerfully— not repining, nor fretting, nor wasting their energies in useless lamentation, but struggling onward manfully, gathering up such flowers as lie along their path.

Let it not for a moment be supposed that men such as those we speak of are weak and unreflective. The largest and most comprehensive natures are generally also the most cheerful, the most loving, the most hopeful, the most trustful. It is the wise man, of large vision, who is the quickest to discern the moral sunshine gleaming through the darkest cloud. In present evil he sees prospective good; in pain, he recognises the effort of nature to restore health; in trials, he finds correction and discipline; and in sorrow and suffering, he gathers courage, knowledge, and the best practical wisdom.

When Jeremy Taylor had lost all—when his house had been plundered, and his family driven out-of-doors, and all his worldly estate had been sequestrated—he could still write thus: "I am fallen into the hands of publicans and sequestrators, and they have taken all from me; what now? Let me look about me. They have left me the sun and moon, a loving wife, and many friends to pity me, and some to relieve me; and I can still discourse, and, unless I list, they have not taken away my merry countenance and my cheerful spirit, and a good conscience; they have still left me the providence of God, and all the promises of the Gospel, and my religion, and my hopes of heaven, and my charity to them, too; and still I sleep and digest, I eat and drink, I read and meditate.... And he that hath so many causes of joy, and so great, is very much in love with sorrow and peevishness, who loves all these pleasures, and chooses to sit down upon his little handful of thorns. " (1)

Although cheerfulness of disposition is very much a matter of inborn temperament, it is also capable of being trained and cultivated like any other habit. We may make the best of life, or we may make the worst of it; and it depends very much upon ourselves whether we extract joy or misery from it. There are always two sides of life on which we can look, according as we choose—the bright side or the gloomy. We can bring the power of the will to bear in making the choice, and thus cultivate the habit of being happy or the reverse. We can encourage the disposition of looking at the brightest side of things, instead of the darkest. And while we see the cloud, let us not shut our eyes to the silver lining.

The beam in the eye sheds brightness, beauty, and joy upon life in all its phases. It shines upon coldness, and warms it; upon suffering, and comforts it; upon ignorance, and enlightens it; upon sorrow, and cheers it. The beam in the eye gives lustre to intellect, and brightens beauty itself. Without it the sunshine of life is not felt, flowers bloom in vain, the marvels of heaven and earth are not seen or acknowledged, and creation is but a dreary, lifeless, soulless blank.

While cheerfulness of disposition is a great source of enjoyment in life, it is also a great safeguard of character. A devotional writer of the present day, in answer to the question, How are we to overcome temptations? says: "Cheerfulness is the first thing, cheerfulness is the second, and cheerfulness is the third. " It furnishes the best soil for the growth of goodness and virtue. It gives brightness of heart and elasticity of spirit. It is the companion of charity, the nurse of patience the mother of wisdom. It is also the best of moral and mental tonics. "The best cordial of all, " said Dr. Marshall Hall to one of his patients, "is cheerfulness. " And Solomon has said that "a merry heart doeth good like a medicine. " When Luther was once applied to for a remedy against melancholy, his advice was: "Gaiety and courage— innocent gaiety, and rational honourable courage— are the best medicine for young men, and for old men, too; for all men against sad thoughts. " (2) Next to music, if not before it, Luther loved children and flowers. The great gnarled man had a heart as tender as a woman's.

Cheerfulness is also an excellent wearing quality. It has been called the bright weather of the heart. It gives harmony of soul, and is a perpetual song without words. It is tantamount to repose. It enables nature to recruit its strength; whereas worry and discontent debilitate it, involving constant wear-and-tear. How is it that we see such men as Lord Palmerston growing old in harness, working on vigorously to the end? Mainly through equanimity of temper and habitual cheerfulness. They have educated themselves in the habit of endurance, of not being easily provoked, of bearing and forbearing, of hearing harsh and even unjust things said of them without indulging in undue resentment, and avoiding worreting, petty, and self-tormenting cares. An intimate friend of Lord Palmerston, who observed him closely for twenty years, has said that he never saw him angry, with perhaps one exception; and that was when the ministry responsible for the calamity in Affghanistan, of which he was one, were unjustly accused by their opponents of falsehood, perjury, and wilful mutilation of public documents.

So far as can be learnt from biography, men of the greatest genius have been for the most part cheerful, contented men—not eager for reputation, money, or power—but relishing life, and keenly susceptible of enjoyment, as we find reflected in their works. Such seem to have been Homer, Horace, Virgil, Montaigne, Shakspeare, Cervantes. Healthy serene cheerfulness is apparent in their great creations. Among the same class of cheerful-minded men may also be mentioned Luther, More, Bacon, Leonardo da Vinci, Raphael, and Michael Angelo. Perhaps they were happy because constantly occupied, and in the pleasantest of all work—that of creating out of the fulness and richness of their great minds.

Milton, too, though a man of many trials and sufferings, must have been a man of great cheerfulness and elasticity of nature. Though overtaken by blindness, deserted by friends, and fallen upon evil days—"darkness before and danger's voice behind" —yet did he not bate heart or hope, but "still bore up and steered right onward. "

Henry Fielding was a man borne down through life by debt, and difficulty, and bodily suffering; and yet Lady Mary Wortley Montague has said of him that, by virtue of his cheerful disposition, she was persuaded he "had known more happy moments than any person on earth. "

Dr. Johnson, through all his trials and sufferings and hard fights with fortune, was a courageous and cheerful-natured man. He manfully made the best of life, and tried to be glad in it. Once, when a clergyman was complaining of the dulness of society in the country, saying "they only talk of runts" (young cows), Johnson felt flattered by the observation of Mrs. Thrale's mother, who said, "Sir, Dr. Johnson would learn to talk of runts"—meaning that he was a man who would make the most of his situation, whatever it was.

Johnson was of opinion that a man grew better as he grew older, and that his nature mellowed with age. This is certainly a much more cheerful view of human nature than that of Lord Chesterfield, who saw life through the eyes of a cynic, and held that "the heart never grows better by age: it only grows harder. " But both sayings may be true according to the point from which life is viewed, and the temper by which a man is governed; for while the good, profiting by experience, and disciplining themselves by self-control, will grow better, the ill-conditioned, uninfluenced by experience, will only grow worse.

Sir Walter Scott was a man full of the milk of human kindness. Everybody loved him. He was never five minutes in a room ere the little pets of the family, whether dumb or lisping, had found out his kindness for all their generation. Scott related to Captain Basil Hall an incident of his boyhood which showed the tenderness of his nature. One day, a dog coming towards him, he took up a big stone, threw it, and hit the dog. The poor creature had strength enough left to crawl up to him and lick his feet, although he saw its leg was broken. The incident, he said, had given him the bitterest remorse in his after-life; but he added, "An early circumstance of that kind, properly reflected on, is calculated to have the best effect on one's character throughout life. "

"Give me an honest laugher, " Scott would say; and he himself laughed the heart's laugh. He had a kind word for everybody, and his kindness acted all round him like a contagion, dispelling the reserve and awe which his great name was calculated to inspire. "He'll come here, " said the keeper of the ruins of Melrose Abbey to Washington Irving—"he'll come here some-times, wi' great folks in his company, and the first I'll know of it is hearing his voice calling out, 'Johnny! Johnny Bower! ' And when I go out I'm sure to be greeted wi' a joke or a pleasant word. He'll stand and crack and laugh wi' me, just like an auld wife; and to think that of a man that has SUCH AN AWFU' KNOWLEDGE O' HISTORY! "

Dr. Arnold was a man of the same hearty cordiality of manner — full of human sympathy. There was not a particle of affectation or pretence of condescension about him. "I never knew such a humble man as the doctor, " said the parish clerk at Laleham; "he comes and shakes us by the hand as if he was one of us. " "He used to come into my house, " said an old woman near Fox How, "and talk to me as if I were a lady. "

Sydney Smith was another illustration of the power of cheerfulness. He was ever ready to look on the bright side of things; the darkest cloud had to him its silver lining. Whether working as country curate, or as parish rector, he was always kind, laborious, patient, and exemplary; exhibiting in every sphere of life the spirit of a Christian, the kindness of a pastor, and the honour of a gentleman. In his leisure he employed his pen on the side of justice, freedom, education, toleration, emancipation; and his writings, though full of common-sense and bright humour, are never vulgar; nor did he ever pander to popularity or prejudice. His good spirits, thanks to his natural vivacity and stamina of constitution, never forsook him; and in his old age, when borne down by disease, he wrote to a friend: "I have gout, asthma, and seven other maladies, but am otherwise very well. " In one of the last letters he wrote to Lady Carlisle, he said: "If you hear of sixteen or eighteen pounds of flesh wanting an owner, they belong to me. I look as if a curate had been taken out of me. "

Great men of science have for the most part been patient, laborious, cheerful-minded men. Such were Galileo, Descartes, Newton, and Laplace. Euler the mathematician, one of the greatest of natural philosophers, was a distinguished instance. Towards the close of his life he became completely blind; but he went on writing as cheerfully as before, supplying the want of sight by various ingenious mechanical devices, and by the increased cultivation of his memory, which became exceedingly tenacious. His chief pleasure was in the society of his grandchildren, to whom he taught their little lessons in the intervals of his severer studies.

In like manner, Professor Robison of Edinburgh, the first editor of the 'Encyclopaedia Britannica, ' when disabled from work by a lingering and painful disorder, found his chief pleasure in the society of his grandchild. "I am infinitely delighted, " he wrote to James Watt, "with observing the growth of its little soul, and particularly with its numberless instincts, which formerly passed unheeded. I thank the French theorists for more forcibly directing my attention to the finger of God, which I discern in every awkward movement and every wayward whim. They are all guardians of his life and growth and power. I regret indeed that I have not time to make infancy and the development of its powers my sole study. "

One of the sorest trials of a man's temper and patience was that which befell Abauzit, the natural philosopher, while residing at Geneva; resembling in many respects a similar calamity which occurred to Newton, and which he bore with equal resignation. Amongst other things, Abauzit devoted much study to the barometer and its variations, with the object of deducing the general laws which regulated atmospheric pressure. During twenty-seven years he made numerous observations daily, recording them on sheets prepared for the purpose. One day, when a new servant was installed in the house, she immediately proceeded to display her zeal by "putting things to-rights. " Abauzit's study, amongst other rooms, was made tidy and set in order. When he entered it, he asked of the servant, "What have you done with the paper that was round the barometer? " "Oh, sir, " was the reply, "it was so dirty that I burnt it, and put in its place this paper, which you will see is quite new. " Abauzit crossed his arms, and after some moments of internal struggle, he said, in a tone of calmness and resignation: "You have destroyed the results of twenty-seven years labour; in future touch nothing whatever in this room. "

The study of natural history more than that of any other branch of science, seems to be accompanied by unusual cheerfulness and equanimity of temper on the part of its votaries; the result of which is, that the life of naturalists is on the whole more prolonged than that of any other class of men of science. A member of the Linnaean Society has informed us that of fourteen members who died in 1870, two were over ninety, five were over eighty, and two were over seventy. The average age of all the members who died in that year was seventy-five.

Adanson, the French botanist, was about seventy years old when the Revolution broke out, and amidst the shock he lost everything— his fortune, his places, and his gardens. But his patience, courage, and resignation never forsook him. He became reduced to the greatest straits, and even wanted food and clothing; yet his ardour of investigation remained the same. Once, when the Institute invited him, as being one of its oldest members, to assist at a SEANCE, his answer was that he regretted he could not attend for want of shoes. "It was a touching sight, " says Cuvier, "to see the poor old man, bent over the embers of a decaying fire, trying to trace characters with a feeble hand on the little bit of paper which he held, forgetting all the pains of life in some new idea in natural history, which came to him like some beneficent fairy to cheer him in his loneliness. " The Directory eventually gave him a small pension, which Napoleon doubled; and at length, easeful death came to his relief in his seventy-ninth year. A clause in his will, as to the manner of his funeral, illustrates the character of the man. He directed that a garland of flowers, provided by fifty-eight families whom he had established in life, should be the only decoration of his coffin—a slight but touching image of the more durable monument which he had erected for himself in his works.

Such are only a few instances, of the cheerful-working-ness of great men, which might, indeed, be multiplied to any extent. All large healthy natures are cheerful as well as hopeful. Their example is also contagious and diffusive, brightening and cheering all who come within reach of their influence. It was said of Sir John Malcolm, when he appeared in a saddened camp in India, that "it was like a gleam of sunlight,.... no man left him without a smile on his face. He was 'boy Malcolm' still. It was impossible to resist the fascination of his genial presence. " (3)

There was the same joyousness of nature about Edmund Burke. Once at a dinner at Sir Joshua Reynolds's, when the conversation turned upon the suitability of liquors for particular temperaments, Johnson said, "Claret is for boys, port for men, and brandy for heroes. " "Then, " said Burke, "let me have claret: I love to be a boy, and to have the careless gaiety of boyish days. " And so it is, that there are old young men, and young old men—some who are as joyous and cheerful as boys in their old age, and others who are as morose and cheerless as saddened old men while still in their boyhood.

In the presence of some priggish youths, we have heard a cheerful old man declare that, apparently, there would soon be nothing but "old boys" left. Cheerfulness, being generous and genial, joyous and hearty, is never the characteristic of prigs. Goethe used to exclaim of goody-goody persons, "Oh! if they had but the heart to commit an absurdity! " This was when he thought they wanted heartiness and nature. "Pretty dolls! " was his expression when speaking of them, and turning away.

The true basis of cheerfulness is love, hope, and patience. Love evokes love, and begets loving kindness. Love cherishes hopeful and generous thoughts of others. It is charitable, gentle, and truthful. It is a discerner of good. It turns to the brightest side of things, and its face is ever directed towards happiness. It sees "the glory in the grass, the sunshine on the flower. " It encourages happy thoughts, and lives in an atmosphere of cheerfulness. It costs nothing, and yet is invaluable; for it blesses its possessor, and grows up in abundant happiness in the bosoms of others. Even its sorrows are linked with pleasures, and its very tears are sweet.

Bentham lays it down as a principle, that a man becomes rich in his own stock of pleasures in proportion to the amount he distributes to others. His kindness will evoke kindness, and his happiness be increased by his own benevolence. "Kind words, " he says, "cost no more than unkind ones. Kind words produce kind actions, not only on the part of him to whom they are addressed, but on the part of him by whom they are employed; and this not incidentally only, but habitually, in virtue of the principle of association. ".... "It may indeed happen, that the effort of beneficence may not benefit those for whom it was intended; but when wisely directed, it MUST benefit the person from whom it emanates. Good and friendly conduct may meet with an unworthy and ungrateful return; but the absence of gratitude on the part of the receiver cannot destroy the self-approbation which recompenses the giver, and we may scatter the seeds of courtesy and kindliness around us at so little expense. Some of them will inevitably fall on good ground, and grow up into benevolence in the minds of others; and all of them will bear fruit of happiness in the bosom whence they spring. Once blest are all the virtues always; twice blest sometimes. " (4)

The poet Rogers used to tell a story of a little girl, a great favourite with every one who knew her. Some one said to her, "Why does everybody love you so much? " She answered, "I think it is because I love everybody so much. " This little story is capable of a very wide application; for our happiness as human beings, generally speaking, will be found to be very much in proportion to the number of things we love, and the number of things that love us. And the greatest worldly success, however honestly achieved, will contribute comparatively little to happiness, unless it be accompanied by a lively benevolence towards every human being.

Kindness is indeed a great power in the world. Leigh Hunt has truly said that "Power itself hath not one half the might of gentleness. " Men are always best governed through their affections. There is a French proverb which says that, "LES HOMMES SE PRENNENT PAR LA DOUCEUR, " and a coarser English one, to the effect that "More wasps are caught by honey than by vinegar. " "Every act of kindness, " says Bentham, "is in fact an exercise of power, and a stock of friendship laid up; and why should not power exercise itself in the production of pleasure as of pain? "

Kindness does not consist in gifts, but in gentleness and generosity of spirit. Men may give their money which comes from the purse, and withhold their kindness which comes from the heart. The kindness that displays itself in giving money, does not amount to much, and often does quite as much harm as good; but the kindness of true sympathy, of thoughtful help, is never without beneficent results.

The good temper that displays itself in kindness must not be confounded with softness or silliness. In its best form, it is not a merely passive but an active condition of being. It is not by any means indifferent, but largely sympathetic. It does not characterise the lowest and most gelatinous forms of human life, but those that are the most highly organized. True kindness cherishes and actively promotes all reasonable instrumentalities for doing practical good in its own time; and, looking into futurity, sees the same spirit working on for the eventual elevation and happiness of the race.

It is the kindly-dispositioned men who are the active men of the world, while the selfish and the sceptical, who have no love but for themselves, are its idlers. Buffon used to say, that he would give nothing for a young man who did not begin life with an enthusiasm of some sort. It showed that at least he had faith in something good, lofty, and generous, even if unattainable.

Egotism, scepticism, and selfishness are always miserable companions in life, and they are especially unnatural in youth. The egotist is next-door to a fanatic. Constantly occupied with self, he has no thought to spare for others. He refers to himself in all things, thinks of himself, and studies himself, until his own little self becomes his own little god.

Worst of all are the grumblers and growlers at fortune—who find that "whatever is is wrong, " and will do nothing to set matters right—who declare all to be barren "from Dan even to Beersheba. " These grumblers are invariably found the least efficient helpers in the school of life. As the worst workmen are usually the readiest to "strike, " so the least industrious members of society are the readiest to complain. The worst wheel of all is the one that creaks.

There is such a thing as the cherishing of discontent until the feeling becomes morbid. The jaundiced see everything about them yellow. The ill-conditioned think all things awry, and the whole world out-of-joint. All is vanity and vexation of spirit. The little girl in PUNCH, who found her doll stuffed with bran, and forthwith declared everything to be hollow and wanted to "go into a nunnery, " had her counterpart in real life. Many full-grown people are quite as morbidly unreasonable. There are those who may be said to "enjoy bad health; " they regard it as a sort of property. They can speak of "MY headache"—"MY backache, " and so forth, until in course of time it becomes their most cherished possession. But perhaps it is the source to them of much coveted sympathy, without which they might find themselves of comparatively little importance in the world.

We have to be on our guard against small troubles, which, by encouraging, we are apt to magnify into great ones. Indeed, the chief source of worry in the world is not real but imaginary evil —small vexations and trivial afflictions. In the presence of a great sorrow, all petty troubles disappear; but we are too ready to take some cherished misery to our bosom, and to pet it there. Very often it is the child of our fancy; and, forgetful of the many means of happiness which lie within our reach, we indulge this spoilt child of ours until it masters us. We shut the door against cheerfulness, and surround ourselves with gloom. The habit gives a colouring to our life. We grow querulous, moody, and unsympathetic. Our conversation becomes full of regrets. We are harsh in our judgment of others. We are unsociable, and think everybody else is so. We make our breast a storehouse of pain, which we inflict upon ourselves as well as upon others.

This disposition is encouraged by selfishness: indeed, it is for the most part selfishness unmingled, without any admixture of sympathy or consideration for the feelings of those about us. It is simply wilfulness in the wrong direction. It is wilful, because it might be avoided. Let the necessitarians argue as they may, freedom of will and action is the possession of every man and woman. It is sometimes our glory, and very often it is our shame: all depends upon the manner in which it is used. We can choose to look at the bright side of things, or at the dark. We can follow good and eschew evil thoughts. We can be wrongheaded and wronghearted, or the reverse, as we ourselves determine. The world will be to each one of us very much what we make it. The cheerful are its real possessors, for the world belongs to those who enjoy it.

It must, however, be admitted that there are cases beyond the reach of the moralist. Once, when a miserable-looking dyspeptic called upon a leading physician and laid his case before him, "Oh! " said the doctor, "you only want a good hearty laugh: go and see Grimaldi. " "Alas! " said the miserable patient, "I am Grimaldi! " So, when Smollett, oppressed by disease, travelled over Europe in the hope of finding health, he saw everything through his own jaundiced eyes. "I'll tell it, " said Smellfungus, "to the world. " "You had better tell it, " said Sterne, "to your physician. " The restless, anxious, dissatisfied temper, that is ever ready to run and meet care half-way, is fatal to all happiness and peace of mind. How often do we see men and women set themselves about as if with stiff bristles, so that one dare scarcely approach them without fear of being pricked! For want of a little occasional command over one's temper, an amount of misery is occasioned in society which is positively frightful. Thus enjoyment is turned into bitterness, and life becomes like a journey barefooted amongst thorns and briers and prickles. "Though sometimes small evils, " says Richard Sharp, "like invisible insects, inflict great pain, and a single hair may stop a vast machine, yet the chief secret of comfort lies in not suffering trifles to vex us; and in prudently cultivating an undergrowth of small pleasures, since very few great ones, alas! are let on long leases. " (5)

St. Francis de Sales treats the same topic from the Christian's point of view. "How carefully, " he says, "we should cherish the little virtues which spring up at the foot of the Cross! " When the saint was asked, "What virtues do you mean? " he replied: "Humility, patience, meekness, benignity, bearing one another's burden, condescension, softness of heart, cheerfulness, cordiality, compassion, forgiving injuries, simplicity, candour— all, in short of that sort of little virtues. They, like unobtrusive violets, love the shade; like them are sustained by dew; and though, like them, they make little show, they shed a sweet odour on all around. " (6)

And again he said: "If you would fall into any extreme, let it be on the side of gentleness. The human mind is so constructed that it resists rigour, and yields to softness. A mild word quenches anger, as water quenches the rage of fire; and by benignity any soil may be rendered fruitful. Truth, uttered with courtesy, is heaping coals of fire on the head—or rather, throwing roses in the face. How can we resist a foe whose weapons are pearls and diamonds? " (7)

Meeting evils by anticipation is not the way to overcome them. If we perpetually carry our burdens about with us, they will soon bear us down under their load. When evil comes, we must deal with it bravely and hopefully. What Perthes wrote to a young man, who seemed to him inclined to take trifles as well as sorrows too much to heart, was doubtless good advice: "Go forward with hope and confidence. This is the advice given thee by an old man, who has had a full share of the burden and heat of life's day. We must ever stand upright, happen what may, and for this end we must cheerfully resign ourselves to the varied influences of this many- coloured life. You may call this levity, and you are partly right; for flowers and colours are but trifles light as air, but such levity is a constituent portion of our human nature, without which it would sink under the weight of time. While on earth we must still play with earth, and with that which blooms and fades upon its breast. The consciousness of this mortal life being but the way to a higher goal, by no means precludes our playing with it cheerfully; and, indeed, we must do so, otherwise our energy in action will entirely fail. " (8)

Cheerfulness also accompanies patience, which is one of the main conditions of happiness and success in life. "He that will be served, " says George Herbert, "must be patient. " It was said of the cheerful and patient King Alfred, that "good fortune accompanied him like a gift of God. " Marlborough's expectant calmness was great, and a principal secret of his success as a general. "Patience will overcome all things, " he wrote to Godolphin, in 1702. In the midst of a great emergency, while baffled and opposed by his allies, he said, "Having done all that is possible, we should submit with patience. "

Last and chiefest of blessings is Hope, the most common of possessions; for, as Thales the philosopher said, "Even those who have nothing else have hope. " Hope is the great helper of the poor. It has even been styled "the poor man's bread. " It is also the sustainer and inspirer of great deeds. It is recorded of Alexander the Great, that when he succeeded to the throne of Macedon, he gave away amongst his friends the greater part of the estates which his father had left him; and when Perdiccas asked him what he reserved for himself, Alexander answered, "The greatest possession of all, — Hope! "

The pleasures of memory, however great, are stale compared with those of hope; for hope is the parent of all effort and endeavour; and "every gift of noble origin is breathed upon by Hope's perpetual breath. " It may be said to be the moral engine that moves the world, and keeps it in action; and at the end of all there stands before us what Robertson of Ellon styled "The Great Hope. " "If it were not for Hope, " said Byron, "where would the Future be? —in hell! It is useless to say where the Present is, for most of us know; and as for the Past, WHAT predominates in memory? —Hope baffled. ERGO, in all human affairs it is Hope, Hope, Hope! " (9)

NOTES

(1) Jeremy Taylor's 'Holy Living. '

(2) 'Michelet's 'Life of Luther, ' pp. 411-12.

(3) Sir John Kaye's 'Lives of Indian Officers. '

(4) 'Deontology, ' pp. 130-1, 144.

(5) 'Letters and Essays, ' p. 67.

(6) 'Beauties of St. Francis de Sales. '

(7) Ibid.

(8) 'Life of Perthes, ' ii. 449.

(9) Moore's 'Life of Byron, ' 8vo. Ed., p. 483.

CHAPTER IX. —MANNER—ART.

"We must be gentle, now we are gentlemen." —SHAKSPEARE.

"Manners are not idle, but the fruit
Of noble nature and of loyal mind." —TENNYSON.

"A beautiful behaviour is better than a beautiful form; it gives a higher pleasure than statues and pictures; it is the finest of the fine arts. " —EMERSON.

"Manners are often too much neglected; they are most important to men, no less than to women.... Life is too short to get over a bad manner; besides, manners are the shadows of virtues. " —THE REV. SIDNEY SMITH.

Manner is one of the principal external graces of character. It is the ornament of action, and often makes the commonest offices beautiful by the way in which it performs them. It is a happy way of doing things, adorning even the smallest details of life, and contributing to render it, as a whole, agreeable and pleasant.

Manner is not so frivolous or unimportant as some may think it to be; for it tends greatly to facilitate the business of life, as well as to sweeten and soften social intercourse. "Virtue itself, " says Bishop Middleton, "offends, when coupled with a forbidding manner. "

Manner has a good deal to do with the estimation in which men are held by the world; and it has often more influence in the government of others than qualities of much greater depth and substance. A manner at once gracious and cordial is among the greatest aids to success, and many there are who fail for want of it. (1) For a great deal depends upon first impressions; and these are usually favourable or otherwise according to a man's courteousness and civility.

While rudeness and gruffness bar doors and shut hearts, kindness and propriety of behaviour, in which good manners consist, act as an "open sesame" everywhere. Doors unbar before them, and they are a passport to the hearts of everybody, young and old.

There is a common saying that "Manners make the man; " but this is not so true as that "Man makes the manners. " A man may be gruff, and even rude, and yet be good at heart and of sterling character; yet he would doubtless be a much more agreeable, and probably a much more useful man, were he to exhibit that suavity of disposition and courtesy of manner which always gives a finish to the true gentleman.

Mrs. Hutchinson, in the noble portraiture of her husband, to which we have already had occasion to refer, thus describes his manly courteousness and affability of disposition: - "I cannot say whether he were more truly magnanimous or less proud; he never disdained the meanest person, nor flattered the greatest; he had a loving and sweet courtesy to the poorest, and would often employ many spare hours with the commonest soldiers and poorest labourers; but still so ordering his familiarity, that it never raised them to a contempt, but entertained still at the same time a reverence and love of him. " (2)

A man's manner, to a certain extent, indicates his character. It is the external exponent of his inner nature. It indicates his taste, his feelings, and his temper, as well as the society to which he has been accustomed. There is a conventional manner, which is of comparatively little importance; but the natural manner, the outcome of natural gifts, improved by careful self- culture, signifies a great deal.

Grace of manner is inspired by sentiment, which is a source of no slight enjoyment to a cultivated mind. Viewed in this light, sentiment is of almost as much importance as talents and acquirements, while it is even more influential in giving the direction to a man s tastes and character. Sympathy is the golden key that unlocks the hearts of others. It not only teaches politeness and courtesy, but gives insight and unfolds wisdom, and may almost be regarded as the crowning grace of humanity.

Artificial rules of politeness are of very little use. What passes by the name of "Etiquette" is often of the essence of unpoliteness and untruthfulness. It consists in a great measure of posture-making, and is easily seen through. Even at best, etiquette is but a substitute for good manners, though it is often but their mere counterfeit.

Good manners consist, for the most part, in courteousness and kindness. Politeness has been described as the art of showing, by external signs, the internal regard we have for others. But one may be perfectly polite to another without necessarily having a special regard for him. Good manners are neither more nor less than beautiful behaviour. It has been well said, that "a beautiful form is better than a beautiful face, and a beautiful behaviour is better than a beautiful form; it gives a higher pleasure than statues or pictures—it is the finest of the fine arts. "

The truest politeness comes of sincerity. It must be the outcome of the heart, or it will make no lasting impression; for no amount of polish can dispense with truthfulness. The natural character must be allowed to appear, freed of its angularities and asperities. Though politeness, in its best form, should (as St. Francis de Sales says) resemble water—"best when clearest, most simple, and without taste, "—yet genius in a man will always cover many defects of manner, and much will be excused to the strong and the original. Without genuineness and individuality, human life would lose much of its interest and variety, as well as its manliness and robustness of character.

True courtesy is kind. It exhibits itself in the disposition to contribute to the happiness of others, and in refraining from all that may annoy them. It is grateful as well as kind, and readily acknowledges kind actions. Curiously enough, Captain Speke found this quality of character recognised even by the natives of Uganda on the shores of Lake Nyanza, in the heart of Africa, where, he says. "Ingratitude, or neglecting to thank a person for a benefit conferred, is punishable. "

True politeness especially exhibits itself in regard for the personality of others. A man will respect the individuality of another if he wishes to be respected himself. He will have due regard for his views and opinions, even though they differ from his own. The well-mannered man pays a compliment to another, and sometimes even secures his respect, by patiently listening to him. He is simply tolerant and forbearant, and refrains from judging harshly; and harsh judgments of others will almost invariably provoke harsh judgments of ourselves.

The unpolite impulsive man will, however, sometimes rather lose his friend than his joke. He may surely be pronounced a very foolish person who secures another's hatred at the price of a moment's gratification. It was a saying of Brunel the engineer— himself one of the kindest-natured of men—that "spite and ill- nature are among the most expensive luxuries in life. " Dr. Johnson once said: "Sir, a man has no more right to SAY an uncivil thing than to ACT one—no more right to say a rude thing to another than to knock him down. "

A sensible polite person does not assume to be better or wiser or richer than his neighbour. He does not boast of his rank, or his birth, or his country; or look down upon others because they have not been born to like privileges with himself. He does not brag of his achievements or of his calling, or "talk shop" whenever he opens his mouth. On the contrary, in all that he says or does, he will be modest, unpretentious, unassuming; exhibiting his true character in performing rather than in boasting, in doing rather than in talking.

Want of respect for the feelings of others usually originates in selfishness, and issues in hardness and repulsiveness of manner. It may not proceed from malignity so much as from want of sympathy and want of delicacy—a want of that perception of, and attention to, those little and apparently trifling things by which pleasure is given or pain occasioned to others. Indeed, it may be said that in self-sacrificingness, so to speak, in the ordinary intercourse of life, mainly consists the difference between being well and ill bred.

Without some degree of self-restraint in society, a man may be found almost insufferable. No one has pleasure in holding intercourse with such a person, and he is a constant source of annoyance to those about him. For want of self-restraint, many men are engaged all their lives in fighting with difficulties of their own making, and rendering success impossible by their own crossgrained ungentleness; whilst others, it may be much less gifted, make their way and achieve success by simple patience, equanimity, and self-control.

It has been said that men succeed in life quite as much by their temper as by their talents. However this may be, it is certain that their happiness depends mainly on their temperament, especially upon their disposition to be cheerful; upon their complaisance, kindliness of manner, and willingness to oblige others—details of conduct which are like the small-change in the intercourse of life, and are always in request.

Men may show their disregard of others in various unpolite ways— as, for instance, by neglect of propriety in dress, by the absence of cleanliness, or by indulging in repulsive habits. The slovenly dirty person, by rendering himself physically disagreeable, sets the tastes and feelings of others at defiance, and is rude and uncivil only under another form.

David Ancillon, a Huguenot preacher of singular attractiveness, who studied and composed his sermons with the greatest care, was accustomed to say "that it was showing too little esteem for the public to take no pains in preparation, and that a man who should appear on a ceremonial-day in his nightcap and dressing-gown, could not commit a greater breach of civility. "

The perfection of manner is ease—that it attracts no man's notice as such, but is natural and unaffected. Artifice is incompatible with courteous frankness of manner. Rochefoucauld has said that "nothing so much prevents our being natural as the desire of appearing so. " Thus we come round again to sincerity and truthfulness, which find their outward expression in graciousness, urbanity, kindliness, and consideration for the feelings of others. The frank and cordial man sets those about him at their ease. He warms and elevates them by his presence, and wins all hearts. Thus manner, in its highest form, like character, becomes a genuine motive power.

"The love and admiration, " says Canon Kingsley, "which that truly brave and loving man, Sir Sydney Smith, won from every one, rich and poor, with whom he came in contact seems to have arisen from the one fact, that without, perhaps, having any such conscious intention, he treated rich and poor, his own servants and the noblemen his guests, alike, and alike courteously, considerately, cheerfully, affectionately—so leaving a blessing, and reaping a blessing, wherever he went. "

Good manners are usually supposed to be the peculiar characteristic of persons gently born and bred, and of persons moving in the higher rather than in the lower spheres of society. And this is no doubt to a great extent true, because of the more favourable surroundings of the former in early life. But there is no reason why the poorest classes should not practise good manners towards each other as well as the richest.

Men who toil with their hands, equally with those who do not, may respect themselves and respect one another; and it is by their demeanour to each other—in other words, by their manners—that self-respect as well as mutual respect are indicated. There is scarcely a moment in their lives, the enjoyment of which might not be enhanced by kindliness of this sort—in the workshop, in the street, or at home. The civil workman will exercise increased power amongst his class, and gradually induce them to imitate him by his persistent steadiness, civility, and kindness. Thus Benjamin Franklin, when a working-man, is said to have reformed the habits of an entire workshop.

One may be polite and gentle with very little money in his purse. Politeness goes far, yet costs nothing. It is the cheapest of all commodities. It is the humblest of the fine arts, yet it is so useful and so pleasure-giving, that it might almost be ranked amongst the humanities.

Every nation may learn something of others; and if there be one thing more than another that the English working-class might afford to copy with advantage from their Continental neighbours, it is their politeness. The French and Germans, of even the humblest classes, are gracious in manner, complaisant, cordial, and well-bred. The foreign workman lifts his cap and respectfully salutes his fellow-workman in passing. There is no sacrifice of manliness in this, but grace and dignity. Even the lowest poverty of the foreign workpeople is not misery, simply because it is cheerful. Though not receiving one-half the income which our working-classes do, they do not sink into wretchedness and drown their troubles in drink; but contrive to make the best of life, and to enjoy it even amidst poverty.

Good taste is a true economist. It may be practised on small means, and sweeten the lot of labour as well as of ease. It is all the more enjoyed, indeed, when associated with industry and the performance of duty. Even the lot of poverty is elevated by taste. It exhibits itself in the economies of the household. It gives brightness and grace to the humblest dwelling. It produces refinement, it engenders goodwill, and creates an atmosphere of cheerfulness. Thus good taste, associated with kindliness, sympathy, and intelligence, may elevate and adorn even the lowliest lot.

The first and best school of manners, as of character, is always the Home, where woman is the teacher. The manners of society at large are but the reflex of the manners of our collective homes, neither better nor worse. Yet, with all the disadvantages of ungenial homes, men may practise self-culture of manner as of intellect, and learn by good examples to cultivate a graceful and agreeable behaviour towards others. Most men are like so many gems in the rough, which need polishing by contact with other and better natures, to bring out their full beauty and lustre. Some have but one side polished, sufficient only to show the delicate graining of the interior; but to bring out the full qualities of the gem needs the discipline of experience, and contact with the best examples of character in the intercourse of daily life.

A good deal of the success of manner consists in tact, and it is because women, on the whole, have greater tact than men, that they prove its most influential teachers. They have more self- restraint than men, and are naturally more gracious and polite. They possess an intuitive quickness and readiness of action, have a keener insight into character, and exhibit greater discrimination and address. In matters of social detail, aptness and dexterity come to them like nature; and hence well-mannered men usually receive their best culture by mixing in the society of gentle and adroit women.

Tact is an intuitive art of manner, which carries one through a difficulty better than either talent or knowledge. "Talent, " says a public writer, "is power: tact is skill. Talent is weight: tact is momentum. Talent knows what to do: tact knows how to do it. Talent makes a man respectable: tact makes him respected. Talent is wealth: tact is ready-money. "

The difference between a man of quick tact and of no tact whatever was exemplified in an interview which once took place between Lord Palmerston and Mr. Behnes, the sculptor. At the last sitting which Lord Palmerston gave him, Behnes opened the conversation with—"Any news, my Lord, from France? How do we stand with Louis Napoleon? " The Foreign Secretary raised his eyebrows for an instant, and quietly replied, "Really, Mr. Behnes, I don't know: I have not seen the newspapers! " Poor Behnes, with many excellent qualities and much real talent, was one of the many men who entirely missed their way in life through want of tact.

Such is the power of manner, combined with tact, that Wilkes, one of the ugliest of men, used to say, that in winning the graces of a lady, there was not more than three days' difference between him and the handsomest man in England.

But this reference to Wilkes reminds us that too much importance must not be attached to manner, for it does not afford any genuine test of character. The well-mannered man may, like Wilkes, be merely acting a part, and that for an immoral purpose. Manner, like other fine arts, gives pleasure, and is exceedingly agreeable to look upon; but it may be assumed as a disguise, as men "assume a virtue though they have it not. " It is but the exterior sign of good conduct, but may be no more than skin-deep. The most highly- polished person may be thoroughly depraved in heart; and his superfine manners may, after all, only consist in pleasing gestures and in fine phrases.

On the other hand, it must be acknowledged that some of the richest and most generous natures have been wanting in the graces of courtesy and politeness. As a rough rind sometimes covers the sweetest fruit, so a rough exterior often conceals a kindly and hearty nature. The blunt man may seem even rude in manner, and yet, at heart, be honest, kind, and gentle.

John Knox and Martin Luther were by no means distinguished for their urbanity. They had work to do which needed strong and determined rather than well-mannered men. Indeed, they were both thought to be unnecessarily harsh and violent in their manner. "And who art thou, " said Mary Queen of Scots to Knox, "that presumest to school the nobles and sovereign of this realm? "— "Madam, " replied Knox, "a subject born within the same. " It is said that his boldness, or roughness, more than once made Queen Mary weep. When Regent Morton heard of this, he said, "Well, 'tis better that women should weep than bearded men. "

As Knox was retiring from the Queen's presence on one occasion, he overheard one of the royal attendants say to another, "He is not afraid! " Turning round upon them, he said: "And why should the pleasing face of a gentleman frighten me? I have looked on the faces of angry men, and yet have not been afraid beyond measure. " When the Reformer, worn-out by excess of labour and anxiety, was at length laid to his rest, the Regent, looking down into the open grave, exclaimed, in words which made a strong impression from their aptness and truth—"There lies he who never feared the face of man!"

Luther also was thought by some to be a mere compound of violence and ruggedness. But, as in the case of Knox, the times in which he lived were rude and violent; and the work he had to do could scarcely have been accomplished with gentleness and suavity. To rouse Europe from its lethargy, he had to speak and to write with force, and even vehemence. Yet Luther's vehemence was only in words. His apparently rude exterior covered a warm heart. In private life he was gentle, loving, and affectionate. He was simple and homely, even to commonness. Fond of all common pleasures and enjoyments, he was anything but an austere man, or a bigot; for he was hearty, genial, and even "jolly. " Luther was the common people's hero in his lifetime, and he remains so in Germany to this day.

Samuel Johnson was rude and often gruff in manner. But he had been brought up in a rough school. Poverty in early life had made him acquainted with strange companions. He had wandered in the streets with Savage for nights together, unable between them to raise money enough to pay for a bed. When his indomitable courage and industry at length secured for him a footing in society, he still bore upon him the scars of his early sorrows and struggles. He was by nature strong and robust, and his experience made him unaccommodating and self-asserting. When he was once asked why he was not invited to dine out as Garrick was, he answered, "Because great lords and ladies did not like to have their mouths stopped; " and Johnson was a notorious mouth-stopper, though what he said was always worth listening to.

Johnson's companions spoke of him as "Ursa Major; " but, as Goldsmith generously said of him, "No man alive has a more tender heart; he has nothing of the bear about him but his skin. " The kindliness of Johnson's nature was shown on one occasion by the manner in which he assisted a supposed lady in crossing Fleet Street. He gave her his arm, and led her across, not observing that she was in liquor at the time. But the spirit of the act was not the less kind on that account. On the other hand, the conduct of the bookseller on whom Johnson once called to solicit employment, and who, regarding his athletic but uncouth person, told him he had better "go buy a porter's knot and carry trunks, " in howsoever bland tones the advice might have been communicated, was simply brutal.

While captiousness of manner, and the habit of disputing and contradicting everything said, is chilling and repulsive, the opposite habit of assenting to, and sympathising with, every statement made, or emotion expressed, is almost equally disagreeable. It is unmanly, and is felt to be dishonest. "It may seem difficult, " says Richard Sharp, "to steer always between bluntness and plain-dealing, between giving merited praise and lavishing indiscriminate flattery;

but it is very easy—good- humour, kindheartedness, and perfect simplicity, being all that are requisite to do what is right in the right way. " (3)

At the same time, many are unpolite—not because they mean to be so, but because they are awkward, and perhaps know no better. Thus, when Gibbon had published the second and third volumes of his 'Decline and Fall, ' the Duke of Cumberland met him one day, and accosted him with, "How do you do, Mr. Gibbon? I see you are always AT IT in the old way—SCRIBBLE, SCRIBBLE, SCRIBBLE! " The Duke probably intended to pay the author a compliment, but did not know how better to do it, than in this blunt and apparently rude way.

Again, many persons are thought to be stiff, reserved, and proud, when they are only shy. Shyness is characteristic of most people of Teutonic race. It has been styled "the English mania, " but it pervades, to a greater or less degree, all the Northern nations. The ordinary Englishman, when he travels abroad, carries his shyness with him. He is stiff, awkward, ungraceful, undemonstrative, and apparently unsympathetic; and though he may assume a brusqueness of manner, the shyness is there, and cannot be wholly concealed. The naturally graceful and intensely social French cannot understand such a character; and the Englishman is their standing joke—the subject of their most ludicrous caricatures. George Sand attributes the rigidity of the natives of Albion to a stock of FLUIDE BRITANNIQUE which they carry about with them, that renders them impassive under all circumstances, and "as impervious to the atmosphere of the regions they traverse as a mouse in the centre of an exhausted receiver. " (4)

The average Frenchman or Irishman excels the average Englishman, German, or American in courtesy and ease of manner, simply because it is his nature. They are more social and less self-dependent than men of Teutonic origin, more demonstrative and less reticent; they are more communicative, conversational, and freer in their intercourse with each other in all respects; whilst men of German race are comparatively stiff, reserved, shy, and awkward. At the same time, a people may exhibit ease, gaiety, and sprightliness of character, and yet possess no deeper qualities calculated to inspire respect. They may have every grace of manner, and yet be heartless, frivolous, selfish. The character may be on the surface only, and without any solid qualities for a foundation.

There can be no doubt as to which of the two sorts of people—the easy and graceful, or the stiff and awkward—it is most agreeable to meet, either in business, in society, or in the casual intercourse of life. Which make the fastest friends, the truest men of their word, the most conscientious performers of their duty, is an entirely different matter.

The dry GAUCHE Englishman—to use the French phrase, L'ANGLAIS EMPETRE—is certainly a somewhat disagreeable person to meet at first. He looks as if he had swallowed a poker. He is shy himself, and the cause of shyness in others. He is stiff, not because he is proud, but because he is shy; and he cannot shake it off, even if he would. Indeed, we should not be surprised to find that even the clever writer who describes the English Philistine in all his enormity of awkward manner and absence of grace, were himself as shy as a bat.

When two shy men meet, they seem like a couple of icicles. They sidle away and turn their backs on each other in a room, or when travelling creep into the opposite corners of a railway-carriage. When shy Englishmen are about to start on a journey by railway, they walk along the train, to discover an empty compartment in which to bestow themselves; and when once ensconced, they inwardly hate the next man who comes in. So; on entering the dining-room of their club, each shy man looks out for an unoccupied table, until sometimes—all the tables in the room are occupied by single diners. All this apparent unsociableness is merely shyness — the national characteristic of the Englishman.

"The disciples of Confucius, " observes Mr. Arthur Helps, "say that when in the presence of the prince, his manner displayed RESPECTFUL UNEASINESS. There could hardly be given any two words which more fitly describe the manner of most Englishmen when in society. " Perhaps it is due to this feeling that Sir Henry Taylor, in his 'Statesman, ' recommends that, in the management of interviews, the minister should be as "near to the door" as possible; and, instead of bowing his visitor out, that he should take refuge, at the end of an interview, in the adjoining room. "Timid and embarrassed men, " he says, "will sit as if they were rooted to the spot, when they are conscious that they have to traverse the length of a room in their retreat. In every case, an interview will find a more easy and pleasing termination WHEN THE DOOR IS AT HAND as the last words are spoken. " (5)

The late Prince Albert, one of the gentlest and most amiable, was also one of the most retiring of men. He struggled much against his sense of shyness, but was never able either to conquer or conceal it. His biographer, in explaining its causes, says: "It was the shyness of a very delicate nature, that is not sure it will please, and is without the confidence and the vanity which often go to form characters that are outwardly more genial. " (6)

But the Prince shared this defect with some of the greatest of Englishmen. Sir Isaac Newton was probably the shyest man of his age. He kept secret for a time some of his greatest discoveries, for fear of the notoriety they might bring him. His discovery of the Binomial Theorem and its most important applications, as well as his still greater discovery of the Law of Gravitation, were not published for years after they were made; and when he communicated to Collins his solution of the theory of the moon's rotation round the earth, he forbade him to insert his name in connection with it in the 'Philosophical Transactions, ' saying: "It would, perhaps, increase my acquaintance—the thing which I chiefly study to decline. "

From all that can be learnt of Shakspeare, it is to be inferred that he was an exceedingly shy man. The manner in which his plays were sent into the world—for it is not known that he edited or authorized the publication of a single one of them—and the dates at which they respectively appeared, are mere matters of conjecture. His appearance in his own plays in second and even third-rate parts—his indifference to reputation, and even his apparent aversion to be held in repute by his contemporaries—his disappearance from London (the seat and centre of English histrionic art) so soon as he had realised a moderate competency— and his retirement about the age of forty, for the remainder of his days, to a life of obscurity in a small town in the midland counties—all seem to unite in proving the shrinking nature of the man, and his unconquerable shyness.

It is also probable that, besides being shy—and his shyness may, like that of Byron, have been increased by his limp—Shakspeare did not possess in any high degree the gift of hope. It is a remarkable circumstance, that whilst the great dramatist has, in the course of his writings, copiously illustrated all other gifts, affections, and virtues, the passages are very rare in which Hope is mentioned, and then it is usually in a desponding and despairing tone, as when he says:

"The miserable hath no other medicine, But only Hope. "

Many of his sonnets breathe the spirit of despair and hopelessness. (7) He laments his lameness; (8) apologizes for his profession as an actor; (9) expresses his "fear of trust" in himself, and his hopeless, perhaps misplaced, affection; (10) anticipates a "coffin'd doom; " and utters his profoundly pathetic cry "for restful death. "

It might naturally be supposed that Shakspeare's profession of an actor, and his repeated appearances in public, would speedily overcome his shyness, did such exist. But inborn shyness, when strong, is not so easily conquered. (11) Who could have believed that the late Charles Mathews, who entertained crowded houses night after night, was naturally one of the shyest of men? He would even make long circuits (lame though he was) along the byelanes of London to avoid recognition. His wife says of him, that he looked "sheepish" and confused if recognised; and that his eyes would fall, and his colour would mount, if he heard his name even whispered in passing along the streets. (12)

Nor would it at first sight have been supposed that Lord Byron was affected with shyness, and yet he was a victim to it; his biographer relating that, while on a visit to Mrs. Pigot, at Southwell, when he saw strangers approaching, he would instantly jump out of the window, and escape on to the lawn to avoid them.

But a still more recent and striking instance is that of the late Archbishop Whately, who, in the early part of his life, was painfully oppressed by the sense of shyness. When at Oxford, his white rough coat and white hat obtained for him the soubriquet of "The White Bear; " and his manners, according to his own account of himself, corresponded with the appellation. He was directed, by way of remedy, to copy the example of the best-mannered men he met in society; but the attempt to do this only increased his shyness, and he failed. He found that he was all the while thinking of himself, rather than of others; whereas thinking of others, rather than of one's self, is of the true essence of politeness.

Finding that he was making no progress, Whately was driven to utter despair; and then he said to himself: "Why should I endure this torture all my life to no purpose? I would bear it still if there was any success to be hoped for; but since there is not, I will die quietly, without taking any more doses. I have tried my very utmost, and find that I must be as awkward as a bear all my life, in spite of it. I will endeavour to think as little about it as a bear, and make up my mind to endure what can't be cured. " From this time forth he struggled to shake off all consciousness as to manner, and to disregard censure as much as possible. In adopting this course, he says: "I succeeded beyond my expectations; for I not only got rid of the personal suffering of shyness, but also of most of those faults of manner which consciousness produces; and acquired at once an easy and natural manner—careless, indeed, in the extreme, from its originating in a stern defiance of opinion, which I had convinced myself must be ever against me; rough and awkward, for smoothness and grace are quite out of my way, and, of course, tutorially pedantic; but unconscious, and therefore giving expression to that goodwill towards men which I really feel; and these, I believe, are the main points. " (13)

Washington, who was an Englishman in his lineage, was also one in his shyness. He is described incidentally by Mr. Josiah Quincy, as "a little stiff in his person, not a little formal in his manner, and not particularly at ease in the presence of strangers. He had the air of a country gentleman not accustomed to mix much in society, perfectly polite, but not easy in his address and conversation, and not graceful in his movements. "

Although we are not accustomed to think of modern Americans as shy, the most distinguished American author of our time was probably the shyest of men. Nathaniel Hawthorne was shy to the extent of morbidity. We have observed him, when a stranger entered the room where he was, turn his back for the purpose of avoiding recognition. And yet, when the crust of his shyness was broken, no man could be more cordial and genial than Hawthorne.

We observe a remark in one of Hawthorne's lately-published 'Notebooks, ' (14) that on one occasion he met Mr. Helps in society, and found him "cold. " And doubtless Mr. Helps thought the same of him. It was only the case of two shy men meeting, each thinking the other stiff and reserved, and parting before their mutual film of shyness had been removed by a little friendly intercourse. Before pronouncing a hasty judgment in such cases, it would be well to bear in mind the motto of Helvetius, which Bentham says proved such a real treasure to him: "POUR AIMER LES HOMMES, IL FAUT ATTENDRE PEU. "

We have thus far spoken of shyness as a defect. But there is another way of looking at it; for even shyness has its bright side, and contains an element of good. Shy men and shy races are ungraceful and undemonstrative, because, as regards society at large, they are comparatively unsociable. They do not possess those elegances of manner, acquired by free intercourse, which distinguish the social races, because their tendency is to shun society rather than to seek it. They are shy in the presence of strangers, and shy even in their own families. They hide their affections under a robe of reserve, and when they do give way to their feelings, it is only in some very hidden inner-chamber. And yet the feelings ARE there, and not the less healthy and genuine that they are not made the subject of exhibition to others.

It was not a little characteristic of the ancient Germans, that the more social and demonstrative peoples by whom they were surrounded should have characterised them as the NIEMEC, or Dumb men. And the same designation might equally apply to the modern English, as compared, for example, with their nimbler, more communicative and vocal, and in all respects more social neighbours, the modern French and Irish.

But there is one characteristic which marks the English people, as it did the races from which they have mainly sprung, and that is their intense love of Home. Give the Englishman a home, and he is comparatively indifferent to society. For the sake of a holding which he can call his own, he will cross the seas, plant himself on the prairie or amidst the primeval forest, and make for himself a home. The solitude of the wilderness has no fears for him; the society of his wife and family is sufficient, and he cares for no other. Hence it is that the people of Germanic origin, from whom the English and Americans have alike sprung, make the best of colonizers, and are now rapidly extending themselves as emigrants and settlers in all parts of the habitable globe.

The French have never made any progress as colonizers, mainly because of their intense social instincts—the secret of their graces of manner, —and because they can never forget that they are Frenchmen. (15) It seemed at one time within the limits of probability that the French would occupy the greater part of the North American continent. From Lower Canada their line of forts extended up the St. Lawrence, and from Fond du Lac on Lake Superior, along the River St. Croix, all down the Mississippi, to its mouth at New Orleans. But the great, self-reliant, industrious "Niemec, " from a fringe of settlements along the seacoast, silently extended westward, settling and planting themselves everywhere solidly upon the soil; and nearly all that now remains of the original French occupation of America, is the French colony of Acadia, in Lower Canada.

And even there we find one of the most striking illustrations of that intense sociability of the French which keeps them together, and prevents their spreading over and planting themselves firmly in a new country, as it is the instinct of the men of Teutonic race to do. While, in Upper Canada, the colonists of English and Scotch descent penetrate the forest and the wilderness, each settler living, it may be, miles apart from his nearest neighbour, the Lower Canadians of French descent continue clustered together in villages, usually consisting of a line of houses on either side of the road, behind which extend their long strips of farm-land, divided and subdivided to an extreme tenuity. They willingly submit to all the inconveniences of this method of farming for the sake of each other's society, rather than betake themselves to the solitary backwoods, as English, Germans, and Americans so readily do. Indeed, not only does the American backwoodsman become accustomed to solitude, but he prefers it. And in the Western States, when settlers come too near him, and the country seems to become "overcrowded, " he retreats before the advance of society, and, packing up his "things" in a waggon, he sets out cheerfully, with his wife and family, to found for himself a new home in the Far West.

Thus the Teuton, because of his very shyness, is the true colonizer. English, Scotch, Germans, and Americans are alike ready to accept solitude, provided they can but establish a home and maintain a family. Thus their comparative indifference to society has tended to spread this race over the earth, to till and to subdue it; while the intense social instincts of the French, though issuing in much greater gracefulness of manner, has stood in their way as colonizers; so that, in the countries in which they have planted themselves—as in Algiers and elsewhere—they have remained little more than garrisons. (16)

There are other qualities besides these, which grow out of the comparative unsociableness of the Englishman. His shyness throws him back upon himself, and renders him self-reliant and self-dependent. Society not being essential to his happiness, he takes refuge in reading, in study, in invention; or he finds pleasure in industrial work, and becomes the best of mechanics. He does not fear to entrust himself to the solitude of the ocean, and he becomes a fisherman, a sailor, a discoverer. Since the early Northmen scoured the northern seas, discovered America, and sent their fleets along the shores of Europe and up the Mediterranean, the seamanship of the men of Teutonic race has always been in the ascendant.

The English are inartistic for the same reason that they are unsociable. They may make good colonists, sailors, and mechanics; but they do not make good singers, dancers, actors, artistes, or modistes. They neither dress well, act well, speak well, nor write well. They want style—they want elegance. What they have to do they do in a straightforward manner, but without grace. This was strikingly exhibited at an International Cattle Exhibition held at Paris a few years ago. At the close of the Exhibition, the competitors came up with the prize animals to receive the prizes. First came a gay and gallant Spaniard, a magnificent man, beautifully dressed, who received a prize of the lowest class with an air and attitude that would have become a grandee of the highest order. Then came Frenchmen and Italians, full of grace, politeness, and CHIC— themselves elegantly dressed, and their animals decorated to the horns with flowers and coloured ribbons harmoniously blended. And last of all came the exhibitor who was to receive the first prize— a slouching man, plainly dressed, with a pair of farmer's gaiters on, and without even a flower in his buttonhole. "Who is he? " asked the spectators. "Why, he is the Englishman, " was the reply. "The Englishman! —that the representative of a great country! " was the general exclamation. But it was the Englishman all over. He was sent there, not to exhibit himself, but to show "the best beast, " and he did it, carrying away the first prize. Yet he would have been nothing the worse for the flower in his buttonhole.

To remedy this admitted defect of grace and want of artistic taste in the English people, a school has sprung up amongst us for the more general diffusion of fine art. The Beautiful has now its teachers and preachers, and by some it is almost regarded in the light of a religion. "The Beautiful is the Good"—"The Beautiful is the True"— "The Beautiful is the priest of the Benevolent, " are among their texts. It is believed that by the study of art the tastes of the people may be improved; that by contemplating objects of beauty their nature will become purified; and that by being thereby withdrawn from sensual enjoyments, their character will be refined and elevated.

But though such culture is calculated to be elevating and purifying in a certain degree, we must not expect too much from it. Grace is a sweetener and embellisher of life, and as such is worthy of cultivation. Music, painting, dancing, and the fine arts, are all sources of pleasure; and though they may not be sensual, yet they are sensuous, and often nothing more. The cultivation of a taste for beauty of form or colour, of sound or attitude, has no necessary effect upon the cultivation of the mind or the development of the character. The contemplation of fine works of art will doubtless improve the taste, and excite admiration; but a single noble action done in the sight of men will more influence the mind, and stimulate the character to imitation, than the sight of miles of statuary or acres of pictures. For it is mind, soul, and heart—not taste or art— that make men great.

It is indeed doubtful whether the cultivation of art—which usually ministers to luxury—has done so much for human progress as is generally supposed. It is even possible that its too exclusive culture may effeminate rather than strengthen the character, by laying it more open to the temptations of the senses. "It is the nature of the imaginative temperament cultivated by the arts, " says Sir Henry Taylor, "to undermine the courage, and, by abating strength of character, to render men more easily subservient—SEQUACES, CEREOS, ET AD MANDATA DUCTILES. " (17) The gift of the artist greatly differs from that of the thinker; his highest idea is to mould his subject—whether it be of painting, or music, or literature—into that perfect grace of form in which thought (it may not be of the deepest) finds its apotheosis and immortality.

Art has usually flourished most during the decadence of nations, when it has been hired by wealth as the minister of luxury. Exquisite art and degrading corruption were contemporary in Greece as well as in Rome. Phidias and Iktinos had scarcely completed the Parthenon, when the glory of Athens had departed; Phidias died in prison; and the Spartans set up in the city the memorials of their own triumph and of Athenian defeat. It was the same in ancient Rome, where art was at its greatest height when the people were in their most degraded condition. Nero was an artist, as well as Domitian, two of the greatest monsters of the Empire. If the "Beautiful" had been the "Good, " Commodus must have been one of the best of men. But according to history he was one of the worst.

Again, the greatest period of modern Roman art was that in which Pope Leo X. flourished, of whose reign it has been said, that "profligacy and licentiousness prevailed amongst the people and clergy, as they had done almost uncontrolled ever since the pontificate of Alexander VI. " In like manner, the period at which art reached its highest point in the Low Countries was that which immediately succeeded the destruction of civil and religious liberty, and the prostration of the national life under the despotism of Spain. If art could elevate a nation, and the contemplation of The Beautiful were calculated to make men The Good—then Paris ought to contain a population of the wisest and best of human beings. Rome also is a great city of art; and yet there, the VIRTUS or valour of the ancient Romans has characteristically degenerated into VERTU, or a taste for knicknacks; whilst, according to recent accounts, the city itself is inexpressibly foul. (18)

Art would sometimes even appear to have a close connection with dirt; and it is said of Mr. Ruskin, that when searching for works of art in Venice, his attendant in his explorations would sniff an ill-odour, and when it was strong would say, "Now we are coming to something very old and fine! "—meaning in art. (19) A little common education in cleanliness, where it is wanting, would probably be much more improving, as well as wholesome, than any amount of education in fine art. Ruffles are all very well, but it is folly to cultivate them to the neglect of the shirt.

Whilst, therefore, grace of manner, politeness of behaviour, elegance of demeanour, and all the arts that contribute to make life pleasant and beautiful, are worthy of cultivation, it must not be at the expense of the more solid and enduring qualities of honesty, sincerity, and truthfulness. The fountain of beauty must be in the heart; more than in the eye, and if art do not tend to produce beautiful life and noble practice, it will be of comparatively little avail. Politeness of manner is not worth much, unless accompanied by polite action. Grace may be but skin- deep—very pleasant and attractive, and yet very heartless. Art is a source of innocent enjoyment, and an important aid to higher culture; but unless it leads to higher culture, it will probably be merely sensuous. And when art is merely sensuous, it is enfeebling and demoralizing rather than strengthening or elevating. Honest courage is of greater worth than any amount of grace; purity is better than elegance; and cleanliness of body, mind, and heart, than any amount of fine art.

In fine, while the cultivation of the graces is not to be neglected, it should ever be held in mind that there is something far higher and nobler to be aimed at—greater than pleasure, greater than art, greater than wealth, greater than power, greater than intellect, greater than genius—and that is, purity and excellence of character. Without a solid sterling basis of individual goodness, all the grace, elegance, and art in the world would fail to save or to elevate a people.

NOTES

(1) Locke thought it of greater importance that an educator of youth should be well-bred and well-tempered, than that he should be either a thorough classicist or man of science. Writing to Lord Peterborough on his son's education, Locke said: "Your Lordship would have your son's tutor a thorough scholar, and I think it not much matter whether he be any scholar or no: if he but understand Latin well, and have a general scheme of the sciences, I think that enough. But I would have him WELL-BRED and WELL-TEMPERED."

(2) Mrs. Hutchinson's 'Memoir of the Life of Lieut. -Colonel Hutchinson, ' p. 32.

(3) 'Letters and Essays, ' p. 59.

(4) 'Lettres d'un Voyageur. '

(5) Sir Henry Taylor's 'Statesman, ' p. 59.

(6) Introduction to the 'Principal Speeches and Addresses of His Royal Highness the Prince Consort, ' 1862.

(7) "When in disgrace with fortune and men's eyes,
    I all alone beween my outcast state,
  And troubled deaf heaven with my bootless cries,
    And look upon myself and curse my fate;
  WISHING ME LIKE TO ONE MORE RICH IN HOPE,
    Featured like him, like him with friends possessed,
  Desiring this man's art, and that man's scope,
    With what I most enjoy, contented least;
  Yet in these thoughts, MYSELF ALMOST DESPISING,
    Haply I think on thee," &c.—SONNET XXIX.

"So I, MADE LAME by sorrow's dearest spite," &c.—SONNET
XXXVI

"So I, MADE LAME by sorrow's dearest spite, " &c. —SONNET
XXXVI

(8) "And strength, by LIMPING sway disabled," &c.—SONNET
LXVI.

"Speak of MY LAMENESS, and I straight will halt."—SONNET
LXXXIX.

(9) "Alas! 'tis true, I have gone here and there,
    And MADE MYSELF A MOTLEY TO THE VIEW,
Gored mine own thoughts, sold cheap what is most dear,
    Made old offences of affections new," &c.—SONNET CX.

"Oh, for my sake do you with fortune chide!
  The guilty goddess of my harmful deeds,
That did not better for my life provide,
  THAN PUBLIC MEANS, WHICH PUBLIC MANNERS BREED;
Thence comes it that my name receives a brand,
  And almost thence my nature is subdued,
To what it works in like the dyer's hand," &c.—SONNET CXI.

(10) "In our two loves there is but one respect,
    Though in our loves a separable spite,
Which though it alter not loves sole effect;
    Yet doth it steal sweet hours from love's delight,
I may not evermore acknowledge thee,
    Lest MY BEWAILED GUILT SHOULD DO THEE SHAME."—
SONNET XXXVI.

(11) It is related of Garrick, that when subpoenaed on Baretti's trial,
and required to give his evidence before the court—though he had
been accustomed for thirty years to act with the greatest self-
possession in the presence of thousands—he became so perplexed
and confused, that he was actually sent from the witness-box by the
judge, as a man from whom no evidence could be obtained.

(12)Mrs. Mathews' 'Life and Correspondence of Charles Mathews, '
(Ed. 1860) p. 232.

(13) Archbishop Whately's 'Commonplace Book. '

(14) Emerson is said to have had Nathaniel Hawthorne in his mind when writing the following passage in his 'Society and Solitude: ' — "The most agreeable compliment you could pay him was, to imply that you had not observed him in a house or a street where you had met him. Whilst he suffered at being seen where he was, he consoled himself with the delicious thought of the inconceivable number of places where he was not. All he wished of his tailor was to provide that sober mean of colour and cut which would never detain the eye for a moment.... He had a remorse, running to despair, of his social GAUCHERIES, and walked miles and miles to get the twitchings out of his face, and the starts and shrugs out of his arms and shoulders. 'God may forgive sins, ' he said, 'but awkwardness has no forgiveness in heaven or earth. '"

(15) In a series of clever articles in the REVUE DES DEUX MONDES, entitled, 'Six mille Lieues a toute Vapeur, ' giving a description of his travels in North America, Maurice Sand keenly observed the comparatively anti-social proclivities of the American compared with the Frenchman. The one, he says, is inspired by the spirit of individuality, the other by the spirit of society. In America he sees the individual absorbing society; as in France he sees society absorbing the individual. "Ce peuple Anglo-Saxon, " he says, "qui trouvait devant lui la terre, l'instrument de travail, sinon inepuisable, du mons inepuise, s'est mis a l'exploiter sous l'inspiration de l'egoisme; et nous autres Francais, nous n'avons rien su en faire, parceque NOUS NE POUVONS RIEN DANS L'ISOLEMENT.... L'Americain supporte la solitude avec un stoicisme admirable, mais effrayant; il ne l'aime pas, il ne songe qu'a la detruire.... Le Francais est tout autre. Il aime son parent, son ami, son compagnon, et jusqu'a son voisin d'omnibus ou de theatre, si sa figure lui est sympathetique. Pourquoi? Parce qu'il le regarde et cherche son ame, parce qu'il vit dans son semblable autant qu'en lui-meme. Quand il est longtemps seul, il deperit, et quand il est toujours seul, it meurt. "

All this is perfectly true, and it explains why the comparatively unsociable Germans, English, and Americans, are spreading over the earth, while the intensely sociable Frenchmen, unable to enjoy life without each other's society, prefer to stay at home, and France fails to extend itself beyond France.

(16) The Irish have, in many respects, the same strong social instincts as the French. In the United States they cluster naturally in the towns, where they have their "Irish Quarters, " as in England. They are even more Irish there than at home, and can no more forget that they are Irishmen than the French can that they are Frenchmen. "I deliberately assert, " says Mr. Maguire, in his recent work on 'The Irish in America, ' "that it is not within the power of language to describe adequately, much less to exaggerate, the evils consequent on the unhappy tendency of the Irish to congregate in the large towns of America. " It is this intense socialism of the Irish that keeps them in a comparatively hand-to- mouth condition in all the States of the Union.

(17) 'The Statesman, ' p. 35.

(18) Nathaniel Hawthorne, in his 'First Impressions of France and Italy, ' says his opinion of the uncleanly character of the modern Romans is so unfavourable that he hardly knows how to express it "But the fact is that through the Forum, and everywhere out of the commonest foot-track and roadway, you must look well to your steps.... Perhaps there is something in the minds of the people of these countries that enables them to dissever small ugliness from great sublimity and beauty. They spit upon the glorious pavement of St. Peter's, and wherever else they like; they place paltry-looking wooden confessionals beneath its sublime arches, and ornament them with cheap little coloured prints of the Crucifixion; they hang tin hearts, and other tinsel and trumpery, at the gorgeous shrines of the saints, in chapels that are encrusted with gems, or marbles almost as precious; they put pasteboard statues of saints beneath the dome of the Pantheon; — in short, they let the sublime and the ridiculous come close together, and are not in the least troubled by the proximity. "

(19) Edwin Chadwick's 'Address to the Economic Science and Statistic Section, ' British Association (Meeting, 1862).

CHAPTER X—COMPANIONSHIP OF BOOKS.

> "Books, we know,
> Are a substantial world, both pure and good,
> Round which, with tendrils strong as flesh and blood,
> Our pastime and our happiness can grow." — WORDSWORTH.

"Not only in the common speech of men, but in all art too—which is or should be the concentrated and conserved essence of what men can speak and show—Biography is almost the one thing needful"
—CARLYLE.

"I read all biographies with intense interest. Even a man without a heart, like Cavendish, I think about, and read about, and dream about, and picture to myself in all possible ways, till he grows into a living being beside me, and I put my feet into his shoes, and become for the time Cavendish, and think as he thought, and do as he did."—GEORGE WILSON.

> "My thoughts are with the dead; with them
> I live in long-past years;
> Their virtues love, their faults condemn;
> Partake their hopes and fears;
> And from their lessons seek and find
> Instruction with a humble mind."—SOUTHEY.

A man may usually be known by the books he reads, as well as by the company he keeps; for there is a companionship of books as well as of men; and one should always live in the best company, whether it be of books or of men.

A good book may be among the best of friends. It is the same to- day that it always was, and it will never change. It is the most patient and cheerful of companions. It does not turn its back upon us in times of adversity or distress. It always receives us with the same kindness; amusing and instructing us in youth, and comforting and consoling us in age.

Men often discover their affinity to each other by the mutual love they have for a book—just as two persons sometimes discover a friend by the admiration which both entertain for a third. There is an old proverb, "Love me, love my dog. " But there is more wisdom in this: "Love me, love my book. " The book is a truer and higher bond of union. Men can think, feel, and sympathise with each other through their favourite author. They live in him together, and he in them.

"Books, " said Hazlitt, "wind into the heart; the poet's verse slides into the current of our blood. We read them when young, we remember them when old. We read there of what has happened to others; we feel that it has happened to ourselves. They are to be had everywhere cheap and good. We breathe but the air of books. We owe everything to their authors, on this side barbarism. "

A good book is often the best urn of a life, enshrining the best thoughts of which that life was capable; for the world of a man's life is, for the most part, but the world of his thoughts. Thus the best books are treasuries of good words and golden thoughts, which, remembered and cherished, become our abiding companions and comforters. "They are never alone, " said Sir Philip Sidney, "that are accompanied by noble thoughts. " The good and true thought may in time of temptation be as an angel of mercy purifying and guarding the soul. It also enshrines the germs of action, for good words almost invariably inspire to good works.

Thus Sir Henry Lawrence prized above all other compositions Wordsworth's 'Character of the Happy Warrior, ' which he endeavoured to embody in his own life. It was ever before him as an exemplar. He thought of it continually, and often quoted it to others. His biographer says: "He tried to conform his own life and to assimilate his own character to it; and he succeeded, as all men succeed who are truly in earnest. " (1)

Books possess an essence of immortality. They are by far the most lasting products of human effort. Temples crumble into ruin; pictures and statues decay; but books survive. Time is of no account with great thoughts, which are as fresh to-day as when they first passed through their authors' minds ages ago. What was then said and thought still speaks to us as vividly as ever from the printed page. The only effect of time has been to sift and winnow out the bad products; for nothing in literature can long survive but what is really good. (2)

Books introduce us into the best society; they bring us into the presence of the greatest minds that have ever lived. We hear what they said and did; we see them as if they were really alive; we are participators in their thoughts; we sympathise with them, enjoy with them, grieve with them; their experience becomes ours, and we feel as if we were in a measure actors with them in the scenes which they describe.

The great and good do not die, even in this world. Embalmed in books their spirits walk abroad. The book is a living voice. It is an intellect to which one still listens. Hence we ever remain under the influence of the great men of old:

> "The dead but sceptred sovrans, who still rule
> Our spirits from their urns."

The imperial intellects of the world are as much alive now as they were ages ago. Homer still lives; and though his personal history is hidden in the mists of antiquity, his poems are as fresh to-day as if they had been newly written. Plato still teaches his transcendent philosophy; Horace, Virgil, and Dante still sing as when they lived; Shakspeare is not dead: his body was buried in 1616, but his mind is as much alive in England now, and his thought as far-reaching, as in the time of the Tudors.

The humblest and poorest may enter the society of these great spirits without being thought intrusive. All who can read have got the ENTREE. Would you laugh? —Cervantes or Rabelais will laugh with you. Do you grieve? —there is Thomas a Kempis or Jeremy Taylor to grieve with and console you. Always it is to books, and the spirits of great men embalmed in them, that we turn, for entertainment, for instruction and solace—in joy and in sorrow, as in prosperity and in adversity.

Man himself is, of all things in the world, the most interesting to man. Whatever relates to human life—its experiences, its joys, its sufferings, and its achievements—has usually attractions for him beyond all else. Each man is more or less interested in all other men as his fellow-creatures—as members of the great family of humankind; and the larger a man's culture, the wider is the range of his sympathies in all that affects the welfare of his race.

Men's interest in each other as individuals manifests itself in a thousand ways—in the portraits which they paint, in the busts which they carve, in the narratives which they relate of each other. "Man, " says Emerson, "can paint, or make, or think, nothing but Man. " Most of all is this interest shown in the fascination which personal history possesses for him. "Man s sociality of nature, " says Carlyle, "evinces itself, in spite of all that can be said, with abundance of evidence, by this one fact, were there no other: the unspeakable delight he takes in Biography. "

Great, indeed, is the human interest felt in biography! What are all the novels that find such multitudes of readers, but so many fictitious biographies? What are the dramas that people crowd to see, but so much acted biography? Strange that the highest genius should be employed on the fictitious biography, and so much commonplace ability on the real!

Yet the authentic picture of any human being's life and experience ought to possess an interest greatly beyond that which is fictitious, inasmuch as it has the charm of reality. Every person may learn something from the recorded life of another; and even comparatively trivial deeds and sayings may be invested with interest, as being the outcome of the lives of such beings as we ourselves are.

The records of the lives of good men are especially useful. They influence our hearts, inspire us with hope, and set before us great examples. And when men have done their duty through life in a great spirit, their influence will never wholly pass away. "The good life, " says George Herbert, "is never out of season. "

Goethe has said that there is no man so commonplace that a wise man may not learn something from him. Sir Walter Scott could not travel in a coach without gleaning some information or discovering some new trait of character in his companions. (3) Dr. Johnson once observed that there was not a person in the streets but he should like to know his biography—his experiences of life, his trials, his difficulties, his successes, and his failures. How much more truly might this be said of the men who have made their mark in the world's history, and have created for us that great inheritance of civilization of which we are the possessors! Whatever relates to such men—to their habits, their manners, their modes of living, their personal history, their conversation, their maxims, their virtues, or their greatness—is always full of interest, of instruction, of encouragement, and of example.

Character

The great lesson of Biography is to show what man can be and do at his best. A noble life put fairly on record acts like an inspiration to others. It exhibits what life is capable of being made. It refreshes our spirit, encourages our hopes, gives us new strength and courage and faith—faith in others as well as in ourselves. It stimulates our aspirations, rouses us to action, and incites us to become co-partners with them in their work. To live with such men in their biographies, and to be inspired by their example, is to live with the best of men, and to mix in the best of company.

At the head of all biographies stands the Great Biography, the Book of Books. And what is the Bible, the most sacred and impressive of all books—the educator of youth, the guide of manhood, and the consoler of age—but a series of biographies of great heroes and patriarchs, prophets, kings, and judges, culminating in the greatest biography of all, the Life embodied in the New Testament? How much have the great examples there set forth done for mankind! How many have drawn from them their truest strength, their highest wisdom, their best nurture and admonition! Truly does a great Roman Catholic writer describe the Bible as a book whose words "live in the ear like a music that can never be forgotten—like the sound of church bells which the convert hardly knows how he can forego. Its felicities often seem to be almost things rather than mere words. It is part of the national mind, and the anchor of national seriousness. The memory of the dead passes into it, The potent traditions of childhood are stereotyped in its verses. The power of all the griefs and trials of man is hidden beneath its words. It is the representative of his best moments, and all that has been about him of soft, and gentle, and pure, and penitent, and good, speaks to him for ever out of his English Bible. It is his sacred thing, which doubt has never dimmed and controversy never soiled. In the length and breadth of the land there is not a Protestant with one spark of religiousness about him whose spiritual biography is not in his Saxon Bible. " (4)

It would, indeed, be difficult to overestimate the influence which the lives of the great and good have exercised upon the elevation of human character. "The best biography, " says Isaac Disraeli, "is a reunion with human existence in its most excellent state. " Indeed, it is impossible for one to read the lives of good men, much less inspired men, without being unconsciously lighted and lifted up in them, and growing insensibly nearer to what they thought and did. And even the lives of humbler persons, of men of faithful and honest spirit, who have done their duty in life well, are not without an elevating influence upon the character of those who come after them.

History itself is best studied in biography. Indeed, history is biography—collective humanity as influenced and governed by individual men. "What is all history, " says Emerson, "but the work of ideas, a record of the incomparable energy which his infinite aspirations infuse into man? " In its pages it is always persons we see more than principles. Historical events are interesting to us mainly in connection with the feelings, the sufferings, and interests of those by whom they are accomplished. In history we are surrounded by men long dead, but whose speech and whose deeds survive. We almost catch the sound of their voices; and what they did constitutes the interest of history. We never feel personally interested in masses of men; but we feel and sympathise with the individual actors, whose biographies afford the finest and most real touches in all great historical dramas.

Among the great writers of the past, probably the two that have been most influential in forming the characters of great men of action and great men of thought, have been Plutarch and Montaigne —the one by presenting heroic models for imitation, the other by probing questions of constant recurrence in which the human mind in all ages has taken the deepest interest. And the works of both are for the most part cast in a biographic form, their most striking illustrations consisting in the exhibitions of character and experience which they contain.

Plutarch's 'Lives, ' though written nearly eighteen hundred years ago, like Homer's 'Iliad, ' still holds its ground as the greatest work of its kind. It was the favourite book of Montaigne; and to Englishmen it possesses the special interest of having been Shakspeare's principal authority in his great classical dramas. Montaigne pronounced Plutarch to be "the greatest master in that kind of writing"—the biographic; and he declared that he "could no sooner cast an eye upon him but he purloined either a leg or a wing."

Alfieri was first drawn with passion to literature by reading Plutarch. "I read, " said he, "the lives of Timoleon, Caesar, Brutus, Pelopidas, more than six times, with cries, with tears, and with such transports, that I was almost furious.... Every time that I met with one of the grand traits of these great men, I was seized with such vehement agitation as to be unable to sit still. " Plutarch was also a favourite with persons of such various minds as Schiller and Benjamin Franklin, Napoleon and Madame Roland. The latter was so fascinated by the book that she carried it to church with her in the guise of a missal, and read it surreptitiously during the service.

It has also been the nurture of heroic souls such as Henry IV. of France, Turenne, and the Napiers. It was one of Sir William Napier's favourite books when a boy. His mind was early imbued by it with a passionate admiration for the great heroes of antiquity; and its influence had, doubtless, much to do with the formation of his character, as well as the direction of his career in life. It is related of him, that in his last illness, when feeble and exhausted, his mind wandered back to Plutarch's heroes; and he descanted for hours to his son-in-law on the mighty deeds of Alexander, Hannibal, and Caesar. Indeed, if it were possible to poll the great body of readers in all ages whose minds have been influenced and directed by books, it is probable that—excepting always the Bible—the immense majority of votes would be cast in favour of Plutarch.

And how is it that Plutarch has succeeded in exciting an interest which continues to attract and rivet the attention of readers of all ages and classes to this day? In the first place, because the subject of his work is great men, who occupied a prominent place in the world's history, and because he had an eye to see and a pen to describe the more prominent events and circumstances in their lives. And not only so, but he possessed the power of portraying the individual character of his heroes; for it is the principle of individuality which gives the charm and interest to all biography. The most engaging side of great men is not so much what they do as what they are, and does not depend upon their power of intellect but on their personal attractiveness. Thus, there are men whose lives are far more eloquent than their speeches, and whose personal character is far greater than their deeds.

It is also to be observed, that while the best and most carefully-drawn of Plutarch's portraits are of life-size, many of them are little more than busts. They are well-proportioned but compact, and within such reasonable compass that the best of them—such as the lives of Caesar and Alexander—may be read in half an hour. Reduced to this measure, they are, however, greatly more imposing than a lifeless Colossus, or an exaggerated giant. They are not overlaid by disquisition and description, but the characters naturally unfold themselves. Montaigne, indeed, complained of Plutarch's brevity. "No doubt, " he added, "but his reputation is the better for it, though in the meantime we are the worse. Plutarch would rather we should applaud his judgment than commend his knowledge, and had rather leave us with an appetite to read more than glutted with what we have already read. He knew very well that a man may say too much even on the best subjects.... Such as have lean and spare bodies stuff themselves out with clothes; so they who are defective in matter, endeavour to make amends with words. (5)

Plutarch possessed the art of delineating the more delicate features of mind and minute peculiarities of conduct, as well as the foibles and defects of his heroes, all of which is necessary to faithful and accurate portraiture. "To see him, " says Montaigne, "pick out a light action in a man's life, or a word, that does not seem to be of any importance, is itself a whole discourse. " He even condescends to inform us of such homely particulars as that Alexander carried his head affectedly on one side; that Alcibiades was a dandy, and had a lisp, which became him, giving a grace and persuasive turn to his discourse; that Cato had red hair and gray eyes, and was a usurer and a screw, selling off his old slaves when they became unfit for hard work; that Caesar was bald and fond of gay dress; and that Cicero (like Lord Brougham) had involuntary twitchings of his nose.

Such minute particulars may by some be thought beneath the dignity of biography, but Plutarch thought them requisite for the due finish of the complete portrait which he set himself to draw; and it is by small details of character—personal traits, features, habits, and characteristics—that we are enabled to see before us the men as they really lived. Plutarch's great merit consists in his attention to these little things, without giving them undue preponderance, or neglecting those which are of greater moment. Sometimes he hits off an individual trait by an anecdote, which throws more light upon the character described than pages of rhetorical description would do. In some cases, he gives us the favourite maxim of his hero; and the maxims of men often reveal their hearts.

Then, as to foibles, the greatest of men are not visually symmetrical. Each has his defect, his twist, his craze; and it is by his faults that the great man reveals his common humanity. We may, at a distance, admire him as a demigod; but as we come nearer to him, we find that he is but a fallible man, and our brother. (6)

Nor are the illustrations of the defects of great men without their uses; for, as Dr. Johnson observed, "If nothing but the bright side of characters were shown, we should sit down in despondency, and think it utterly impossible to imitate them in anything. "

Plutarch, himself justifies his method of portraiture by averring that his design was not to write histories, but lives. "The most glorious exploits, " he says, "do not always furnish us with the clearest discoveries of virtue or of vice in men. Sometimes a matter of much less moment, an expression or a jest, better informs us of their characters and inclinations than battles with the slaughter of tens of thousands, and the greatest arrays of armies or sieges of cities. Therefore, as portrait-painters are more exact in their lines and features of the face and the expression of the eyes, in which the character is seen, without troubling themselves about the other parts of the body, so I must be allowed to give my more particular attention to the signs and indications of the souls of men; and while I endeavour by these means to portray their lives, I leave important events and great battles to be described by others. "

Things apparently trifling may stand for much in biography as well as history, and slight circumstances may influence great results. Pascal has remarked, that if Cleopatra's nose had been shorter, the whole face of the world would probably have been changed. But for the amours of Pepin the Fat, the Saracens might have overrun Europe; as it was his illegitimate son, Charles Martel, who overthrew them at Tours, and eventually drove them out of France.

That Sir Walter Scott should have sprained his foot in running round the room when a child, may seem unworthy of notice in his biography; yet 'Ivanhoe, ' 'Old Mortality, ' and all the Waverley novels depended upon it. When his son intimated a desire to enter the army, Scott wrote to Southey, "I have no title to combat a choice which would have been my own, had not my lameness prevented. " So that, had not Scott been lame, he might have fought all through the Peninsular War, and had his breast covered with medals; but we should probably have had none of those works of his which have made his name immortal, and shed so much glory upon his country. Talleyrand also was kept out of the army, for which he had been destined, by his lameness; but directing his attention to the study of books, and eventually of men, he at length took rank amongst the greatest diplomatists of his time.

Byron's clubfoot had probably not a little to do with determining his destiny as a poet. Had not his mind been embittered and made morbid by his deformity, he might never have written a line—he might have been the noblest fop of his day. But his misshapen foot stimulated his mind, roused his ardour, threw him upon his own resources—and we know with what result.

So, too, of Scarron, to whose hunchback we probably owe his cynical verse; and of Pope, whose satire was in a measure the outcome of his deformity—for he was, as Johnson described him, "protuberant behind and before. " What Lord Bacon said of deformity is doubtless, to a great extent, true. "Whoever, " said he, "hath anything fixed in his person that doth induce contempt, hath also a perpetual spur in himself to rescue and deliver himself from scorn; therefore, all deformed persons are extremely bold. "

As in portraiture, so in biography, there must be light and shade. The portrait-painter does not pose his sitter so as to bring out his deformities; nor does the biographer give undue prominence to the defects of the character he portrays. Not many men are so outspoken as Cromwell was when he sat to Cooper for his miniature: "Paint me as I am, " said he, "warts and all. " Yet, if we would have a faithful likeness of faces and characters, they must be painted as they are. "Biography, " said Sir Walter Scott, "the most interesting of every species of composition, loses all its interest with me when the shades and lights of the principal characters are not accurately and faithfully detailed. I can no more sympathise with a mere eulogist, than I can with a ranting hero on the stage. " (7)

Addison liked to know as much as possible about the person and character of his authors, inasmuch as it increased the pleasure and satisfaction which he derived from the perusal of their books. What was their history, their experience, their temper and disposition? Did their lives resemble their books? They thought nobly—did they act nobly? "Should we not delight, " says Sir Egerton Brydges, "to have the frank story of the lives and feelings of Wordsworth, Southey, Coleridge, Campbell, Rogers, Moore, and Wilson, related by themselves? —with whom they lived early; how their bent took a decided course; their likes and dislikes; their difficulties and obstacles; their tastes, their passions; the rocks they were conscious of having split upon; their regrets, their complacencies, and their self- justifications? " (8)

When Mason was reproached for publishing the private letters of Gray, he answered, "Would you always have my friends appear in full-dress? " Johnson was of opinion that to write a man's life truly, it is necessary that the biographer should have personally known him. But this condition has been wanting in some of the best writers of biographies extant. (9) In the case of Lord Campbell, his personal intimacy with Lords Lyndhurst and Brougham seems to have been a positive disadvantage, leading him to dwarf the excellences and to magnify the blots in their characters. Again, Johnson says: "If a man profess to write a life, he must write it really as it was. A man's peculiarities, and even his vices, should be mentioned, because they mark his character. " But there is always this difficulty, —that while minute details of conduct, favourable or otherwise, can best be given from personal knowledge, they cannot always be published, out of regard for the living; and when the time arrives when they may at length be told, they are then no longer remembered. Johnson himself expressed this reluctance to tell all he knew of those poets who had been his contemporaries, saying that he felt as if "walking upon ashes under which the fire was not extinguished. "

For this reason, amongst others, we rarely obtain an unvarnished picture of character from the near relatives of distinguished men; and, interesting though all autobiography is, still less can we expect it from the men themselves. In writing his own memoirs, a man will not tell all that he knows about himself. Augustine was a rare exception, but few there are who will, as he did in his 'Confessions, ' lay bare their innate viciousness, deceitfulness, and selfishness. There is a Highland proverb which says, that if the best man's faults were written on his forehead he would pull his bonnet over his brow. "There is no man, " said Voltaire, "who has not something hateful in him—no man who has not some of the wild beast in him. But there are few who will honestly tell us how they manage their wild beast. " Rousseau pretended to unbosom himself in his 'Confessions; ' but it is manifest that he held back far more than he revealed. Even Chamfort, one of the last men to fear what his contemporaries might think or say of him, once observed: - "It seems to me impossible, in the actual state of society, for any man to exhibit his secret heart, the details of his character as known to himself, and, above all, his weaknesses and his vices, to even his best friend. "

An autobiography may be true so far as it goes; but in communicating only part of the truth, it may convey an impression that is really false. It may be a disguise—sometimes it is an apology—exhibiting not so much what a man really was, as what he would have liked to be. A portrait in profile may be correct, but who knows whether some scar on the off-cheek, or some squint in the eye that is not seen, might not have entirely altered the expression of the face if brought into sight? Scott, Moore, Southey, all began autobiographies, but the task of continuing them was doubtless felt to be too difficult as well as delicate, and they were abandoned.

French literature is especially rich in a class of biographic memoirs, of which we have few counterparts in English. We refer to their MEMOIRES POUR SERVIR, such as those of Sully, De Comines, Lauzun, De Retz, De Thou, Rochefoucalt, &c., in which we have recorded an immense mass of minute and circumstantial information relative to many great personages of history. They are full of anecdotes illustrative of life and character, and of details which might be called frivolous, but that they throw a flood of light on the social habits and general civilisation of the periods to which they relate. The MEMOIRES of Saint-Simon are something more: they are marvellous dissections of character, and constitute the most extraordinary collection of anatomical biography that has ever been brought together.

Saint-Simon might almost be regarded in the light of a posthumous court-spy of Louis the Fourteenth. He was possessed by a passion for reading character, and endeavouring to decipher motives and intentions in the faces, expressions, conversation, and byplay of those about him. "I examine all my personages closely, " said he— "watch their mouth, eyes, and ears constantly. " And what he heard and saw he noted down with extraordinary vividness and dash. Acute, keen, and observant, he pierced the masks of the courtiers, and detected their secrets. The ardour with which he prosecuted his favourite study of character seemed insatiable, and even cruel. "The eager anatomist, " says Sainte-Beuve, "was not more ready to plunge the scalpel into the still-palpitating bosom in search of the disease that had baffled him. "

La Bruyere possessed the same gift of accurate and penetrating observation of character. He watched and studied everybody about him. He sought to read their secrets; and, retiring to his chamber, he deliberately painted their portraits, returning to them from time to time to correct some prominent feature—hanging over them as fondly as an artist over some favourite study— adding trait to trait, and touch to touch, until at length the picture was complete and the likeness perfect.

It may be said that much of the interest of biography, especially of the more familiar sort, is of the nature of gossip; as that of the MEMOIRES POUR SERVIR is of the nature of scandal, which is no doubt true. But both gossip and scandal illustrate the strength of the interest which men and women take in each other's personality; and which, exhibited in the form of biography, is capable of communicating the highest pleasure, and yielding the best instruction. Indeed biography, because it is instinct of humanity, is the branch of literature which—whether in the form of fiction, of anecdotal recollection, or of personal narrative— is the one that invariably commends itself to by far the largest class of readers.

There is no room for doubt that the surpassing interest which fiction, whether in poetry or prose, possesses for most minds, arises mainly from the biographic element which it contains. Homer's 'Iliad' owes its marvellous popularity to the genius which its author displayed in the portrayal of heroic character. Yet he does not so much describe his personages in detail as make them develope themselves by their actions. "There are in Homer, " said Dr. Johnson, "such characters of heroes and combination of qualities of heroes, that the united powers of mankind ever since have not produced any but what are to be found there. "

The genius of Shakspeare also was displayed in the powerful delineation of character, and the dramatic evolution of human passions. His personages seem to be real—living and breathing before us. So too with Cervantes, whose Sancho Panza, though homely and vulgar, is intensely human. The characters in Le Sage's 'Gil Blas, ' in Goldsmith's 'Vicar of Wakefield, ' and in Scott's marvellous muster-roll, seem to us almost as real as persons whom we have actually known; and De Foe's greatest works are but so many biographies, painted in minute detail, with reality so apparently stamped upon every page, that it is difficult to believe his Robinson Crusoe and Colonel Jack to have been fictitious instead of real persons.

Though the richest romance lies enclosed in actual human life, and though biography, because it describes beings who have actually felt the joys and sorrows, and experienced the difficulties and triumphs, of real life, is capable of being made more attractive, than the most perfect fictions ever woven, it is remarkable that so few men of genius have been attracted to the composition of works of this kind. Great works of fiction abound, but great biographies may be counted on the fingers. It may be for the same reason that a great painter of portraits, the late John Philip, R.A., explained his preference for subject-painting, because, said he, "Portrait-painting does not pay. " Biographic portraiture involves laborious investigation and careful collection of facts, judicious rejection and skilful condensation, as well as the art of presenting the character portrayed in the most attractive and lifelike form; whereas, in the work of fiction, the writer's imagination is free to create and to portray character, without being trammelled by references, or held down by the actual details of real life.

There is, indeed, no want among us of ponderous but lifeless memoirs, many of them little better than inventories, put together with the help of the scissors as much as of the pen. What Constable said of the portraits of an inferior artist—"He takes all the bones and brains out of his heads"—applies to a large class of portraiture, written as well as painted. They have no more life in them than a piece of waxwork, or a clothes-dummy at a tailor's door. What we want is a picture of a man as he lived, and lo! we have an exhibition of the biographer himself. We expect an embalmed heart, and we find only clothes.

There is doubtless as high art displayed in painting a portrait in words, as there is in painting one in colours. To do either well requires the seeing eye and the skilful pen or brush. A common artist sees only the features of a face, and copies them; but the great artist sees the living soul shining through the features, and places it on the canvas. Johnson was once asked to assist the chaplain of a deceased bishop in writing a memoir of his lordship; but when he proceeded to inquire for information, the chaplain could scarcely tell him anything. Hence Johnson was led to observe that "few people who have lived with a man know what to remark about him. "

In the case of Johnson's own life, it was the seeing eye of Boswell that enabled him to note and treasure up those minute details of habit and conversation in which so much of the interest of biography consists. Boswell, because of his simple love and admiration of his hero, succeeded where probably greater men would have failed. He descended to apparently insignificant, but yet most characteristic, particulars. Thus he apologizes for informing the reader that

Johnson, when journeying, "carried in his hand a large English oak-stick: " adding, "I remember Dr. Adam Smith, in his rhetorical lectures at Glasgow, told us he was glad to know that Milton wore latchets in his shoes instead of buckles. " Boswell lets us know how Johnson looked, what dress he wore, what was his talk, what were his prejudices. He painted him with all his scars, and a wonderful portrait it is—perhaps the most complete picture of a great man ever limned in words.

But for the accident of the Scotch advocate's intimacy with Johnson, and his devoted admiration of him, the latter would not probably have stood nearly so high in literature as he now does. It is in the pages of Boswell that Johnson really lives; and but for Boswell, he might have remained little more than a name. Others there are who have bequeathed great works to posterity, but of whose lives next to nothing is known. What would we not give to have a Boswell's account of Shakspeare? We positively know more of the personal history of Socrates, of Horace, of Cicero, of Augustine, than we do of that of Shakspeare. We do not know what was his religion, what were his politics, what were his experiences, what were his relations to his contemporaries. The men of his own time do not seem to have recognised his greatness; and Ben Jonson, the court poet, whose blank-verse Shakspeare was content to commit to memory and recite as an actor, stood higher in popular estimation. We only know that he was a successful theatrical manager, and that in the prime of life he retired to his native place, where he died, and had the honours of a village funeral. The greater part of the biography which has been constructed respecting him has been the result, not of contemporary observation or of record, but of inference. The best inner biography of the man is to be found in his sonnets.

Men do not always take an accurate measure of their contemporaries. The statesman, the general, the monarch of to-day fills all eyes and ears, though to the next generation he may be as if he had never been. "And who is king to-day? " the painter Greuze would ask of his daughter, during the throes of the first French Revolution, when men, great for the time, were suddenly thrown to the surface, and as suddenly dropt out of sight again, never to reappear. "And who is king to-day? After all, " Greuze would add, "Citizen Homer and Citizen Raphael will outlive those great citizens of ours, whose names I have never before heard of. " Yet of the personal history of Homer nothing is known, and of Raphael comparatively little. Even Plutarch, who wrote the lives of others: so well, has no biography, none of the eminent Roman writers who were his contemporaries having so much as mentioned his name. And so of Correggio, who delineated the features of others so well, there is not known to exist an authentic portrait.

There have been men who greatly influenced the life of their time, whose reputation has been much greater with posterity than it was with their contemporaries. Of Wickliffe, the patriarch of the Reformation, our knowledge is extremely small. He was but as a voice crying in the wilderness. We do not really know who was the author of 'The Imitation of Christ' —a book that has had an immense circulation, and exercised a vast religious influence in all Christian countries. It is usually attributed to Thomas a Kempis but there is reason to believe that he was merely its translator, and the book that is really known to be his, (10) is in all respects so inferior, that it is difficult to believe that 'The Imitation' proceeded from the same pen. It is considered more probable that the real author was John Gerson, Chancellor of the University of Paris, a most learned and devout man, who died in 1429.

Some of the greatest men of genius have had the shortest biographies. Of Plato, one of the great fathers of moral philosophy, we have no personal account. If he had wife and children, we hear nothing of them. About the life of Aristotle there is the greatest diversity of opinion. One says he was a Jew; another, that he only got his information from a Jew: one says he kept an apothecary's shop; another, that he was only the son of a physician: one alleges that he was an atheist; another, that he was a Trinitarian, and so forth. But we know almost as little with respect to many men of comparatively modern times. Thus, how little do we know of the lives of Spenser, author of 'The Faerie Queen, ' and of Butler, the author of 'Hudibras, ' beyond the fact that they lived in comparative obscurity, and died in extreme poverty! How little, comparatively, do we know of the life of Jeremy Taylor, the golden preacher, of whom we should like to have known so much!

The author of 'Philip Van Artevelde' has said that "the world knows nothing of its greatest men. " And doubtless oblivion has enwrapt in its folds many great men who have done great deeds, and been forgotten. Augustine speaks of Romanianus as the greatest genius that ever lived, and yet we know nothing of him but his name; he is as much forgotten as the builders of the Pyramids. Gordiani's epitaph was written in five languages, yet it sufficed not to rescue him from oblivion.

Many, indeed, are the lives worthy of record that have remained unwritten. Men who have written books have been the most fortunate in this respect, because they possess an attraction for literary men which those whose lives have been embodied in deeds do not possess. Thus there have been lives written of Poets Laureate who were mere men of their time, and of their time only. Dr. Johnson includes some of them in his 'Lives of the Poets, ' such as Edmund Smith and others, whose poems are now no longer known. The lives of some men of letters—such as Goldsmith, Swift, Sterne, and Steele—have been written again and again, whilst great men of action, men of science, and men of industry, are left without a record. (11)

We have said that a man may be known by the company he keeps in his books. Let us mention a few of the favourites of the best- known men. Plutarch's admirers have already been referred to. Montaigne also has been the companion of most meditative men. Although Shakspeare must have studied Plutarch carefully, inasmuch as he copied from him freely, even to his very words, it is remarkable that Montaigne is the only book which we certainly know to have been in the poet's library; one of Shakspeare's existing autographs having been found in a copy of Florio's translation of 'The Essays, ' which also contains, on the flyleaf, the autograph of Ben Jonson.

Milton's favourite books were Homer, Ovid, and Euripides. The latter book was also the favourite of Charles James Fox, who regarded the study of it as especially useful to a public speaker. On the other hand, Pitt took especial delight in Milton—whom Fox did not appreciate—taking pleasure in reciting, from 'Paradise Lost, ' the grand speech of Belial before the assembled powers of Pandemonium. Another of Pitt's, favourite books was Newton's 'Principia. ' Again, the Earl of Chatham's favourite book was 'Barrow's Sermons, ' which he read so often as to be able to repeat them from memory; while Burke's companions were Demosthenes, Milton, Bolingbroke, and Young's 'Night Thoughts. '

Curran's favourite was Homer, which he read through once a year. Virgil was another of his favourites; his biographer, Phillips, saying that he once saw him reading the 'Aeneid' in the cabin of a Holyhead packet, while every one about him was prostrate by seasickness.

Of the poets, Dante's favourite was Virgil; Corneille's was Lucan; Schiller's was Shakspeare; Gray's was Spenser; whilst Coleridge admired Collins and Bowles. Dante himself was a favourite with most great poets, from Chaucer to Byron and Tennyson. Lord Brougham, Macaulay, and Carlyle have alike admired and eulogized the great Italian. The former advised the students at Glasgow that, next to Demosthenes, the study of Dante was the best preparative for the eloquence of the pulpit or the bar. Robert Hall sought relief in Dante from the racking pains of spinal disease; and Sydney Smith took to the same poet for comfort and solace in his old age. It was characteristic of Goethe that his favourite book should have been Spinoza's 'Ethics, ' in which he said he had found a peace and consolation such as he had been able to find in no other work. (12)

Barrow's favourite was St. Chrysostom; Bossuet's was Homer. Bunyan's was the old legend of Sir Bevis of Southampton, which in all probability gave him the first idea of his 'Pilgrim's Progress. ' One of the best prelates that ever sat on the English bench, Dr. John Sharp, said—"Shakspeare and the Bible have made me Archbishop of York. " The two books which most impressed John Wesley when a young man, were 'The Imitation of Christ' and Jeremy Taylor's 'Holy Living and Dying. ' Yet Wesley was accustomed to caution his young friends against overmuch reading. "Beware you be not swallowed up in books, " he would say to them; "an ounce of love is worth a pound of knowledge. "

Wesley's own Life has been a great favourite with many thoughtful readers. Coleridge says, in his preface to Southey's 'Life of Wesley, ' that it was more often in his hands than any other in his ragged book-regiment. "To this work, and to the Life of Richard Baxter, " he says, "I was used to resort whenever sickness and languor made me feel the want of an old friend of whose company I could never be tired. How many and many an hour of self-oblivion do I owe to this Life of Wesley; and how often have I argued with it, questioned, remonstrated, been peevish, and asked pardon; then again listened, and cried, 'Right! Excellent! ' and in yet heavier hours entreated it, as it were, to continue talking to me; for that I heard and listened, and was soothed, though I could make no reply! " (13)

Soumet had only a very few hooks in his library, but they were of the best—Homer, Virgil, Dante, Camoens, Tasso, and Milton. De Quincey's favourite few were Donne, Chillingworth, Jeremy Taylor, Milton, South, Barrow, and Sir Thomas Browne. He described these writers as "a pleiad or constellation of seven golden stars, such as in their class no literature can match, " and from whose works he would undertake "to build up an entire body of philosophy. "

Frederick the Great of Prussia manifested his strong French leanings in his choice of books; his principal favourites being Bayle, Rousseau, Voltaire, Rollin, Fleury, Malebranche, and one English author — Locke. His especial favourite was Bayle's Dictionary, which was the first book that laid hold of his mind; and he thought so highly of it, that he himself made an abridgment and translation of it into German, which was published. It was a saying of Frederick's, that "books make up no small part of true happiness. " In his old age he said, "My latest passion will be for literature. "

It seems odd that Marshal Blucher's favourite book should have been Klopstock's 'Messiah, ' and Napoleon Buonaparte's favourites, Ossian's 'Poems' and the 'Sorrows of Werther. ' But Napoleon's range of reading was very extensive. It included Homer, Virgil, Tasso; novels of all countries; histories of all times; mathematics, legislation, and theology. He detested what he called "the bombast and tinsel" of Voltaire. The praises of Homer and Ossian he was never wearied of sounding. "Read again, " he said to an officer on board the BELLEROPHO—"read again the poet of Achilles; devour Ossian. Those are the poets who lift up the soul, and give to man a colossal greatness. " (14)

The Duke of Wellington was an extensive reader; his principal favourites were Clarendon, Bishop Butler, Smith's 'Wealth of Nations, ' Hume, the Archduke Charles, Leslie, and the Bible. He was also particularly interested by French and English memoirs — more especially the French MEMOIRES POUR SERVIR of all kinds. When at Walmer, Mr. Gleig says, the Bible, the Prayer Book, Taylor's 'Holy Living and Dying, ' and Caesar's 'Commentaries, ' lay within the Duke's reach; and, judging by the marks of use on them, they must have been much read and often consulted.

While books are among the best companions of old age, they are often the best inspirers of youth. The first book that makes a deep impression on a young man's mind, often constitutes an epoch in his life. It may fire the heart, stimulate the enthusiasm, and by directing his efforts into unexpected channels, permanently influence his character. The new book, in which we form an intimacy with a new friend, whose mind is wiser and riper than our own, may thus form an important starting-point in the history of a life. It may sometimes almost be regarded in the light of a new birth.

From the day when James Edward Smith was presented with his first botanical lesson-book, and Sir Joseph Banks fell in with Gerard's 'Herbal'—from the time when Alfieri first read Plutarch, and Schiller made his first acquaintance with Shakspeare, and Gibbon devoured the first volume of 'The Universal History'—each dated an inspiration so exalted, that they felt as if their real lives had only then begun.

In the earlier part of his youth, La Fontaine was distinguished for his idleness, but hearing an ode by Malherbe read, he is said to have exclaimed, "I too am a poet, " and his genius was awakened. Charles Bossuet's mind was first fired to study by reading, at an early age, Fontenelle's 'Eloges' of men of science. Another work of Fontenelle's—'On the Plurality of Worlds'—influenced the mind of Lalande in making choice of a profession. "It is with pleasure, " says Lalande himself in a preface to the book, which be afterwards edited, "that I acknowledge my obligation to it for that devouring activity which its perusal first excited in me at the age of sixteen, and which I have since retained. "

In like manner, Lacepede was directed to the study of natural history by the perusal of Buffon's 'Histoire Naturelle, ' which he found in his father's library, and read over and over again until he almost knew it by heart. Goethe was greatly influenced by the reading of Goldsmith's 'Vicar of Wakefield, ' just at the critical moment of his mental development; and he attributed to it much of his best education. The reading of a prose 'Life of Gotz vou Berlichingen' afterwards stimulated him to delineate his character in a poetic form. "The figure of a rude, well-meaning self-helper, " he said, "in a wild anarchic time, excited my deepest sympathy. "

Keats was an insatiable reader when a boy; but it was the perusal of the 'Faerie Queen, ' at the age of seventeen, that first lit the fire of his genius. The same poem is also said to have been the inspirer of Cowley, who found a copy of it accidentally lying on the window of his mother's apartment; and reading and admiring it, he became, as he relates, irrecoverably a poet.

Coleridge speaks of the great influence which the poems of Bowles had in forming his own mind. The works of a past age, says he, seem to a young man to be things of another race; but the writings of a contemporary "possess a reality for him, and inspire an actual friendship as of a man for a man. His very admiration is the wind which fans and feeds his hope. The poems themselves assume the properties of flesh and blood. " (15)

But men have not merely been stimulated to undertake special literary pursuits by the perusal of particular books; they have been also stimulated by them to enter upon particular lines of action in the serious business of life. Thus Henry Martyn was powerfully influenced to enter upon his heroic career as a missionary by perusing the Lives of Henry Brainerd and Dr. Carey, who had opened up the furrows in which he went forth to sow the seed.

Bentham has described the extraordinary influence which the perusal of 'Telemachus' exercised upon his mind in boyhood. "Another book, " said he, "and of far higher character (than a collection of Fairy Tales, to which he refers), was placed in my hands. It was 'Telemachus. ' In my own imagination, and at the age of six or seven, I identified my own personality with that of the hero, who seemed to me a model of perfect virtue; and in my walk of life, whatever it may come to be, why (said I to myself every now and then)—why should not I be a Telemachus? .... That romance may be regarded as THE FOUNDATION-STONE OF MY WHOLE CHARACTER—the starting-post from whence my career of life commenced. The first dawning in my mind of the 'Principles of Utility' may, I think, be traced to it. " (16)

Cobbett's first favourite, because his only book, which he bought for threepence, was Swift's 'Tale of a Tub, ' the repeated perusal of which had, doubtless, much to do with the formation of his pithy, straightforward, and hard-hitting style of writing. The delight with which Pope, when a schoolboy, read Ogilvy's 'Homer' was, most probably, the origin of the English 'Iliad; ' as the 'Percy Reliques' fired the juvenile mind of Scott, and stimulated him to enter upon the collection and composition of his 'Border Ballads. ' Keightley's first reading of 'Paradise Lost, ' when a boy, led to his afterwards undertaking his Life of the poet. "The reading, " he says, "of 'Paradise Lost' for the first time forms, or should form, an era in the life of every one possessed of taste and poetic feeling. To my mind, that time is ever present.... Ever since, the poetry of Milton has formed my constant study—a source of delight in prosperity, of strength and consolation in adversity. "

Good books are thus among the best of companions; and, by elevating the thoughts and aspirations, they act as preservatives against low associations. "A natural turn for reading and intellectual pursuits, " says Thomas Hood, "probably preserved me from the moral shipwreck so apt to befal those who are deprived in early life of their parental pilotage. My books kept me from the ring, the dogpit, the tavern, the saloon. The closet associate of Pope and Addison, the mind accustomed to the noble though silent discourse of Shakspeare and Milton, will hardly seek or put up with low company and slaves. "

It has been truly said, that the best books are those which most resemble good actions. They are purifying, elevating, and sustaining; they enlarge and liberalize the mind; they preserve it against vulgar worldliness; they tend to produce highminded cheerfulness and equanimity of character; they fashion, and shape, and humanize the mind. In the Northern universities, the schools in which the ancient classics are studied, are appropriately styled "The Humanity Classes." (17)

Erasmus, the great scholar, was even of opinion that books were the necessaries of life, and clothes the luxuries; and he frequently postponed buying the latter until he had supplied himself with the former. His greatest favourites were the works of Cicero, which he says he always felt himself the better for reading. "I can never, " he says, "read the works of Cicero on 'Old Age, ' or 'Friendship, ' or his 'Tusculan Disputations, ' without fervently pressing them to my lips, without being penetrated with veneration for a mind little short of inspired by God himself. " It was the accidental perusal of Cicero's 'Hortensius' which first detached St. Augustine—until then a profligate and abandoned sensualist—from his immoral life, and started him upon the course of inquiry and study which led to his becoming the greatest among the Fathers of the Early Church. Sir William Jones made it a practice to read through, once a year, the writings of Cicero, "whose life indeed, " says his biographer, was the great exemplar of his own. "

When the good old Puritan Baxter came to enumerate the valuable and delightful things of which death would deprive him, his mind reverted to the pleasures he had derived from books and study. "When I die, " he said, "I must depart, not only from sensual delights, but from the more manly pleasures of my studies, knowledge, and converse with many wise and godly men, and from all my pleasure in reading, hearing, public and private exercises of religion, and such like. I must leave my library, and turn over those pleasant books no more. I must no more come among the living, nor see the faces of my faithful friends, nor be seen of man; houses, and cities, and fields, and countries, gardens, and walks, will be as nothing to me. I shall no more hear of the affairs of the world, of man, or wars, or other news; nor see what becomes of that beloved interest of wisdom, piety, and peace, which I desire may prosper. "

It is unnecessary to speak of the enormous moral influence which books have exercised upon the general civilization of mankind, from the Bible downwards. They contain the treasured knowledge of the human race. They are the record of all labours, achievements, speculations, successes, and failures, in science, philosophy, religion, and morals. They have been the greatest motive powers in all times. "From the Gospel to the Contrat Social, " says De Bonald, "it is books that have made revolutions. " Indeed, a great book is often a greater thing than a great battle. Even works of fiction have occasionally exercised immense power on society. Thus Rabelais in France, and Cervantes in Spain, overturned at the same time the dominion of monkery and chivalry, employing no other weapons but ridicule, the natural contrast of human terror. The people laughed, and felt reassured. So 'Telemachus' appeared, and recalled men back to the harmonies of nature.

"Poets, " says Hazlitt, "are a longer-lived race than heroes: they breathe more of the air of immortality. They survive more entire in their thoughts and acts. We have all that Virgil or Homer did, as much as if we had lived at the same time with them. We can hold their works in our hands, or lay them on our pillows, or put them to our lips. Scarcely a trace of what the others did is left upon the earth, so as to be visible to common eyes. The one, the dead authors, are living men, still breathing and moving in their writings; the others, the conquerors of the world, are but the ashes in an urn. The sympathy (so to speak) between thought and thought is more intimate and vital than that between thought and action. Thought is linked to thought as flame kindles into flame; the tribute of admiration to the MANES of departed heroism is like burning incense in a marble monument. Words, ideas, feelings, with the progress of time harden into substances: things, bodies, actions, moulder away, or melt into a sound—into thin air.... Not only a man's actions are effaced and vanish with him; his virtues and generous qualities die with him also. His intellect only is immortal, and bequeathed unimpaired to posterity. Words are the only things that last for ever. " (18)

NOTES

(1) 'Kaye's 'Lives of Indian Officers. '

(2) Emerson, in his 'Society and Solitude, ' says "In contemporaries, it is not so easy to distinguish between notoriety and fame. Be sure, then, to read no mean books. Shun the spawn of the press or the gossip of the hour.... The three practical rules I have to offer are these: - 1. Never read a book that is not a year old; 2. Never read any but famed books; 3. Never read any but what you like. " Lord Lytton's maxim is: "In science, read by preference the newest books; in literature, the oldest. "

(3) A friend of Sir Walter Scott, who had the same habit, and prided himself on his powers of conversation, one day tried to "draw out" a fellow-passenger who sat beside him on the outside of a coach, but with indifferent success. At length the conversationalist descended to expostulation. "I have talked to you, my friend, " said he, "on all the ordinary subjects—literature, farming, merchandise, gaming, game-laws, horse-races, suits at law, politics, and swindling, and blasphemy, and philosophy: is there any one subject that you will favour me by opening upon? " The wight writhed his countenance into a grin: "Sir, " said he, "can you say anything clever about BEND-LEATHER? " As might be expected, the conversationalist was completely nonplussed.

(4) Coleridge, in his 'Lay Sermon, ' points out, as a fact of history, how large a part of our present knowledge and civilization is owing, directly or indirectly, to the Bible; that the Bible has been the main lever by which the moral and intellectual character of Europe has been raised to its present comparative height; and he specifies the marked and prominent difference of this book from the works which it is the fashion to quote as guides and authorities in morals, politics, and history. "In the Bible, " he says, "every agent appears and acts as a self-substituting individual: each has a life of its own, and yet all are in life. The elements of necessity and freewill are reconciled in the higher power of an omnipresent Providence, that predestinates the whole in the moral freedom of the integral parts. Of this the Bible never suffers us to lose sight. The root is never detached from the ground, it is God everywhere; and all creatures conform to His

decrees—the righteous by performance of the law, the disobedient by the sufferance of the penalty. "

(5) Montaigne's Essay (Book I. chap. xxv.)—'Of the Education of Children. '

(6) "Tant il est vrai, " says Voltaire, "que les hommes, qui sont audessus des autres par les talents, s'en RAPPROCHENT PRESQUE TOUJOURS PAR LES FAIBLESSES; car pourquoi les talents nous mettraient-ils audessous de l'humanite. "—VIE DE MOLIERE.

(7) 'Life, ' 8vo Ed., p. 102.

(8) 'Autobiography of Sir Egerton Brydges, Bart., ' vol. i. p. 91.

(9) It was wanting in Plutarch, in Southey ('Life of Nelson'), and in Forster ('Life of Goldsmith'); yet it must be acknowledged that personal knowledge gives the principal charm to Tacitus's 'Agricola, ' Roper's 'Life of More, ' Johnson's 'Lives of Savage and Pope, ' Boswell's 'Johnson, ' Lockhart's 'Scott, ' Carlyle's 'Sterling, ' and Moore's 'Byron, '

(10) The 'Dialogus Novitiorum de Contemptu Mundi. '

(11) The Life of Sir Charles Bell, one of our greatest physiologists, was left to be written by Amedee Pichot, a Frenchman; and though Sir Charles Bell's letters to his brother have since been published, his Life still remains to be written. It may also be added that the best Life of Goethe has been written by an Englishman, and the best Life of Frederick the Great by a Scotchman.

(12) It is not a little remarkable that the pious Schleiermacher should have concurred in opinion with Goethe as to the merits of Spinoza, though he was a man excommunicated by the Jews, to whom he belonged, and denounced by the Christians as a man little better than an atheist. "The Great Spirit of the world, " says Schleiermacher, in his REDE UBER DIE RELIGION, "penetrated the holy but repudiated Spinoza; the Infinite was his beginning and his end; the universe his only and eternal love. He was filled with religion and religious feeling: and therefore is it that he stands alone unapproachable, the master in his art, but elevated above the profane world, without adherents, and without even citizenship. "

Cousin also says of Spinoza: - "The author whom this pretended atheist most resembles is the unknown author of 'The Imitation of Jesus Christ. '"

(13) Preface to Southeys 'Life of Wesley' (1864).

(14) Napoleon also read Milton carefully, and it has been related of him by Sir Colin Campbell, who resided with Napoleon at Elba, that when speaking of the Battle of Austerlitz, he said that a particular disposition of his artillery, which, in its results, had a decisive effect in winning the battle, was suggested to his mind by the recollection of four lines in Milton. The lines occur in the sixth book, and are descriptive of Satan's artifice during the war with Heaven

> "In hollow cube
> Training his devilish engin'ry, impal'd
> On every side WITH SHADOWING SQUADRONS DEEP
> TO HIDE THE FRAUD."

"The indubitable fact, " says Mr. Edwards, in his book 'On Libraries,' "that these lines have a certain appositeness to an important manoeuvre at Austerlitz, gives an independent interest to the story; but it is highly imaginative to ascribe the victory to that manoeuvre. And for the other preliminaries of the tale, it is unfortunate that Napoleon had learned a good deal about war long before he had learned anything about Milton. "

(15) 'Biographia Literaria, ' chap. i.

(16) Sir John Bowring's 'Memoirs of Bentham, ' p. 10.

(17) Notwithstanding recent censures of classical studies as a useless waste of time, there can be no doubt that they give the highest finish to intellectual culture. The ancient classics contain the most consummate models of literary art; and the greatest writers have been their most diligent students. Classical culture was the instrument with which Erasmus and the Reformers purified Europe. It distinguished the great patriots of the seventeenth century; and it has ever since characterised our greatest statesmen. "I know not how it is, " says an English writer, "but their commerce with the ancients appears to me to produce, in those who constantly practise it, a steadying and composing effect upon their judgment, not of literary works only, but of men and events in general. They are like persons

who have had a weighty and impressive experience; they are more truly than others under the empire of facts, and more independent of the language current among those with whom they live. "

(18) Hazlitt's TABLE TALK: 'On Thought and Action. '

CHAPTER XI. —COMPANIONSHIP IN MARRIAGE.

"Kindness in women, not their beauteous looks,
Shall win my love."—SHAKSPEARE.

"In the husband Wisdom, In the wife Gentleness. "—GEORGE HERBERT.

"If God had designed woman as man's master, He would have taken her from his head; If as his slave, He would have taken her from his feet; but as He designed her for his companion and equal, He took her from his side. "—SAINT AUGUSTINE. —'DE CIVITATE DEI. '

"Who can find a virtuous woman? for her price is far above rubies.... Her husband is known in the gates, and he sitteth among the elders of the land.... Strength and honour are her clothing, and she shall rejoice in time to come. She openeth her mouth with wisdom, and in her tongue is the law of kindness. She looketh well to the ways of her husband, and eateth not the bread of idleness. Her children arise up and call her blessed; her husband also, and he praiseth her. "— PROVERBS OF SOLOMON.

THE character of men, as of women, is powerfully influenced by their companionship in all the stages of life. We have already spoken of the influence of the mother in forming the character of her children. She makes the moral atmosphere in which they live, and by which their minds and souls are nourished, as their bodies are by the physical atmosphere they breathe. And while woman is the natural cherisher of infancy and the instructor of childhood, she is also the guide and counsellor of youth, and the confidant and companion of manhood, in her various relations of mother, sister, lover, and wife. In short, the influence of woman more or less affects, for good or for evil, the entire destinies of man.

The respective social functions and duties of men and women are clearly defined by nature. God created man AND woman, each to do their proper work, each to fill their proper sphere. Neither can occupy the position, nor perform the functions, of the other. Their several vocations are perfectly distinct. Woman exists on her own account, as man does on his, at the same time that each has intimate relations with the other. Humanity needs both for the purposes of the race, and in every consideration of social progress both must necessarily be included.

Though companions and equals, yet, as regards the measure of their powers, they are unequal. Man is stronger, more muscular, and of rougher fibre; woman is more delicate, sensitive, and nervous. The one excels in power of brain, the other in qualities of heart; and though the head may rule, it is the heart that influences. Both are alike adapted for the respective functions they have to perform in life; and to attempt to impose woman's work upon man would be quite as absurd as to attempt to impose man's work upon woman. Men are sometimes womanlike, and women are sometimes manlike; but these are only exceptions which prove the rule.

Although man's qualities belong more to the head, and woman's more to the heart—yet it is not less necessary that man's heart should be cultivated as well as his head, and woman's head cultivated as well as her heart. A heartless man is as much out- of- keeping in civilized society as a stupid and unintelligent woman. The cultivation of all parts of the moral and intellectual nature is requisite to form the man or woman of healthy and well- balanced character. Without sympathy or consideration for others, man were a poor, stunted, sordid, selfish being; and without cultivated intelligence, the most beautiful woman were little better than a well-dressed doll.

It used to be a favourite notion about woman, that her weakness and dependency upon others constituted her principal claim to admiration. "If we were to form an image of dignity in a man, " said Sir Richard Steele, "we should give him wisdom and valour, as being essential to the character of manhood. In like manner, if you describe a right woman in a laudable sense, she should have gentle softness, tender fear, and all those parts of life which distinguish her from the other sex, with some subordination to it, but an inferiority which makes her lovely. " Thus, her weakness was to be cultivated, rather than her strength; her folly, rather than her wisdom. She was to be a weak, fearful, tearful, characterless, inferior creature, with just sense enough to understand the soft nothings addressed to her by the "superior" sex. She was to be educated as an ornamental appanage of man, rather as an independent intelligence—or as a wife, mother, companion, or friend.

Pope, in one of his 'Moral Essays, ' asserts that "most women have no characters at all; " and again he says: -

> "Ladies, like variegated tulips, show:
> 'Tis to their changes half their charms we owe,
> Fine by defect and delicately weak."

This satire characteristically occurs in the poet's 'Epistle to Martha Blount, ' the housekeeper who so tyrannically ruled him; and in the same verses he spitefully girds at Lady Mary Wortley Montague, at whose feet he had thrown himself as a lover, and been contemptuously rejected. But Pope was no judge of women, nor was he even a very wise or tolerant judge of men.

It is still too much the practice to cultivate the weakness of woman rather than her strength, and to render her attractive rather than self-reliant. Her sensibilities are developed at the expense of her health of body as well as of mind. She lives, moves, and has her being in the sympathy of others. She dresses that she may attract, and is burdened with accomplishments that she may be chosen. Weak, trembling, and dependent, she incurs the risk of becoming a living embodiment of the Italian proverb—"so good that she is good for nothing. "

On the other hand, the education of young men too often errs on the side of selfishness. While the boy is incited to trust mainly to his own efforts in pushing his way in the world, the girl is encouraged to rely almost entirely upon others. He is educated with too exclusive reference to himself and she is educated with too exclusive reference to him. He is taught to be self-reliant and self-dependent, while she is taught to be distrustful of herself, dependent, and self-sacrificing in all things. Thus, the intellect of the one is cultivated at the expense of the affections, and the affections of the other at the expense of the intellect.

It is unquestionable that the highest qualities of woman are displayed in her relationship to others, through the medium of her affections. She is the nurse whom nature has given to all humankind. She takes charge of the helpless, and nourishes and cherishes those we love. She is the presiding genius of the fireside, where she creates an atmosphere of serenity and contentment suitable for the nurture and growth of character in its best forms. She is by her very constitution compassionate, gentle, patient, and self-denying.

Loving, hopeful, trustful, her eye sheds brightness everywhere. It shines upon coldness and warms it, upon suffering and relieves it, upon sorrow and cheers it: —

"Her silver flow
  Of subtle-paced counsel in distress,
  Right to the heart and brain, though undescried,
    Winning its way with extreme gentleness
  Through all the outworks of suspicion's pride."

Woman has been styled "the angel of the unfortunate. " She is ready to help the weak, to raise the fallen, to comfort the suffering. It was characteristic of woman, that she should have been the first to build and endow an hospital. It has been said that wherever a human being is in suffering, his sighs call a woman to his side. When Mungo Park, lonely, friendless, and famished, after being driven forth from an African village by the men, was preparing to spend the night under a tree, exposed to the rain and the wild beasts which there abounded, a poor negro woman, returning from the labours of the field, took compassion upon him, conducted him into her hut, and there gave him food, succour, and shelter. (1)

But while the most characteristic qualities of woman are displayed through her sympathies and affections, it is also necessary for her own happiness, as a self-dependent being, to develope and strengthen her character, by due self-culture, self-reliance, and self-control. It is not desirable, even were it possible, to close the beautiful avenues of the heart. Self-reliance of the best kind does not involve any limitation in the range of human sympathy. But the happiness of woman, as of man, depends in a great measure upon her individual completeness of character. And that self-dependence which springs from the due cultivation of the intellectual powers, conjoined with a proper discipline of the heart and conscience, will enable her to be more useful in life as well as happy; to dispense blessings intelligently as well as to enjoy them; and most of all those which spring from mutual dependence and social sympathy.

To maintain a high standard of purity in society, the culture of both sexes must be in harmony, and keep equal pace. A pure womanhood must be accompanied by a pure manhood. The same moral law applies alike to both. It would be loosening the foundations of virtue, to countenance the notion that because of a difference in sex, man were at liberty to set morality at defiance, and to do that with impunity, which, if done by a woman, would stain her character for life. To maintain a pure and virtuous condition of society, therefore, man as well as woman must be pure and virtuous; both alike shunning all acts impinging on the heart, character, and conscience—shunning them as poison, which, once imbibed, can never be entirely thrown out again, but mentally embitters, to a greater or less extent, the happiness of after-life.

And here we would venture to touch upon a delicate topic. Though it is one of universal and engrossing human interest, the moralist avoids it, the educator shuns it, and parents taboo it. It is almost considered indelicate to refer to Love as between the sexes; and young persons are left to gather their only notions of it from the impossible love-stories that fill the shelves of circulating libraries. This strong and absorbing feeling, this BESOIN D'AIMER—which nature has for wise purposes made so strong in woman that it colours her whole life and history, though it may form but an episode in the life of man—is usually left to follow its own inclinations, and to grow up for the most part unchecked, without any guidance or direction whatever.

Although nature spurns all formal rules and directions in affairs of love, it might at all events be possible to implant in young minds such views of Character as should enable them to discriminate between the true and the false, and to accustom them to hold in esteem those qualities of moral purity and integrity, without which life is but a scene of folly and misery. It may not be possible to teach young people to love wisely, but they may at least be guarded by parental advice against the frivolous and despicable passions which so often usurp its name. "Love, " it has been said, "in the common acceptation of the term, is folly; but love, in its purity, its loftiness, its unselfishness, is not only a consequence, but a proof, of our moral excellence. The sensibility to moral beauty, the forgetfulness of self in the admiration engendered by it, all prove its claim to a high moral influence. It is the triumph of the unselfish over the selfish part of our nature. "

It is by means of this divine passion that the world is kept ever fresh and young. It is the perpetual melody of humanity. It sheds an effulgence upon youth, and throws a halo round age. It glorifies the present by the light it casts backward, and it lightens the future by the beams it casts forward. The love which is the outcome of esteem and admiration, has an elevating and purifying effect on the character. It tends to emancipate one from the slavery of self. It is altogether unsordid; itself is its only price. It inspires gentleness, sympathy, mutual faith, and confidence. True love also in a measure elevates the intellect. "All love renders wise in a degree, " says the poet Browning, and the most gifted minds have been the sincerest lovers. Great souls make all affections great; they elevate and consecrate all true delights. The sentiment even brings to light qualities before lying dormant and unsuspected. It elevates the aspirations, expands the soul, and stimulates the mental powers. One of the finest compliments ever paid to a woman was that of Steele, when he said of Lady Elizabeth Hastings, "that to have loved her was a liberal education. " Viewed in this light, woman is an educator in the highest sense, because, above all other educators, she educates humanly and lovingly.

It has been said that no man and no woman can be regarded as complete in their experience of life, until they have been subdued into union with the world through their affections. As woman is not woman until she has known love, neither is man man. Both are requisite to each other's completeness. Plato entertained the idea that lovers each sought a likeness in the other, and that love was only the divorced half of the original human being entering into union with its counterpart. But philosophy would here seem to be at fault, for affection quite as often springs from unlikeness as from likeness in its object.

The true union must needs be one of mind as well as of heart, and based on mutual esteem as well as mutual affection. "No true and enduring love, " says Fichte, "can exist without esteem; every other draws regret after it, and is unworthy of any noble human soul. " One cannot really love the bad, but always something that we esteem and respect as well as admire. In short, true union must rest on qualities of character, which rule in domestic as in public life.

But there is something far more than mere respect and esteem in the union between man and wife. The feeling on which it rests is far deeper and tenderer—such, indeed, as never exists between men or between women. "In matters of affection, " says Nathaniel Hawthorne, "there is always an impassable gulf between man and man. They can never quite grasp each other's hands, and therefore man never derives any intimate help, any heart-sustenance, from his brother man, but from woman—his mother, his sister, or his wife."(2)

Man enters a new world of joy, and sympathy, and human interest, through the porch of love. He enters a new world in his home— the home of his own making—altogether different from the home of his boyhood, where each day brings with it a succession of new joys and experiences. He enters also, it may be, a new world of trials and sorrows, in which he often gathers his best culture and discipline. "Family life, " says Sainte-Beuve, "may be full of thorns and cares; but they are fruitful: all others are dry thorns. " And again: "If a man's home, at a certain period of life, does not contain children, it will probably be found filled with follies or with vices. " (3)

A life exclusively occupied in affairs of business insensibly tends to narrow and harden the character. It is mainly occupied with self-watching for advantages, and guarding against sharp practice on the part of others. Thus the character unconsciously tends to grow suspicious and ungenerous. The best corrective of such influences is always the domestic; by withdrawing the mind from thoughts that are wholly gainful, by taking it out of its daily rut, and bringing it back to the sanctuary of home for refreshment and rest:

> "That truest, rarest light of social joy,
> Which gleams upon the man of many cares."

"Business, " says Sir Henry Taylor, "does but lay waste the approaches to the heart, whilst marriage garrisons the fortress. " And however the head may be occupied, by labours of ambition or of business—if the heart be not occupied by affection for others and sympathy with them—life, though it may appear to the outer world to be a success, will probably be no success at all, but a failure. (4)

A man's real character will always be more visible in his household than anywhere else; and his practical wisdom will be better exhibited by the manner in which he bears rule there, than even in the larger affairs of business or public life. His whole mind may be in his business; but, if he would be happy, his whole heart must be in his home. It is there that his genuine qualities most surely display themselves—there that he shows his truthfulness, his love, his sympathy, his consideration for others, his uprightness, his manliness—in a word, his character. If affection be not the governing principle in a household, domestic life may be the most intolerable of despotisms. Without justice, also, there can be neither love, confidence, nor respect, on which all true domestic rule is founded.

Erasmus speaks of Sir Thomas More's home as "a school and exercise of the Christian religion. " "No wrangling, no angry word was heard in it; no one was idle; every one did his duty with alacrity, and not without a temperate cheerfulness. " Sir Thomas won all hearts to obedience by his gentleness. He was a man clothed in household goodness; and he ruled so gently and wisely, that his home was pervaded by an atmosphere of love and duty. He himself spoke of the hourly interchange of the smaller acts of kindness with the several members of his family, as having a claim upon his time as strong as those other public occupations of his life which seemed to others so much more serious and important.

But the man whose affections are quickened by home-life, does not confine his sympathies within that comparatively narrow sphere. His love enlarges in the family, and through the family it expands into the world. "Love, " says Emerson, "is a fire that, kindling its first embers in the narrow nook of a private bosom, caught from a wandering spark out of another private heart, glows and enlarges until it warms and beams upon multitudes of men and women, upon the universal heart of all, and so lights up the whole world and nature with its generous flames. "

It is by the regimen of domestic affection that the heart of man is best composed and regulated. The home is the woman's kingdom, her state, her world—where she governs by affection, by kindness, by the power of gentleness. There is nothing which so settles the turbulence of a man's nature as his union in life with a highminded woman. There he finds rest, contentment, and happiness—rest of brain and peace of spirit. He will also often find in her his best counsellor, for her instinctive tact will usually lead him right when his own unaided reason might be apt to go wrong. The true wife is a staff to lean upon in times of trial and difficulty; and she is never wanting in sympathy and solace when distress occurs or fortune frowns. In the time of youth, she is a comfort and an ornament of man's life; and she remains a faithful helpmate in maturer years, when life has ceased to be an anticipation, and we live in its realities.

What a happy man must Edmund Burke have been, when he could say of his home, "Every care vanishes the moment I enter under my own roof! " And Luther, a man full of human affection, speaking of his wife, said, "I would not exchange my poverty with her for all the riches of Croesus without her. " Of marriage he observed: "The utmost blessing that God can confer on a man is the possession of a good and pious wife, with whom he may live in peace and tranquillity—to whom he may confide his whole possessions, even his life and welfare. " And again he said, "To rise betimes, and to marry young, are what no man ever repents of doing. "

For a man to enjoy true repose and happiness in marriage, he must have in his wife a soul-mate as well as a helpmate. But it is not requisite that she should be merely a pale copy of himself. A man no more desires in his wife a manly woman, than the woman desires in her husband a feminine man. A woman's best qualities do not reside in her intellect, but in her affections. She gives refreshment by her sympathies, rather than by her knowledge. "The brain-women, " says Oliver Wendell Holmes, "never interest us like the heart-women. " (5) Men are often so wearied with themselves, that they are rather predisposed to admire qualities and tastes in others different from their own. "If I were suddenly asked, " says Mr. Helps, "to give a proof of the goodness of God to us, I think I should say that it is most manifest in the exquisite difference He has made between the souls of men and women, so as to create the possibility of the most comforting and charming companionship that the mind of man can imagine. " (6) But though no man may love a woman for her understanding, it is not the less necessary for her to cultivate it on that account. (7) There may be difference in character, but there must be harmony of mind and sentiment— two intelligent souls as well as two loving hearts:

> "Two heads in council, two beside the hearth,
> Two in the tangled business of the world,
> Two in the liberal offices of life."

There are few men who have written so wisely on the subject of marriage as Sir Henry Taylor. What he says about the influence of a happy union in its relation to successful statesmanship, applies to all conditions of life. The true wife, he says, should possess such qualities as will tend to make home as much as may be a place of repose. To this end, she should have sense enough or worth enough to exempt her husband as much as possible from the troubles of family management, and more especially from all possibility of debt. "She should be pleasing to his eyes and to his taste: the taste goes deep into the nature of all men—love is hardly apart from it; and in a life of care and excitement, that home which is not the seat of love cannot be a place of repose; rest for the brain, and peace for the spirit, being only to be had through the softening of the affections.

He should look for a clear understanding, cheerfulness, and alacrity of mind, rather than gaiety and brilliancy, and for a gentle tenderness of disposition in preference to an impassioned nature. Lively talents are too stimulating in a tired man's house—passion is too disturbing....

"Her love should be
A love that clings not, nor is exigent,
Encumbers not the active purposes,
Nor drains their source; but profers with free grace
Pleasure at pleasure touched, at pleasure waived,
A washing of the weary traveller's feet,
A quenching of his thirst, a sweet repose,
Alternate and preparative; in groves
Where, loving much the flower that loves the shade,
And loving much the shade that that flower loves,
He yet is unbewildered, unenslaved,
Thence starting light, and pleasantly let go
When serious service calls. (8)

Some persons are disappointed in marriage, because they expect too much from it; but many more, because they do not bring into the co-partnership their fair share of cheerfulness, kindliness, forbearance, and common sense. Their imagination has perhaps pictured a condition never experienced on this side Heaven; and when real life comes, with its troubles and cares, there is a sudden waking-up as from a dream. Or they look for something approaching perfection in their chosen companion, and discover by experience that the fairest of characters have their weaknesses. Yet it is often the very imperfection of human nature, rather than its perfection, that makes the strongest claims on the forbearance and sympathy of others, and, in affectionate and sensible natures, tends to produce the closest unions.

The golden rule of married life is, "Bear and forbear. " Marriage, like government, is a series of compromises. One must give and take, refrain and restrain, endure and be patient. One may not be blind to another's failings, but they may be borne with good- natured forbearance. Of all qualities, good temper is the one that wears and works the best in married life. Conjoined with self-control, it gives patience—the patience to bear and forbear, to listen without retort, to refrain until the angry flash has passed. How true it is in marriage, that "the soft answer turneth away wrath! "

Burns the poet, in speaking of the qualities of a good wife, divided them into ten parts. Four of these he gave to good temper, two to good sense, one to wit, one to beauty—such as a sweet face, eloquent eyes, a fine person, a graceful carriage; and the other two parts he divided amongst the other qualities belonging to or attending on a wife—such as fortune, connections, education (that is, of a higher standard than ordinary), family blood, &c. ; but he said: "Divide those two degrees as you please, only remember that all these minor proportions must be expressed by fractions, for there is not any one of them that is entitled to the dignity of an integer. "

It has been said that girls are very good at making nets, but that it would be better still if they would learn to make cages. Men are often as easily caught as birds, but as difficult to keep. If the wife cannot make her home bright and happy, so that it shall be the cleanest, sweetest, cheerfulest place that her husband can find refuge in—a retreat from the toils and troubles of the outer world—then God help the poor man, for he is virtually homeless!

No wise person will marry for beauty mainly. It may exercise a powerful attraction in the first place, but it is found to be of comparatively little consequence afterwards. Not that beauty of person is to be underestimated, for, other things being equal, handsomeness of form and beauty of features are the outward manifestations of health. But to marry a handsome figure without character, fine features unbeautified by sentiment or good-nature, is the most deplorable of mistakes. As even the finest landscape, seen daily, becomes monotonous, so does the most beautiful face, unless a beautiful nature shines through it. The beauty of to-day becomes commonplace to-morrow; whereas goodness, displayed through the most ordinary features, is perennially lovely. Moreover, this kind of beauty improves with age, and time ripens rather than destroys it. After the first year, married people rarely think of each other's features, and whether they be classically beautiful or otherwise. But they never fail to be cognisant of each other's temper. "When I see a man, " says Addison, "with a sour rivelled face, I cannot forbear pitying his wife; and when I meet with an open ingenuous countenance, I think of the happiness of his friends, his family, and his relations. "

We have given the views of the poet Burns as to the qualities necessary in a good wife. Let us add the advice given by Lord Burleigh to his son, embodying the experience of a wise statesman and practised man of the world. "When it shall please God, " said he, "to bring thee to man's estate, use great providence and circumspection in choosing thy wife; for from thence will spring all thy future good or evil. And it is an action of thy life, like unto a stratagem of war, wherein a man can err but once.... Enquire diligently of her disposition, and how her parents have been inclined in their youth. (9) Let her not be poor, how generous (well-born) soever; for a man can buy nothing in the market with gentility. Nor choose a base and uncomely creature altogether for wealth; for it will cause contempt in others, and loathing in thee. Neither make choice of a dwarf, or a fool; for by the one thou shalt beget a race of pigmies, while the other will be thy continual disgrace, and it will yirke (irk) thee to hear her talk. For thou shalt find it to thy great grief, that there is nothing more fulsome (disgusting) than a she-fool."

A man's moral character is, necessarily, powerfully influenced by his wife. A lower nature will drag him down, as a higher will lift him up. The former will deaden his sympathies, dissipate his energies, and distort his life; while the latter, by satisfying his affections, will strengthen his moral nature, and by giving him repose, tend to energise his intellect. Not only so, but a woman of high principles will insensibly elevate the aims and purposes of her husband, as one of low principles will unconsciously degrade them. De Tocqueville was profoundly impressed by this truth. He entertained the opinion that man could have no such mainstay in life as the companionship of a wife of good temper and high principle. He says that in the course of his life, he had seen even weak men display real public virtue, because they had by their side a woman of noble character, who sustained them in their career, and exercised a fortifying influence on their views of public duty; whilst, on the contrary, he had still oftener seen men of great and generous instincts transformed into vulgar self-seekers, by contact with women of narrow natures, devoted to an imbecile love of pleasure, and from whose minds the grand motive of Duty was altogether absent.

De Tocqueville himself had the good fortune to be blessed with an admirable wife: (10) and in his letters to his intimate friends, he spoke most gratefully of the comfort and support he derived from her sustaining courage, her equanimity of temper, and her nobility of character. The more, indeed, that De Tocqueville saw of the world and of practical life, the more convinced he became of the necessity of healthy domestic conditions for a man's growth in virtue and goodness. (11) Especially did he regard marriage as of inestimable importance in regard to a man's true happiness; and he was accustomed to speak of his own as the wisest action of his life. "Many external circumstances of happiness, " he said, "have been granted to me. But more than all, I have to thank Heaven for having bestowed on me true domestic happiness, the first of human blessings. As I grow older, the portion of my life which in my youth I used to look down upon, every day becomes more important in my eyes, and would now easily console me for the loss of all the rest. " And again, writing to his bosom-friend, De Kergorlay, he said: "Of all the blessings which God has given to me, the greatest of all in my eyes is to have lighted on Marie. You cannot imagine what she is in great trials. Usually so gentle, she then becomes strong and energetic. She watches me without my knowing it; she softens, calms, and strengthens me in difficulties which disturb ME, but leave her serene. " (12) In another letter he says: "I cannot describe to you the happiness yielded in the long run by the habitual society of a woman in whose soul all that is good in your own is reflected naturally, and even improved. When I say or do a thing which seems to me to be perfectly right, I read immediately in Marie's countenance an expression of proud satisfaction which elevates me. And so, when my conscience reproaches me, her face instantly clouds over. Although I have great power over her mind, I see with pleasure that she awes me; and so long as I love her as I do now, I am sure that I shall never allow myself to be drawn into anything that is wrong. "

In the retired life which De Tocqueville led as a literary man— political life being closed against him by the inflexible independence of his character—his health failed, and he became ill, irritable, and querulous. While proceeding with his last work, 'L'Ancien Regime et la Revolution, ' he wrote: "After sitting at my desk for five or six hours, I can write no longer; the machine refuses to act. I am in great want of rest, and of a long rest. If you add all the perplexities that besiege an author towards the end of his work, you will be able to imagine a very wretched life. I could not go on with my task if it were not for the refreshing calm of Marie's companionship. It would be impossible to find a disposition forming a happier contrast to my own. In my perpetual irritability of body and mind, she is a providential resource that never fails me. " (13)

M. Guizot was, in like manner, sustained and encouraged, amidst his many vicissitudes and disappointments, by his noble wife. If he was treated with harshness by his political enemies, his consolation was in the tender affection which filled his home with sunshine. Though his public life was bracing and stimulating, he felt, nevertheless, that it was cold and calculating, and neither filled the soul nor elevated the character. "Man longs for a happiness, " he says in his 'Memoires, ' more complete and more tender than that which all the labours and triumphs of active exertion and public importance can bestow. What I know to-day, at the end of my race, I have felt when it began, and during its continuance. Even in the midst of great undertakings, domestic affections form the basis of life; and the most brilliant career has only superficial and incomplete enjoyments, if a stranger to the happy ties of family and friendship. "

The circumstances connected with M. Guizot's courtship and marriage are curious and interesting. While a young man living by his pen in Paris, writing books, reviews, and translations, he formed a casual acquaintance with Mademoiselle Pauline de Meulan, a lady of great ability, then editor of the PUBLICISTE. A severe domestic calamity having befallen her, she fell ill, and was unable for a time to carry on the heavy literary work connected with her journal. At this juncture a letter without any signature reached her one day, offering a supply of articles, which the writer hoped would be worthy of the reputation of the PUBLICISTE. The articles duly arrived, were accepted, and published. They dealt with a great variety of subjects—art, literature, theatricals, and general criticism. When the editor at length recovered from her illness, the writer of the articles disclosed himself: it was M. Guizot. An intimacy sprang up between them, which ripened into mutual affection, and before long Mademoiselle de Meulan became his wife.

From that time forward, she shared in all her husband's joys and sorrows, as well as in many of his labours. Before they became united, he asked her if she thought she should ever become dismayed at the vicissitudes of his destiny, which he then saw looming before him. She replied that he might assure himself that she would always passionately enjoy his triumphs, but never heave a sigh over his defeats. When M. Guizot became first minister of Louis Philippe, she wrote to a friend: "I now see my husband much less than I desire, but still I see him.... If God spares us to each other, I shall always be, in the midst of every trial and apprehension, the happiest of beings. " Little more than six months after these words were written, the devoted wife was laid in her grave; and her sorrowing husband was left thenceforth to tread the journey of life alone.

Burke was especially happy in his union with Miss Nugent, a beautiful, affectionate, and highminded woman. The agitation and anxiety of his public life was more than compensated by his domestic happiness, which seems to have been complete. It was a saying of Burke, thoroughly illustrative of his character, that "to love the little platoon we belong to in society is the germ of all public affections. " His description of his wife, in her youth, is probably one of the finest word-portraits in the language: —

"She is handsome; but it is a beauty not arising from features, from complexion, or from shape. She has all three in a high degree, but it is not by these she touches the heart; it is all that sweetness of temper, benevolence, innocence, and sensibility, which a face can express, that forms her beauty. She has a face that just raises your attention at first sight; it grows on you every moment, and you wonder it did no more than raise your attention at first.

"Her eyes have a mild light, but they awe when she pleases; they command, like a good man out of office, not by authority, but by virtue.

"Her stature is not tall; she is not made to be the admiration of everybody, but the happiness of one.

"She has all the firmness that does not exclude delicacy; she has all the softness that does not imply weakness.

"Her voice is a soft low music—not formed to rule in public assemblies, but to charm those who can distinguish a company from a crowd; it has this advantage—YOU MUST COME CLOSE TO HER TO HEAR IT.

"To describe her body describes her mind—one is the transcript of the other; her understanding is not shown in the variety of matters it exerts itself on, but in the goodness of the choice she makes.

"She does not display it so much in saying or doing striking things, as in avoiding such as she ought not to say or do.

"No person of so few years can know the world better; no person was ever less corrupted by the knowledge of it.

"Her politeness flows rather from a natural disposition to oblige, than from any rules on that subject, and therefore never fails to strike those who understand good breeding and those who do not.

"She has a steady and firm mind, which takes no more from the solidity of the female character than the solidity of marble does from its polish and lustre. She has such virtues as make us value the truly great of our own sex. She has all the winning graces that make us love even the faults we see in the weak and beautiful, in hers. "

Let us give, as a companion picture, the not less beautiful delineation of a husband, that of Colonel Hutchinson, the Commonwealth man, by his widow. Shortly before his death, he enjoined her "not to grieve at the common rate of desolate women. " And, faithful to his injunction, instead of lamenting his loss, she indulged her noble sorrow in depicting her husband as he had lived.

"They who dote on mortal excellences, " she says, in her Introduction to the 'Life, ' "when, by the inevitable fate of all things frail, their adored idols are taken from them, may let loose the winds of passion to bring in a flood of sorrow, whose ebbing tides carry away the dear memory of what they have lost; and when comfort is essayed to such mourners, commonly all objects are removed out of their view which may with their remembrance renew the grief; and in time these remedies succeed, and oblivion's curtain is by degrees drawn over the dead face; and things less lovely are liked, while they are not viewed together with that which was most excellent. But I, that am under a command not to grieve at the common rate of desolate women, (14) while I am studying which way to moderate my woe, and if it were possible to augment my love, I can for the present find out none more just to your dear father, nor consolatory to myself, than the preservation of his memory, which I need not gild with such flattering commendations as hired preachers do equally give to the truly and titularly honourable. A naked undressed narrative, speaking the simple truth of him, will deck him with more substantial glory, than all the panegyrics the best pens could ever consecrate to the virtues of the best men. "

The following is the wife's portrait of Colonel Hutchinson as a husband: —

"For conjugal affection to his wife, it was such in him as whosoever would draw out a rule of honour, kindness, and religion, to be practised in that estate, need no more but exactly draw out his example. Never man had a greater passion for a woman, nor a more honourable esteem of a wife: yet he was not uxorious, nor remitted he that just rule which it was her honour to obey, but managed the reins of government with such prudence and affection, that she who could not delight in such an honourable and advantageable subjection, must have wanted a reasonable soul.

"He governed by persuasion, which he never employed but to things honourable and profitable to herself; he loved her soul and her honour more than her outside, and yet he had ever for her person a constant indulgence, exceeding the common temporary passion of the most uxorious fools. If he esteemed her at a higher rate than she in herself could have deserved, he was the author of that virtue he doated on, while she only reflected his own glories upon him. All that she was, was HIM, while he was here, and all that she is now, at best, is but his pale shade.

"So liberal was he to her, and of so generous a temper, that he hated the mention of severed purses, his estate being so much at her disposal that he never would receive an account of anything she expended. So constant was he in his love, that when she ceased to be young and lovely he began to show most fondness. He loved her at such a kind and generous rate as words cannot express. Yet even this, which was the highest love he or any man could have, was bounded by a superior: he loved her in the Lord as his fellow-creature, not his idol; but in such a manner as showed that an affection, founded on the just rules of duty, far exceeds every way all the irregular passions in the world. He loved God above her, and all the other dear pledges of his heart, and for his glory cheerfully resigned them. " (15)

Lady Rachel Russell is another of the women of history celebrated for her devotion and faithfulness as a wife. She laboured and pleaded for her husband's release so long as she could do so with honour; but when she saw that all was in vain, she collected her courage, and strove by her example to strengthen the resolution of her dear lord. And when his last hour had nearly come, and his wife and children waited to receive his parting embrace, she, brave to the end, that she might not add to his distress, concealed the agony of her grief under a seeming composure; and they parted, after a tender adieu, in silence. After she had gone, Lord William said, "Now the bitterness of death is passed! " (16)

We have spoken of the influence of a wife upon a man's character. There are few men strong enough to resist the influence of a lower character in a wife. If she do not sustain and elevate what is highest in his nature, she will speedily reduce him to her own level. Thus a wife may be the making or the unmaking of the best of men. An illustration of this power is furnished in the life of Bunyan. The profligate tinker had the good fortune to marry, in early life, a worthy young woman of good parentage. "My mercy, " he himself says, "was to light upon a wife whose father and mother were accounted godly. This woman and I, though we came together as poor as poor might be (not having so much household stuff as a dish or a spoon betwixt us both), yet she had for her part, 'The Plain Man's Pathway to Heaven, ' and 'The Practice of Piety, ' which her father had left her when he died. " And by reading these and other good books; helped by the kindly influence of his wife, Bunyan was gradually reclaimed from his evil ways, and led gently into the paths of peace.

Richard Baxter, the Nonconformist divine, was far advanced in life before he met the excellent woman who eventually became his wife. He was too laboriously occupied in his vocation of minister to have any time to spare for courtship; and his marriage was, as in the case of Calvin, as much a matter of convenience as of love. Miss Charlton, the lady of his choice, was the owner of property in her own right; but lest it should be thought that Baxter married her for "covetousness, " he requested, first, that she should give over to her relatives the principal part of her fortune, and that "he should have nothing that before her marriage was hers; " secondly, that she should so arrange her affairs "as that he might be entangled in no lawsuits; " and, thirdly, "that she should expect none of the time that his ministerial work might require. " These several conditions the bride having complied with, the marriage took place, and proved a happy one. "We lived, " said Baxter, "in inviolated love and mutual complacency, sensible of the benefit of mutual help, nearly nineteen years. " Yet the life of Baxter was one of great trials and troubles, arising from the unsettled state of the times in which he lived. He was hunted about from one part of the country to another, and for several years he had no settled dwelling-place. "The women, he gently remarks in his 'Life, ' "have most of that sort of trouble, but my wife easily bore it all. " In the sixth year of his marriage Baxter was brought before the magistrates at Brentford, for holding a conventicle at Acton, and was sentenced by them to be imprisoned in Clerkenwell Gaol. There he was joined by his wife, who affectionately nursed him during his confinement. "She was never so cheerful a companion to me, " he says, "as in prison, and was very much against me seeking to be released. " At length he was set at liberty by the judges of the Court of Common Pleas, to whom he had appealed against the sentence of the magistrates. At the death of Mrs. Baxter, after a very troubled yet happy and cheerful life, her husband left a touching portrait of the graces, virtues, and Christian character of this excellent woman—one of the most charming things to be found in his works.

The noble Count Zinzendorf was united to an equally noble woman, who bore him up through life by her great spirit, and sustained him in all his labours by her unfailing courage. "Twenty-four years' experience has shown me, " he said, "that just the helpmate whom I have is the only one that could suit my vocation. Who else could have so carried through my family affairs? —who lived so spotlessly before the world? Who so wisely aided me in my rejection of a dry morality?.... Who would, like she, without a murmur, have seen her husband encounter such dangers by land and sea? —who undertaken with him, and sustained, such astonishing pilgrimages? Who, amid such difficulties, could have held up her head and supported me?.... And finally, who, of all human beings, could so well understand and interpret to others my inner and outer being as this one, of such nobleness in her way of thinking, such great intellectual capacity, and free from the theological perplexities that so often enveloped me?

One of the brave Dr. Livingstone's greatest trials during his travels in South Africa was the death of his affectionate wife, who had shared his dangers, and accompanied him in so many of his wanderings. In communicating the intelligence of her decease at Shupanga, on the River Zambesi, to his friend Sir Roderick Murchison, Dr. Livingstone said: "I must confess that this heavy stroke quite takes the heart out of me. Everything else that has happened only made me more determined to overcome all difficulties; but after this sad stroke I feel crushed and void of strength. Only three short months of her society, after four years separation! I married her for love, and the longer I lived with her I loved her the more. A good wife, and a good, brave, kindhearted mother was she, deserving all the praises you bestowed upon her at our parting dinner, for teaching her own and the native children, too, at Kolobeng. I try to bow to the blow as from our Heavenly Father, who orders all things for us.... I shall do my duty still, but it is with a darkened horizon that I again set about it. "

Sir Samuel Romilly left behind him, in his Autobiography, a touching picture of his wife, to whom he attributed no small measure of the success and happiness that accompanied him through life. "For the last fifteen years, " he said, "my happiness has been the constant study of the most excellent of wives: a woman in whom a strong understanding, the noblest and most elevated sentiments, and the most courageous virtue, are united to the warmest affection, and to the utmost delicacy of mind and heart; and all these intellectual perfections are graced by the most splendid beauty that human eyes ever beheld. " (17) Romilly's affection and admiration for this noble woman endured to the end; and when she died, the shock proved greater than his sensitive nature could bear. Sleep left his eyelids, his mind became unhinged, and three days after her death the sad event occurred which brought his own valued life to a close. (18)

Sir Francis Burdett, to whom Romilly had been often politically opposed, fell into such a state of profound melancholy on the death of his wife, that he persistently refused nourishment of any kind, and died before the removal of her remains from the house; and husband and wife were laid side by side in the same grave.

It was grief for the loss of his wife that sent Sir Thomas Graham into the army at the age of forty-three. Every one knows the picture of the newly-wedded pair by Gainsborough—one of the most exquisite of that painter's works. They lived happily together for eighteen years, and then she died, leaving him inconsolable. To forget his sorrow — and, as some thought, to get rid of the weariness of his life without her—Graham joined Lord Hood as a volunteer, and distinguished himself by the recklessness of his bravery at the siege of Toulon. He served all through the Peninsular War, first under Sir John Moore, and afterwards under Wellington; rising through the various grades of the service, until he rose to be second in command. He was commonly known as the "hero of Barossa, " because of his famous victory at that place; and he was eventually raised to the peerage as Lord Lynedoch, ending his days peacefully at a very advanced age. But to the last he tenderly cherished the memory of his dead wife, to the love of whom he may be said to have owed all his glory.

"Never," said Sheridan of him, when pronouncing his eulogy in the House of Commons—"never was there seated a loftier spirit in a braver heart. "

And so have noble wives cherished the memory of their husbands. There is a celebrated monument in Vienna, erected to the memory of one of the best generals of the Austrian army, on which there is an inscription, setting forth his great services during the Seven Years' War, concluding with the words, "NON PATRIA, NEC IMPERATOR, SED CONJUX POSUIT. " When Sir Albert Morton died, his wife's grief was such that she shortly followed him, and was laid by his side. Wotton's two lines on the event have been celebrated as containing a volume in seventeen words:

> "He first deceased; she for a little tried
> To live without him, liked it not, and died."

So, when Washington's wife was informed that her dear lord had suffered his last agony—had drawn his last breath, and departed — she said: "'Tis well; all is now over. I shall soon follow him; I have no more trials to pass through. "

Not only have women been the best companions, friends, and consolers, but they have in many cases been the most effective helpers of their husbands in their special lines of work. Galvani was especially happy in his wife. She was the daughter of Professor Galeazzi; and it is said to have been through her quick observation of the circumstance of the leg of a frog, placed near an electrical machine, becoming convulsed when touched by a knife, that her husband was first led to investigate the science which has since become identified with his name. Lavoisier's wife also was a woman of real scientific ability, who not only shared in her husband's pursuits, but even undertook the task of engraving the plates that accompanied his 'Elements. '

The late Dr. Buckland had another true helper in his wife, who assisted him with her pen, prepared and mended his fossils, and furnished many of the drawings and illustrations of his published works. "Notwithstanding her devotion to her husband's pursuits, " says her son, Frank Buckland, in the preface to one of his father's works, "she did not neglect the education of her children, but occupied her mornings in superintending their instruction in sound and useful knowledge. The sterling value of her labours they now, in after-life, fully appreciate, and feel most thankful that they were blessed with so good a mother. " (19)

A still more remarkable instance of helpfulness in a wife is presented in the case of Huber, the Geneva naturalist. Huber was blind from his seventeenth year, and yet he found means to study and master a branch of natural history demanding the closest observation and the keenest eyesight. It was through the eyes of his wife that his mind worked as if they had been his own. She encouraged her husband's studies as a means of alleviating his privation, which at length he came to forget; and his life was as prolonged and happy as is usual with most naturalists. He even went so far as to declare that he should be miserable were he to regain his eyesight. "I should not know, " he said, "to what extent a person in my situation could be beloved; besides, to me my wife is always young, fresh, and pretty, which is no light matter. " Huber's great work on 'Bees' is still regarded as a masterpiece, embodying a vast amount of original observation on their habits and natural history. Indeed, while reading his descriptions, one would suppose that they were the work of a singularly keensighted man, rather than of one who had been entirely blind for twenty-five years at the time at which he wrote them.

Not less touching was the devotion of Lady Hamilton to the service of her husband, the late Sir William Hamilton, Professor of Logic and Metaphysics in the University of Edinburgh. After he had been stricken by paralysis through overwork at the age of fifty-six, she became hands, eyes, mind, and everything to him. She identified herself with his work, read and consulted books for him, copied out and corrected his lectures, and relieved him of all business which she felt herself competent to undertake. Indeed, her conduct as a wife was nothing short of heroic; and it is probable that but for her devoted and more than wifely help, and her rare practical ability, the greatest of her husband's works would never have seen the light. He was by nature unmethodical and disorderly, and she supplied him with method and orderliness. His temperament was studious but indolent, while she was active and energetic. She abounded in the qualities which he most lacked. He had the genius, to which her vigorous nature gave the force and impulse.

When Sir William Hamilton was elected to his Professorship, after a severe and even bitter contest, his opponents, professing to regard him as a visionary, predicted that he could never teach a class of students, and that his appointment would prove a total failure. He determined, with the help of his wife, to justify the choice of his supporters, and to prove that his enemies were false prophets. Having no stock of lectures on hand, each lecture of the first course was written out day by day, as it was to be delivered on the following morning. His wife sat up with him night after night, to write out a fair copy of the lectures from the rough sheets, which he drafted in the adjoining room. "On some occasions, " says his biographer, "the subject of the lectures would prove less easily managed than on others; and then Sir William would be found writing as late as nine o'clock in the morning, while his faithful but wearied amanuensis had fallen asleep on a sofa. " (20)

Sometimes the finishing touches to the lecture were left to be given just before the class-hour. Thus helped, Sir William completed his course; his reputation as a lecturer was established; and he eventually became recognised throughout Europe as one of the leading intellects of his time. (21)

The woman who soothes anxiety by her presence, who charms and allays irritability by her sweetness of temper, is a consoler as well as a true helper. Niebuhr always spoke of his wife as a fellow-worker with him in this sense. Without the peace and consolation which be found in her society, his nature would have fretted in comparative uselessness. "Her sweetness of temper and her love, " said he, "raise me above the earth, and in a manner separate me from this life. " But she was a helper in another and more direct way. Niebuhr was accustomed to discuss with his wife every historical discovery, every political event, every novelty in literature; and it was mainly for her pleasure and approbation, in the first instance, that he laboured while preparing himself for the instruction of the world at large.

The wife of John Stuart Mill was another worthy helper of her husband, though in a more abstruse department of study, as we learn from his touching dedication of the treatise 'On Liberty': — "To the beloved and deplored memory of her who was the inspirer, and in part the author, of all that is best in my writings—the friend and wife, whose exalted sense of truth and right was my strongest incitement, and whose approbation was my chief reward, I dedicate this volume. " Not less touching is the testimony borne by another great living writer to the character of his wife, in the inscription upon the tombstone of Mrs. Carlyle in Haddington Churchyard, where are inscribed these words: - "In her bright existence, she had more sorrows than are common, but also a soft amiability, a capacity of discernment, and a noble loyalty of heart, which are rare. For forty years she was the true and loving helpmate of her husband, and by act and word unweariedly forwarded him as none else could, in all of worthy that he did or attempted"

The married life of Faraday was eminently happy. In his wife he found, at the same time, a true helpmate and soul-mate. She supported, cheered, and strengthened him on his way through life, giving him "the clear contentment of a heart at ease. " In his diary he speaks of his marriage as "a source of honour and happiness far exceeding all the rest. " After twentyeight years' experience, he spoke of it as "an event which, more than any other, had contributed to his earthly happiness and healthy state of mind.... The union (said he) has in nowise changed, except only in the depth and strength of its character. " And for six- and-forty years did the union continue unbroken; the love of the old man remaining as fresh, as earnest, as heart-whole, as in the days of his impetuous youth. In this case, marriage was as—

"A golden chain let down from heaven, Whose links are bright and even; That falls like sleep on lovers, and combines The soft and sweetest minds In equal knots. "

Besides being a helper, woman is emphatically a consoler. Her sympathy is unfailing. She soothes, cheers, and comforts. Never was this more true than in the case of the wife of Tom Hood, whose tender devotion to him, during a life that was a prolonged illness, is one of the most affecting things in biography. A woman of excellent good sense, she appreciated her husband's genius, and, by encouragement and sympathy, cheered and heartened him to renewed effort in many a weary struggle for life. She created about him an atmosphere of hope and cheerfulness, and nowhere did the sunshine of her love seem so bright as when lighting up the couch of her invalid husband.

Nor was he unconscious of her worth. In one of his letters to her, when absent from his side, Hood said: "I never was anything, Dearest, till I knew you; and I have been a better, happier, and more prosperous man ever since. Lay by that truth in lavender, Sweetest, and remind me of it when I fail. I am writing warmly and fondly, but not without good cause. First, your own affectionate letter, lately received; next, the remembrance of our dear children, pledges—

what darling ones! —of our old familiar love; then, a delicious impulse to pour out the overflowings of my heart into yours; and last, not least, the knowledge that your dear eyes will read what my hand is now writing. Perhaps there is an afterthought that, whatever may befall me, the wife of my bosom will have the acknowledgment of her tenderness, worth, excellence —all that is wifely or womanly, from my pen. " In another letter, also written to his wife during a brief absence, there is a natural touch, showing his deep affection for her: "I went and retraced our walk in the park, and sat down on the same seat, and felt happier and better. "

But not only was Mrs. Hood a consoler, she was also a helper of her husband in his special work. He had such confidence in her judgment, that he read, and re-read, and corrected with her assistance all that he wrote. Many of his pieces were first dedicated to her; and her ready memory often supplied him with the necessary references and quotations. Thus, in the roll of noble wives of men of genius, Mrs. Hood will always be entitled to take a foremost place.

Not less effective as a literary helper was Lady Napier, the wife of Sir William Napier, historian of the Peninsular War. She encouraged him to undertake the work, and without her help he would have experienced great difficulty in completing it. She translated and epitomized the immense mass of original documents, many of them in cipher, on which it was in a great measure founded. When the Duke of Wellington was told of the art and industry she had displayed in deciphering King Joseph's portfolio, and the immense mass of correspondence taken at Vittoria, he at first would hardly believe it, adding—"I would have given 20,000L. to any person who could have done this for me in the Peninsula. " Sir William Napier's handwriting being almost illegible, Lady Napier made out his rough interlined manuscript, which he himself could scarcely read, and wrote out a full fair copy for the printer; and all this vast labour she undertook and accomplished, according to the testimony of her husband, without having for a moment neglected the care and education of a large family. When Sir William lay on his deathbed, Lady Napier was at the same time dangerously ill; but she was wheeled into his room on a sofa, and the two took their silent farewell of each other. The husband died first; in a few weeks the wife followed him, and they sleep side by side in the same grave.

Many other similar truehearted wives rise up in the memory, to recite whose praises would more than fill up our remaining space—

such as Flaxman's wife, Ann Denham, who cheered and encouraged her husband through life in the prosecution of his art, accompanying him to Rome, sharing in his labours and anxieties, and finally in his triumphs, and to whom Flaxman, in the fortieth year of their married life, dedicated his beautiful designs illustrative of Faith, Hope, and Charity, in token of his deep and undimmed affection; —such as Katherine Boutcher, "dark-eyed Kate, " the wife of William Blake, who believed her husband to be the first genius on earth, worked off the impressions of his plates and coloured them beautifully with her own hand, bore with him in all his erratic ways, sympathised with him in his sorrows and joys for forty-five years, and comforted him until his dying hour—his last sketch, made in his seventy-first year, being a likeness of himself, before making which, seeing his wife crying by his side, he said, "Stay, Kate! just keep as you are; I will draw your portrait, for you have ever been an angel to me; "—such again as Lady Franklin, the true and noble woman, who never rested in her endeavours to penetrate the secret of the Polar Sea and prosecute the search for her long-lost husband—undaunted by failure, and persevering in her determination with a devotion and singleness of purpose altogether unparalleled; —or such again as the wife of Zimmermann, whose intense melancholy she strove in vain to assuage, sympathizing with him, listening to him, and endeavouring to understand him—and to whom, when on her deathbed, about to leave him for ever, she addressed the touching words, "My poor Zimmermann! who will now understand thee? "

Wives have actively helped their husbands in other ways. Before Weinsberg surrendered to its besiegers, the women of the place asked permission of the captors to remove their valuables. The permission was granted, and shortly after, the women were seen issuing from the gates carrying their husbands on their shoulders. Lord Nithsdale owed his escape from prison to the address of his wife, who changed garments with him, sending him forth in her stead, and herself remaining prisoner, —an example which was successfully repeated by Madame de Lavalette.

But the most remarkable instance of the release of a husband through the devotion of a wife, was that of the celebrated Grotius. He had lain for nearly twenty months in the strong fortress of Loevestein, near Gorcum, having been condemned by the government of the United Provinces to perpetual imprisonment. His wife, having been allowed to share his cell, greatly relieved his solitude. She was permitted to go into the town twice a week, and bring her husband books, of which he required a large number to enable him to prosecute his studies. At length a large chest was required to hold them. This the sentries at first examined with great strictness, but, finding that it only contained books (amongst others Arminian books) and linen, they at length gave up the search, and it was allowed to pass out and in as a matter of course. This led Grotius' wife to conceive the idea of releasing him; and she persuaded him one day to deposit himself in the chest instead of the outgoing books. When the two soldiers appointed to remove it took it up, they felt it to be considerably heavier than usual, and one of them asked, jestingly, "Have we got the Arminian himself here? " to which the ready-witted wife replied, "Yes, perhaps some Arminian books. " The chest reached Gorcum in safety; the captive was released; and Grotius escaped across the frontier into Brabant, and afterwards into France, where he was rejoined by his wife.

Trial and suffering are the tests of married life. They bring out the real character, and often tend to produce the closest union. They may even be the spring of the purest happiness. Uninterrupted joy, like uninterrupted success, is not good for either man or woman. When Heine's wife died, he began to reflect upon the loss he had sustained. They had both known poverty, and struggled through it hand-in-hand; and it was his greatest sorrow that she was taken from him at the moment when fortune was beginning to smile upon him, but too late for her to share in his prosperity. "Alas I" said he, "amongst my griefs must I reckon even her love—the strongest, truest, that ever inspired the heart of woman—which made me the happiest of mortals, and yet was to me a fountain of a thousand distresses, inquietudes, and cares? To entire cheerfulness, perhaps, she never attained; but for what unspeakable sweetness, what exalted, enrapturing joys, is not love indebted to sorrow! Amidst growing anxieties, with the torture of anguish in my heart, I have been made, even by the loss which caused me this anguish and these anxieties, inexpressibly happy! When tears flowed over our cheeks, did not a nameless, seldom-felt delight stream through my breast, oppressed equally by joy and sorrow! "

There is a degree of sentiment in German love which seems strange to English readers, —such as we find depicted in the lives of Novalis, Jung Stilling, Fichte, Jean Paul, and others that might be named. The German betrothal is a ceremony of almost equal importance to the marriage itself; and in that state the sentiments are allowed free play, whilst English lovers are restrained, shy, and as if ashamed of their feelings. Take, for instance, the case of Herder, whom his future wife first saw in the pulpit. "I heard, " she says, "the voice of an angel, and soul's words such as I had never heard before. In the afternoon I saw him, and stammered out my thanks to him; from this time forth our souls were one. " They were betrothed long before their means would permit them to marry; but at length they were united. "We were married, " says Caroline, the wife, "by the rose-light of a beautiful evening. We were one heart, one soul. " Herder was equally ecstatic in his language. "I have a wife, " he wrote to Jacobi, "that is the tree, the consolation, and the happiness of my life. Even in flying transient thoughts (which often surprise us), we are one! "

Take, again, the case of Fichte, in whose history his courtship and marriage form a beautiful episode. He was a poor German student, living with a family at Zurich in the capacity of tutor, when he first made the acquaintance of Johanna Maria Hahn, a niece of Klopstock. Her position in life was higher than that of Fichte; nevertheless, she regarded him with sincere admiration. When Fichte was about to leave Zurich, his troth plighted to her, she, knowing him to be very poor, offered him a gift of money before setting out. He was inexpressibly hurt by the offer, and, at first, even doubted whether she could really love him; but, on second thoughts, he wrote to her, expressing his deep thanks, but, at the same time, the impossibility of his accepting such a gift from her. He succeeded in reaching his destination, though entirely destitute of means. After a long and hard struggle with the world, extending over many years, Fichte was at length earning money enough to enable him to marry. In one of his charming letters to his betrothed he said: —"And so, dearest, I solemnly devote myself to thee, and thank thee that thou hast thought me not unworthy to be thy companion on the journey of life.... There is no land of happiness here below—I know it now—but a land of toil, where every joy but strengthens us for greater labour. Hand-in-hand we shall traverse it, and encourage and strengthen each other, until our spirits—oh, may it be together! —shall rise to the eternal fountain of all peace. "

The married life of Fichte was very happy. His wife proved a true and highminded helpmate. During the War of Liberation she was assiduous in her attention to the wounded in the hospitals, where she caught a malignant fever, which nearly carried her off. Fichte himself caught the same disease, and was for a time completely prostrated; but he lived for a few more years and died at the early age of fifty-two, consumed by his own fire.

What a contrast does the courtship and married life of the blunt and practical William Cobbett present to the aesthetical and sentimental love of these highly refined Germans! Not less honest, not less true, but, as some would think, comparatively coarse and vulgar. When he first set eyes upon the girl that was afterwards to become his wife, she was only thirteen years old, and he was twenty-one—a sergeant-major in a foot regiment stationed at St. John's in New Brunswick. He was passing the door of her father's house one day in winter, and saw the girl out in the snow, scrubbing a washing-tub. He said at once to himself, "That's the girl for me. " He made her acquaintance, and resolved that she should be his wife so soon as he could get discharged from the army.

On the eve of the girl's return to Woolwich with her father, who was a sergeant-major in the artillery, Cobbett sent her a hundred and fifty guineas which he had saved, in order that she might be able to live without hard work until his return to England. The girl departed, taking with her the money; and five years later Cobbett obtained his discharge. On reaching London, he made haste to call upon the sergeant-major's daughter. "I found, " he says, "my little girl a servant-of-all-work (and hard work it was), at five pounds a year, in the house of a Captain Brisac; and, without hardly saying a word about the matter, she put into my hands the whole of my hundred and fifty guineas, unbroken. " Admiration of her conduct was now added to love of her person, and Cobbett shortly after married the girl, who proved an excellent wife. He was, indeed, never tired of speaking her praises, and it was his pride to attribute to her all the comfort and much of the success of his after-life.

Though Cobbett was regarded by many in his lifetime as a coarse, hard, practical man, full of prejudices, there was yet a strong undercurrent of poetry in his nature; and, while he declaimed against sentiment, there were few men more thoroughly imbued with sentiment of the best kind. He had the tenderest regard for the character of woman. He respected her purity and her virtue, and in his 'Advice to Young Men, ' he has painted the true womanly woman—the helpful, cheerful, affectionate wife—with a vividness and brightness, and, at the same time, a force of good sense, that has never been surpassed by any English writer. Cobbett was anything but refined, in the conventional sense of the word; but he was pure, temperate, self-denying, industrious, vigorous, and energetic, in an eminent degree. Many of his views were, no doubt, wrong, but they were his own, for he insisted on thinking for himself in everything.

Though few men took a firmer grasp of the real than he did, perhaps still fewer were more swayed by the ideal. In word-pictures of his own emotions, he is unsurpassed. Indeed, Cobbett might almost be regarded as one of the greatest prose poets of English real life.

NOTES

(1) Mungo Park declared that he was more affected by this incident than by any other that befel him in the course of his travels. As he lay down to sleep on the mat spread for him on the floor of the hut, his benefactress called to the female part of the family to resume their task of spinning cotton, in which they continued employed far into the night. "They lightened their labour with songs, " says the traveller, "one of which was composed extempore, for I was myself the subject of it; it was sung by one of the young women, the rest joining in a chorus. The air was sweet and plaintive, and the words, literally translated, were these: 'The winds roared, and the rains fell. The poor white man, faint and weary, came and sat under our tree. He has no mother to bring him milk, no wife to grind his corn. ' Chorus—'Let us pity the white man, no mother has he! ' Trifling as this recital may appear, to a person in my situation the circumstance was affecting in the highest degree. I was so oppressed by such unexpected kindness, that sleep fled before my eyes. "

(2)'Transformation, or Monte Beni. '

(3) 'Portraits Contemporains, ' iii. 519.

(4) Mr. Arthur Helps, in one of his Essays, has wisely said: "You observe a man becoming day by day richer, or advancing in station, or increasing in professional reputation, and you set him down as a successful man in life. But if his home is an ill-regulated one, where no links of affection extend throughout the family— whose former domestics (and he has had more of them than he can well remember) look back upon their sojourn with him as one unblessed by kind words or deeds—I contend that that man has not been successful. Whatever good fortune he may have in the world, it is to be remembered that he has always left one important fortress untaken behind him. That man's life does not surely read well whose benevolence has found no central home. It may have sent forth rays in various directions, but there should have been a warm focus of love—that home-nest which is formed round a good mans heart. "— CLAIMS OF LABOUR.

(5) "The red heart sends all its instincts up to the white brain, to be analysed, chilled, blanched, and so become pure reason—which is just exactly what we do NOT want of women as women. The current should run the other way. The nice, calm, cold thought, which, in women, shapes itself so rapidly that they hardly know it as thought, should always travel to the lips VIA the heart. It does so in those women whom all love and admire.... The brain-women never interest us like the heart-women; white roses please less than red."— THE PROFESSOR AT THE BREAKFAST TABLE, by Oliver Wendell Holmes.

(6) 'The War and General Culture, ' 1871.

(7) "Depend upon it, men set more value on the cultivated minds than on the accomplishments of women, which they are rarely able to appreciate. It is a common error, but it is an error, that literature unfits women for the everyday business of life. It is not so with men. You see those of the most cultivated minds constantly devoting their time and attention to the most homely objects. Literature gives women a real and proper weight in society, but then they must use it with discretion. " —THE REV. SYDNEY SMITH.

(8) 'The Statesman, ' pp. 73-75.

(9) Fuller, the Church historian, with his usual homely mother-wit, speaking of the choice of a wife, said briefly, "Take the daughter of a good mother. "

(10) She was an Englishwoman—a Miss Motley. It maybe mentioned that amongst other distinguished Frenchmen who have married English wives, were Sismondi, Alfred de Vigny, and Lamartine.

(11) "Plus je roule dans ce monde, et plus je suis amene a penser qu'il n'y a que le bonheur domestique qui signifie quelque chose. " — OEUVRES ET CORRESPONDENCE.

(12) De Tocqueville's 'Memoir and Remains, ' vol. i. p. 408.

(13) De Tocqueville's 'Memoir and Remains, ' vol. ii. p. 48.

(14) Colonel Hutchinson was an uncompromising republican, thoroughly brave, highminded, and pious. At the Restoration, he was discharged from Parliament, and from all offices of state for

ever. He retired to his estate at Owthorp, near Nottingham, but was shortly after arrested and imprisoned in the Tower. From thence he was removed to Sandown Castle, near Deal, where he lay for eleven months, and died on September 11th, 1664. The wife petitioned for leave to share his prison, but was refused. When he felt himself dying, knowing the deep sorrow which his death would occasion to his wife, he left this message, which was conveyed to her: "Let her, as she is above other women, show herself on this occasion a good Christian, and above the pitch of ordinary women. " Hence the wife's allusion to her husband's "command" in the above passage.

(15) Mrs. Lucy Hutchinson to her children concerning their father: 'Memoirs of the Life of Col. Hutchinson' (Bohn's Ed.), pp. 29-30.

(16) On the Declaration of American Independence, the first John Adams, afterwards President of the United States, bought a copy of the 'Life and Letters of Lady Russell, ' and presented it to his wife, "with an express intent and desire" (as stated by himself), "that she should consider it a mirror in which to contemplate herself; for, at that time, I thought it extremely probable, from the daring and dangerous career I was determined to run, that she would one day find herself in the situation of Lady Russell, her husband without a head: " Speaking of his wife in connection with the fact, Mr. Adams added: "Like Lady Russell, she never, by word or look, discouraged me from running all hazards for the salvation of my country's liberties. She was willing to share with me, and that her children should share with us both, in all the dangerous consequences we had to hazard. "

(17) 'Memoirs of the Life of Sir Samuel Romily, ' vol. i. p. 41.

(18) It is a singular circumstance that in the parish church of St. Bride, Fleet Street, there is a tablet on the wall with an inscription to the memory of Isaac Romilly, F.R. S., who died in 1759, of a broken heart, seven days after the decease of a beloved wife—CHAMBERS' BOOK OF DAYS, vol. ii. p. 539.

(19) Mr. Frank Buckland says "During the long period that Dr. Buckland was engaged in writing the book which I now have the honour of editing, my mother sat up night after night, for weeks and months consecutively, writing to my father's dictation; and this often till the sun's rays, shining through the shutters at early morn, warned the husband to cease from thinking, and the wife to rest her

weary hand. Not only with her pen did she render material assistance, but her natural talent in the use of her pencil enabled her to give accurate illustrations and finished drawings, many of which are perpetuated in Dr. Buckland's works. She was also particularly clever and neat in mending broken fossils; and there are many specimens in the Oxford Museum, now exhibiting their natural forms and beauty, which were restored by her perseverance to shape from a mass of broken and almost comminuted fragments. "

(20) Veitch's 'Memoirs of Sir William Hamilton. '

(21) The following extract from Mr. Veitch's biography will give one an idea of the extraordinary labours of Lady Hamilton, to whose unfailing devotion to the service of her husband the world of intellect has been so much indebted: "The number of pages in her handwriting, " says Mr. Veitch, —"filled with abstruse metaphysical matter, original and quoted, bristling with proportional and syllogistic formulae—that are still preserved, is perfectly marvellous. Everything that was sent to the press, and all the courses of lectures, were written by her, either to dictation, or from a copy. This work she did in the truest spirit of love and devotion. She had a power, moreover, of keeping her husband up to what he had to do. She contended wisely against a sort of energetic indolence which characterised him, and which, while he was always labouring, made him apt to put aside the task actually before him—sometimes diverted by subjects of inquiry suggested in the course of study on the matter in hand, sometimes discouraged by the difficulty of reducing to order the immense mass of materials he had accumulated in connection with it. Then her resolution and cheerful disposition sustained and refreshed him, and never more so than when, during the last twelve years of his life, his bodily strength was broken, and his spirit, though languid, yet ceased not from mental toil. The truth is, that Sir William's marriage, his comparatively limited circumstances, and the character of his wife, supplied to a nature that would have been contented to spend its mighty energies in work that brought no reward but in the doing of it, and that might never have been made publicly known or available, the practical force and impulse which enabled him to accomplish what he actually did in literature and philosophy. It was this influence, without doubt, which saved him from utter absorption in his world of rare, noble, and elevated, but ever-increasingly unattainable ideas. But for it, the serene sea of abstract thought might have held him becalmed for life; and in the absence of all utterance of definite

knowledge of his conclusions, the world might have been left to an ignorant and mysterious wonder about the unprofitable scholar. "

CHAPTER XII—THE DISCIPLINE OF EXPERIENCE.

"I would the great would grow like thee.
  Who grewest not alone in power
  And knowledge, but by year and hour
In reverence and in charity."—TENNYSON.

"Not to be unhappy is unhappynesse,
And misery not t'have known miserie;
For the best way unto discretion is
The way that leades us by adversitie;
And men are better shew'd what is amisse,
By th'expert finger of calamitie,
Than they can be with all that fortune brings,
Who never shewes them the true face of things."—DANIEL.

"A lump of wo affliction is,
Yet thence I borrow lumps of bliss;
Though few can see a blessing in't,
It is my furnace and my mint."
      —ERSKINE'S GOSPEL SONNETS.

"Crosses grow anchors, bear as thou shouldst so
Thy cross, and that cross grows an anchor too."—DONNE.

  "Be the day weary, or be the day long,
  At length it ringeth to Evensong."—ANCIENT COUPLET.

Practical wisdom is only to be learnt in the school of experience. Precepts and instructions are useful so far as they go, but, without the discipline of real life, they remain of the nature of theory only. The hard facts of existence have to be faced, to give that touch of truth to character which can never be imparted by reading or tuition, but only by contact with the broad instincts of common men and women.

To be worth anything, character must be capable of standing firm upon its feet in the world of daily work, temptation, and trial; and able to bear the wear-and-tear of actual life. Cloistered virtues do not count for much. The life that rejoices in solitude may be only rejoicing in selfishness. Seclusion may indicate contempt for others; though more usually it means indolence, cowardice, or self-indulgence. To every human being belongs his fair share of manful toil and human duty; and it cannot be shirked without loss to the individual himself, as well as to the community to which he belongs. It is only by mixing in the daily life of the world, and taking part in its affairs, that practical knowledge can be acquired, and wisdom learnt. It is there that we find our chief sphere of duty, that we learn the discipline of work, and that we educate ourselves in that patience, diligence, and endurance which shape and consolidate the character. There we encounter the difficulties, trials, and temptations which, according as we deal with them, give a colour to our entire after- life; and there, too, we become subject to the great discipline of suffering, from which we learn far more than from the safe seclusion of the study or the cloister.

Contact with others is also requisite to enable a man to know himself. It is only by mixing freely in the world that one can form a proper estimate of his own capacity. Without such experience, one is apt to become conceited, puffed-up, and arrogant; at all events, he will remain ignorant of himself, though he may heretofore have enjoyed no other company.

Swift once said: "It is an uncontroverted truth, that no man ever made an ill-figure who understood his own talents, nor a good one who mistook them. " Many persons, however, are readier to take measure of the capacity of others than of themselves. "Bring him to me, " said a certain Dr. Tronchin, of Geneva, speaking of Rousseau"Bring him to me, that I may see whether he has got anything in him! "—the probability being that Rousseau, who knew himself better, was much more likely to take measure of Tronchin than Tronchin was to take measure of him.

A due amount of self-knowledge is, therefore, necessary for those who would BE anything or DO anything in the world. It is also one of the first essentials to the formation of distinct personal convictions. Frederic Perthes once said to a young friend: "You know only too well what you CAN do; but till you have learned what you CANNOT do, you will neither accomplish anything of moment, nor know inward peace. "

Any one who would profit by experience will never be above asking for help. He who thinks himself already too wise to learn of others, will never succeed in doing anything either good or great. We have to keep our minds and hearts open, and never be ashamed to learn, with the assistance of those who are wiser and more experienced than ourselves.

The man made wise by experience endeavours to judge correctly of the thugs which come under his observation, and form the subject of his daily life. What we call common sense is, for the most part, but the result of common experience wisely improved. Nor is great ability necessary to acquire it, so much as patience, accuracy, and watchfulness. Hazlitt thought the most sensible people to be met with are intelligent men of business and of the world, who argue from what they see and know, instead of spinning cobweb distinctions of what things ought to be.

For the same reason, women often display more good sense than men, having fewer pretensions, and judging of things naturally, by the involuntary impression they make on the mind. Their intuitive powers are quicker, their perceptions more acute, their sympathies more lively, and their manners more adaptive to particular ends. Hence their greater tact as displayed in the management of others, women of apparently slender intellectual powers often contriving to control and regulate the conduct of men of even the most impracticable nature. Pope paid a high compliment to the tact and good sense of Mary, Queen of William III., when he described her as possessing, not a science, but (what was worth all else) prudence.

The whole of life may be regarded as a great school of experience, in which men and women are the pupils. As in a school, many of the lessons learnt there must needs be taken on trust. We may not understand them, and may possibly think it hard that we have to learn them, especially where the teachers are trials, sorrows, temptations, and difficulties; and yet we must not only accept their lessons, but recognise them as being divinely appointed.

To what extent have the pupils profited by their experience in the school of life? What advantage have they taken of their opportunities for learning? What have they gained in discipline of heart and mind? —how much in growth of wisdom, courage, self- control? Have they preserved their integrity amidst prosperity, and enjoyed life in temperance and moderation? Or, has life been with them a mere feast of selfishness, without care or thought for others? What have they learnt from trial and adversity? Have they learnt patience, submission, and trust in God? —or have they learnt nothing but impatience, querulousness, and discontent?

The results of experience are, of course, only to be achieved by living; and living is a question of time. The man of experience learns to rely upon Time as his helper. "Time and I against any two, " was a maxim of Cardinal Mazarin. Time has been described as a beautifier and as a consoler; but it is also a teacher. It is the food of experience, the soil of wisdom. It may be the friend or the enemy of youth; and Time will sit beside the old as a consoler or as a tormentor, according as it has been used or misused, and the past life has been well or ill spent.

Time, " says George Herbert, "is the rider that breaks youth. " To the young, how bright the new world looks! —how full of novelty, of enjoyment, of pleasure! But as years pass, we find the world to be a place of sorrow as well as of joy. As we proceed through life, many dark vistas open upon us—of toil, suffering, difficulty, perhaps misfortune and failure. Happy they who can pass through and amidst such trials with a firm mind and pure heart, encountering trials with cheerfulness, and standing erect beneath even the heaviest burden!

A little youthful ardour is a great help in life, and is useful as an energetic motive power. It is gradually cooled down by Time, no matter how glowing it has been, while it is trained and subdued by experience. But it is a healthy and hopeful indication of character, — to be encouraged in a right direction, and not to be sneered down and repressed. It is a sign of a vigorous unselfish nature, as egotism is of a narrow and selfish one; and to begin life with egotism and self-sufficiency is fatal to all breadth and vigour of character. Life, in such a case, would be like a year in which there was no spring. Without a generous seedtime, there will be an unflowering summer and an unproductive harvest. And youth is the springtime of life, in which, if there be not a fair share of enthusiasm, little will be attempted, and still less done. It also considerably helps the working quality, inspiring confidence and hope, and carrying one through the dry details of business and duty with cheerfulness and joy.

"It is the due admixture of romance and reality, " said Sir Henry Lawrence, "that best carries a man through life... The quality of romance or enthusiasm is to be valued as an energy imparted to the human mind to prompt and sustain its noblest efforts. " Sir Henry always urged upon young men, not that they should repress enthusiasm, but sedulously cultivate and direct the feeling, as one implanted for wise and noble purposes. "When the two faculties of romance and reality, " he said, "are duly blended, reality pursues a straight rough path to a desirable and practicable result; while romance beguiles the road by pointing out its beauties—by bestowing a deep and practical conviction that, even in this dark and material existence, there may be found a joy with which a stranger intermeddleth not—a light that shineth more and more unto the perfect day. " (1)

It was characteristic of Joseph Lancaster, when a boy of only fourteen years of age, after reading 'Clarkson on the Slave Trade, ' to form the resolution of leaving his home and going out to the West Indies to teach the poor blacks to read the Bible. And he actually set out with a Bible and 'Pilgrim's Progress' in his bundle, and only a few shillings in his purse. He even succeeded in reaching the West Indies, doubtless very much at a loss how to set about his proposed work; but in the meantime his distressed parents, having discovered whither he had gone, had him speedily brought back, yet with his enthusiasm unabated; and from that time forward he unceasingly devoted himself to the truly philanthropic work of educating the destitute poor. (2)

There needs all the force that enthusiasm can give to enable a man to succeed in any great enterprise of life. Without it, the obstruction and difficulty he has to encounter on every side might compel him to succumb; but with courage and perseverance, inspired by enthusiasm, a man feels strong enough to face any danger, to grapple with any difficulty. What an enthusiasm was that of Columbus, who, believing in the existence of a new world, braved the dangers of unknown seas; and when those about him despaired and rose up against him, threatening to cast him into the sea, still stood firm upon his hope and courage until the great new world at length rose upon the horizon!

The brave man will not be baffled, but tries and tries again until he succeeds. The tree does not fall at the first stroke, but only by repeated strokes and after great labour. We may see the visible success at which a man has arrived, but forget the toil and suffering and peril through which it has been achieved. When a friend of Marshal Lefevre was complimenting him on his possessions and good fortune, the Marshal said: "You envy me, do you? Well, you shall have these things at a better bargain than I had. Come into the court: I'll fire at you with a gun twenty times at thirty paces, and if I don't kill you, all shall be your own. What! you won't! Very well;

recollect, then, that I have been shot at more than a thousand times, and much nearer, before I arrived at the state in which you now find me! "

The apprenticeship of difficulty is one which the greatest of men have had to serve. It is usually the best stimulus and discipline of character. It often evokes powers of action that, but for it, would have remained dormant. As comets are sometimes revealed by eclipses, so heroes are brought to light by sudden calamity. It seems as if, in certain cases, genius, like iron struck by the flint, needed the sharp and sudden blow of adversity to bring out the divine spark. There are natures which blossom and ripen amidst trials, which would only wither and decay in an atmosphere of ease and comfort.

Thus it is good for men to be roused into action and stiffened into self-reliance by difficulty, rather than to slumber away their lives in useless apathy and indolence. (3) It is the struggle that is the condition of victory. If there were no difficulties, there would be no need of efforts; if there were no temptations, there would be no training in self-control, and but little merit in virtue; if there were no trial and suffering, there would be no education in patience and resignation. Thus difficulty, adversity, and suffering are not all evil, but often the best source of strength, discipline, and virtue.

For the same reason, it is often of advantage for a man to be under the necessity of having to struggle with poverty and conquer it. "He who has battled, " says Carlyle, "were it only with poverty and hard toil, will be found stronger and more expert than he who could stay at home from the battle, concealed among the provision waggons, or even rest unwatchfully 'abiding by the stuff. '"

Scholars have found poverty tolerable compared with the privation of intellectual food. Riches weigh much more heavily upon the mind. "I cannot but choose say to Poverty, " said Richter, "Be welcome! so that thou come not too late in life. " Poverty, Horace tells us, drove him to poetry, and poetry introduced him to Varus and Virgil and Maecenas. "Obstacles, " says Michelet, "are great incentives. I lived for whole years upon a Virgil, and found myself well off. An odd volume of Racine, purchased by chance at a stall on the quay, created the poet of Toulon. "

The Spaniards are even said to have meanly rejoiced the poverty of Cervantes, but for which they supposed the production of his great works might have been prevented. When the Archbishop of Toledo visited the French ambassador at Madrid, the gentlemen in the suite of the latter expressed their high admiration of the writings of the author of 'Don Quixote, ' and intimated their desire of becoming acquainted with one who had given them so much pleasure. The answer they received was, that Cervantes had borne arms in the service of his country, and was now old and poor. 'What! " exclaimed one of the Frenchmen, "is not Senor Cervantes in good circumstances? Why is he not maintained, then, out of the public treasury? " "Heaven forbid! " was the reply, "that his necessities should be ever relieved, if it is those which make him write; since it is his poverty that makes the world rich! " (4)

It is not prosperity so much as adversity, not wealth so much as poverty, that stimulates the perseverance of strong and healthy natures, rouses their energy and developes their character. Burke said of himself: "I was not rocked, and swaddled, and dandled into a legislator. 'NITOR IN ADVERSUM' is the motto for a man like you." Some men only require a great difficulty set in their way to exhibit the force of their character and genius; and that difficulty once conquered becomes one of the greatest incentives to their further progress.

It is a mistake to suppose that men succeed through success; they much oftener succeed through failure. By far the best experience of men is made up of their remembered failures in dealing with others in the affairs of life. Such failures, in sensible men, incite to better self-management, and greater tact and self- control, as a means of avoiding them in the future. Ask the diplomatist, and he will tell you that he has learned his art through being baffled, defeated, thwarted, and circumvented, far more than from having succeeded. Precept, study, advice, and example could never have taught them so well as failure has done. It has disciplined them experimentally, and taught them what to do as well as what NOT to do—which is often still more important in diplomacy.

Many have to make up their minds to encounter failure again and again before they succeed; but if they have pluck, the failure will only serve to rouse their courage, and stimulate them to renewed efforts. Talma, the greatest of actors, was hissed off the stage when he first appeared on it. Lacordaire, one of the greatest preachers of modern times, only acquired celebrity after repeated failures. Montalembert said of his first public appearance in the Church of St.

Roch: "He failed completely, and on coming out every one said, 'Though he may be a man of talent, he will never be a preacher. '" Again and again he tried until he succeeded; and only two years after his DEBUT, Lacordaire was preaching in Notre Dame to audiences such as few French orators have addressed since the time of Bossuet and Massillon.

When Mr. Cobden first appeared as a speaker, at a public meeting in Manchester, he completely broke down, and the chairman apologized for his failure. Sir James Graham and Mr. Disraeli failed and were derided at first, and only succeeded by dint of great labour and application. At one time Sir James Graham had almost given up public speaking in despair. He said to his friend Sir Francis Baring: "I have tried it every way—extempore, from notes, and committing all to memory—and I can't do it. I don't know why it is, but I am afraid I shall never succeed. " Yet, by dint of perseverance, Graham, like Disraeli, lived to become one of the most effective and impressive of parliamentary speakers.

Failures in one direction have sometimes had the effect of forcing the farseeing student to apply himself in another. Thus Prideaux's failure as a candidate for the post of parish-clerk of Ugboro, in Devon, led to his applying himself to learning, and to his eventual elevation to the bishopric of Worcester. When Boileau, educated for the bar, pleaded his first cause, he broke down amidst shouts of laughter. He next tried the pulpit, and failed there too. And then he tried poetry, and succeeded. Fontenelle and Voltaire both failed at the bar. So Cowper, through his diffidence and shyness, broke down when pleading his first cause, though he lived to revive the poetic art in England. Montesquieu and Bentham both failed as lawyers, and forsook the bar for more congenial pursuits—the latter leaving behind him a treasury of legislative procedure for all time. Goldsmith failed in passing as a surgeon; but he wrote the 'Deserted Village' and the 'Vicar of Wakefield; ' whilst Addison failed as a speaker, but succeeded in writing 'Sir Roger de Coverley, ' and his many famous papers in the 'Spectator. '

Even the privation of some important bodily sense, such as sight or hearing, has not been sufficient to deter courageous men from zealously pursuing the struggle of life. Milton, when struck by blindness, "still bore up and steered right onward. " His greatest works were produced during that period of his life in which be suffered most—when he was poor, sick, old, blind, slandered, and persecuted.

The lives of some of the greatest men have been a continuous struggle with difficulty and apparent defeat. Dante produced his greatest work in penury and exile. Banished from his native city by the local faction to which he was opposed, his house was given up to plunder, and he was sentenced in his absence to be burnt alive. When informed by a friend that he might return to Florence, if he would consent to ask for pardon and absolution, he replied: "No! This is not the way that shall lead me back to my country. I will return with hasty steps if you, or any other, can open to me a way that shall not derogate from the fame or the honour of Dante; but if by no such way Florence can be entered, then to Florence I shall never return. " His enemies remaining implacable, Dante, after a banishment of twenty years, died in exile. They even pursued him after death, when his book, 'De Monarchia, ' was publicly burnt at Bologna by order of the Papal Legate.

Camoens also wrote his great poems mostly in banishment. Tired of solitude at Santarem, he joined an expedition against the Moors, in which he distinguished himself by his bravery. He lost an eye when boarding an enemy's ship in a sea-fight. At Goa, in the East Indies, he witnessed with indignation the cruelty practised by the Portuguese on the natives, and expostulated with the governor against it. He was in consequence banished from the settlement, and sent to China. In the course of his subsequent adventures and misfortunes, Camoens suffered shipwreck, escaping only with his life and the manuscript of his 'Lusiad. ' Persecution and hardship seemed everywhere to pursue him. At Macao he was thrown into prison. Escaping from it, he set sail for Lisbon, where he arrived, after sixteen years' absence, poor and friendless. His 'Lusiad, ' which was shortly after published, brought him much fame, but no money. But for his old Indian slave Antonio, who begged for his master in the streets, Camoens must have perished. (5) As it was, he died in a public almshouse, worn out by disease and hardship. An inscription was placed over his grave: —"Here lies Luis de Camoens: he excelled all the poets of his time: he lived poor and miserable; and he died so, MDLXXIX. " This record, disgraceful but truthful, has since been removed; and a lying and pompous epitaph, in honour of the great national poet of Portugal, has been substituted in its stead.

Even Michael Angelo was exposed, during the greater part of his life, to the persecutions of the envious—vulgar nobles, vulgar priests, and sordid men of every degree, who could neither sympathise with him, nor comprehend his genius. When Paul IV. condemned some of his work in 'The Last Judgment, ' the artist observed that "The Pope would do better to occupy himself with correcting the disorders and indecencies which disgrace the world, than with any such hypercriticisms upon his art. "

Tasso also was the victim of almost continual persecution and calumny. After lying in a madhouse for seven years, he became a wanderer over Italy; and when on his deathbed, he wrote: "I will not complain of the malignity of fortune, because I do not choose to speak of the ingratitude of men who have succeeded in dragging me to the tomb of a mendicant"

But Time brings about strange revenges. The persecutors and the persecuted often change places; it is the latter who are great— the former who are infamous. Even the names of the persecutors would probably long ago have been forgotten, but for their connection with the history of the men whom they have persecuted. Thus, who would now have known of Duke Alfonso of Ferrara, but for his imprisonment of Tasso? Or, who would have heard of the existence of the Grand Duke of Wurtemburg of some ninety years back, but for his petty persecution of Schiller?

Science also has had its martyrs, who have fought their way to light through difficulty, persecution, and suffering. We need not refer again to the cases of Bruno, Galileo, and others, (6) persecuted because of the supposed heterodoxy of their views. But there have been other unfortunates amongst men of science, whose genius has been unable to save them from the fury of their enemies. Thus Bailly, the celebrated French astronomer (who had been mayor of Paris), and Lavoisier, the great chemist, were both guillotined in the first French Revolution. When the latter, after being sentenced to death by the Commune, asked for a few days' respite, to enable him to ascertain the result of some experiments he had made during his confinement, the tribunal refused his appeal, and ordered him for immediate execution—one of the judges saying, that "the Republic had no need of philosophers. " In England also, about the same time, Dr. Priestley, the father of modern chemistry, had his house burnt over his head, and his library destroyed, amidst shouts of "No philosophers! " and he fled from his native country to lay his bones in a foreign land.

The work of some of the greatest discoverers has been done in the midst of persecution, difficulty, and suffering. Columbus, who discovered the New World and gave it as a heritage to the Old, was in his lifetime persecuted, maligned, and plundered by those whom he had enriched. Mungo Park's drowning agony in the African river he had discovered, but which he was not to live to describe; Clapperton's perishing of fever on the banks of the great lake, in the heart of the same continent, which was afterwards to be rediscovered and described by other explorers; Franklin's perishing in the snow—it might be after he had solved the long- sought problem of the North-west Passage—are among the most melancholy events in the history of enterprise and genius.

The case of Flinders the navigator, who suffered a six years' imprisonment in the Isle of France, was one of peculiar hardship. In 1801, he set sail from England in the INVESTIGATOR, on a voyage of discovery and survey, provided with a French pass, requiring all French governors (notwithstanding that England and France were at war) to give him protection and succour in the sacred name of science. In the course of his voyage he surveyed great part of Australia, Van Diemen's Land, and the neighbouring islands. The INVESTIGATOR, being found leaky and rotten, was condemned, and the navigator embarked as passenger in the PORPOISE for England, to lay the results of his three years' labours before the Admiralty. On the voyage home the PORPOISE was wrecked on a reef in the South Seas, and Flinders, with part of the crew, in an open boat, made for Port Jackson, which they safely reached, though distant from the scene of the wreck not less than 750 miles. There he procured a small schooner, the CUMBERLAND, no larger than a Gravesend sailing-boat, and returned for the remainder of the crew, who had been left on the reef. Having rescued them, he set sail for England, making for the Isle of France, which the CUMBERLAND reached in a sinking condition, being a wretched little craft badly found. To his surprise, he was made a prisoner with all his crew, and thrown into prison, where he was treated with brutal harshness, his French pass proving no protection to him. What aggravated the horrors of Flinders' confinement was, that he knew that Baudin, the French navigator, whom he had encountered while making his survey of the Australian coasts, would reach Europe first, and claim the merit of all the discoveries he had made. It turned out as he had expected; and while Flinders was still imprisoned in the Isle of France, the French Atlas of the new discoveries was published, all the points named by Flinders and his precursors being named afresh. Flinders was at length liberated, after six years' imprisonment, his health completely broken; but he continued correcting his maps, and writing out his descriptions to the last. He only lived long enough to correct his final sheet for the press, and died on the very day that his work was published!

Courageous men have often turned enforced solitude to account in executing works of great pith and moment. It is in solitude that the passion for spiritual perfection best nurses itself. The soul communes with itself in loneliness until its energy often becomes intense. But whether a man profits by solitude or not will mainly depend upon his own temperament, training, and character. While, in a large-natured man, solitude will make the pure heart purer, in the small-natured man it will only serve to make the hard heart still harder: for though solitude may be the nurse of great spirits, it is the torment of small ones.

It was in prison that Boetius wrote his 'Consolations of Philosophy, ' and Grotius his 'Commentary on St. Matthew, ' regarded as his masterwork in Biblical Criticism. Buchanan composed his beautiful 'Paraphrases on the Psalms' while imprisoned in the cell of a Portuguese monastery. Campanella, the Italian patriot monk, suspected of treason, was immured for twenty-seven years in a Neapolitan dungeon, during which, deprived of the sun's light, he sought higher light, and there created his 'Civitas Solis, ' which has been so often reprinted and reproduced in translations in most European languages. During his thirteen years' imprisonment in the Tower, Raleigh wrote his 'History of the World, ' a project of vast extent, of which he was only able to finish the first five books. Luther occupied his prison hours in the Castle of Wartburg in translating the Bible, and in writing the famous tracts and treatises with which he inundated all Germany.

It was to the circumstance of John Bunyan having been cast into gaol that we probably owe the 'Pilgrim's Progress. ' He was thus driven in upon himself; having no opportunity for action, his active mind found vent in earnest thinking and meditation; and indeed, after his enlargement, his life as an author virtually ceased. His 'Grace Abounding' and the 'Holy War' were also written in prison. Bunyan lay in Bedford Gaol, with a few intervals of precarious liberty, during not less than twelve years; (7) and it was most probably to his prolonged imprisonment that we owe what Macaulay has characterised as the finest allegory in the world.

All the political parties of the times in which Bunyan lived, imprisoned their opponents when they had the opportunity and the power. Bunyan's prison experiences were principally in the time of Charles II. But in the preceding reign of Charles I., as well as during the Commonwealth, illustrious prisoners were very numerous. The prisoners of the former included Sir John Eliot, Hampden, Selden, Prynne (8) (a most voluminous prison-writer), and many more. It was while under strict confinement in the Tower, that Eliot composed his noble treatise, 'The Monarchy of Man. ' George Wither, the poet, was another prisoner of Charles the First, and it was while confined in the Marshalsea that he wrote his famous 'Satire to the King. ' At the Restoration he was again imprisoned in Newgate, from which he was transferred to the Tower, and he is supposed by some to have died there.

The Commonwealth also had its prisoners. Sir William Davenant, because of his loyalty, was for some time confined a prisoner in Cowes Castle, where he wrote the greater part of his poem of 'Gondibert': and it is said that his life was saved principally through the generous intercession of Milton. He lived to repay the debt, and to save Milton's life when "Charles enjoyed his own again. " Lovelace, the poet and cavalier, was also imprisoned by the Roundheads, and was only liberated from the Gatehouse on giving an enormous bail. Though he suffered and lost all for the Stuarts, he was forgotten by them at the Restoration, and died in extreme poverty.

Besides Wither and Bunyan, Charles II. imprisoned Baxter, Harrington (the author of 'Oceana'), Penn, and many more. All these men solaced their prison hours with writing. Baxter wrote some of the most remarkable passages of his 'Life and Times' while lying in the King's Bench Prison; and Penn wrote his 'No Cross no Crown' while imprisoned in the Tower. In the reign of Queen Anne, Matthew Prior was in confinement on a vamped-up charge of treason for two years, during which he wrote his 'Alma, or Progress of the Soul. '

Since then, political prisoners of eminence in England have been comparatively few in number. Among the most illustrious were De

Foe, who, besides standing three times in the pillory, spent much of his time in prison, writing 'Robinson Crusoe' there, and many of his best political pamphlets. There also he wrote his 'Hymn to the Pillory, ' and corrected for the press a collection of his voluminous writings. (9) Smollett wrote his 'Sir Lancelot Greaves' in prison, while undergoing confinement for libel. Of recent prison-writers in England, the best known are James Montgomery, who wrote his first volume of poems while a prisoner in York Castle; and Thomas Cooper, the Chartist, who wrote his 'Purgatory of Suicide' in Stafford Gaol.

Silvio Pellico was one of the latest and most illustrious of the prison writers of Italy. He lay confined in Austrian gaols for ten years, eight of which he passed in the Castle of Spielberg in Moravia. It was there that he composed his charming 'Memoirs, ' the only materials for which were furnished by his fresh living habit of observation; and out of even the transient visits of his gaoler's daughter, and the colourless events of his monotonous daily life, he contrived to make for himself a little world of thought and healthy human interest.

Kazinsky, the great reviver of Hungarian literature, spent seven years of his life in the dungeons of Buda, Brunne, Kufstein, and Munkacs, during which he wrote a 'Diary of his Imprisonment, ' and amongst other things translated Sterno's 'Sentimental Journey; ' whilst Kossuth beguiled his two years' imprisonment at Buda in studying English, so as to be able to read Shakspeare in the original.

Men who, like these, suffer the penalty of law, and seem to fail, at least for a time, do not really fail. Many, who have seemed to fail utterly, have often exercised a more potent and enduring influence upon their race, than those whose career has been a course of uninterupted success. The character of a man does not depend on whether his efforts are immediately followed by failure or by success. The martyr is not a failure if the truth for which he suffered acquires a fresh lustre through his sacrifice. (10) The patriot who lays down his life for his cause, may thereby hasten its triumph; and those who seem to throw their lives away in the van of a great movement, often open a way for those who follow them, and pass over their dead bodies to victory. The triumph of a just cause may come late; but when it does come, it is due as much to those who failed in their first efforts, as to those who succeeded in their last.

The example of a great death may be an inspiration to others, as well as the example of a good life. A great act does not perish with the life of him who performs it, but lives and grows up into like acts in those who survive the doer thereof and cherish his memory. Of some great men, it might almost be said that they have not begun to live until they have died.

The names of the men who have suffered in the cause of religion, of science, and of truth, are the men of all others whose memories are held in the greatest esteem and reverence by mankind. They perished, but their truth survived. They seemed to fail, and yet they eventually succeeded. (11) Prisons may have held them, but their thoughts were not to be confined by prison-walls. They have burst through, and defied the power of their persecutors. It was Lovelace, a prisoner, who wrote:

> "Stone walls do not a prison make,
>   Nor iron bars a cage;
>   Minds innocent and quiet take
>   That for a hermitage."

It was a saying of Milton that, "who best can suffer best can do. " The work of many of the greatest men, inspired by duty, has been done amidst suffering and trial and difficulty. They have struggled against the tide, and reached the shore exhausted, only to grasp the sand and expire. They have done their duty, and been content to die. But death hath no power over such men; their hallowed memories still survive, to soothe and purify and bless us. "Life, " said Goethe, "to us all is suffering. Who save God alone shall call us to our reckoning? Let not reproaches fall on the departed. Not what they have failed in, nor what they have suffered, but what they have done, ought to occupy the survivors. "

Thus, it is not ease and facility that tries men, and brings out the good that is in them, so much as trial and difficulty. Adversity is the touchstone of character. As some herbs need to be crushed to give forth their sweetest odour, so some natures need to be tried by suffering to evoke the excellence that is in them. Hence trials often unmask virtues, and bring to light hidden graces. Men apparently useless and purposeless, when placed in positions of difficulty and responsibility, have exhibited powers of character before unsuspected; and where we before saw only pliancy and self-indulgence, we now see strength, valour, and self-denial.

As there are no blessings which may not he perverted into evils, so there are no trials which may not be converted into blessings. All depends on the manner in which we profit by them or otherwise. Perfect happiness is not to be looked for in this world. If it could be secured, it would be found profitless. The hollowest of all gospels is the gospel of ease and comfort. Difficulty, and even failure, are far better teachers. Sir Humphry Davy said: "Even in private life, too much prosperity either injures the moral man, and occasions conduct which ends in suffering; or it is accompanied by the workings of envy, calumny, and malevolence of others. "

Failure improves tempers and strengthens the nature. Even sorrow is in some mysterious way linked with joy and associated with tenderness. John Bunyan once said how, "if it were lawful, he could even pray for greater trouble, for the greater comfort's sake. " When surprise was expressed at the patience of a poor Arabian woman under heavy affliction, she said, "When we look on God's face we do not feel His hand. "

Suffering is doubtless as divinely appointed as joy, while it is much more influential as a discipline of character. It chastens and sweetens the nature, teaches patience and resignation, and promotes the deepest as well as the most exalted thought. (12)

> "The best of men
> That e'er wore earth about Him was a sufferer;
> A soft, meek, patient, humble, tranquil spirit
> The first true gentleman that ever breathed." (13)

Suffering may be the appointed means by which the highest nature of man is to be disciplined and developed. Assuming happiness to be the end of being, sorrow may be the indispensable condition through which it is to be reached. Hence St. Paul's noble paradox descriptive of the Christian life, —"as chastened, and not killed; as sorrowful, yet always rejoicing; as poor, yet making many rich; as having nothing, and yet possessing all things. "

Even pain is not all painful. On one side it is related to suffering, and on the other to happiness. For pain is remedial as well as sorrowful. Suffering is a misfortune as viewed from the one side, and a discipline as viewed from the other. But for suffering, the best part of many men's nature would sleep a deep sleep. Indeed, it might almost be said that pain and sorrow were the indispensable conditions of some men's success, and the necessary means to evoke the highest development of their genius. Shelley has said of poets:

"Most wretched men are cradled into poetry by wrong,
They learn in suffering what they teach in song."

Does any one suppose that Burns would have sung as he did, had he been rich, respectable, and "kept a gig; " or Byron, if he had been a prosperous, happily-married Lord Privy Seal or Postmaster-General?

Sometimes a heartbreak rouses an impassive nature to life. "What does he know, " said a sage, "who has not suffered? " When Dumas asked Reboul, "What made you a poet? " his answer was, "Suffering!" It was the death, first of his wife, and then of his child, that drove him into solitude for the indulgence of his grief, and eventually led him to seek and find relief in verse. (14) It was also to a domestic affliction that we owe the beautiful writings of Mrs. Gaskell. "It was as a recreation, in the highest sense of the word, " says a recent writer, speaking from personal knowledge, "as an escape from the great void of a life from which a cherished presence had been taken, that she began that series of exquisite creations which has served to multiply the number of our acquaintances, and to enlarge even the circle of our friendships. " (15)

Much of the best and most useful work done by men and women has been done amidst affliction—sometimes as a relief from it, sometimes from a sense of duty overpowering personal sorrow. "If I had not been so great an invalid, " said Dr. Darwin to a friend, "I should not have done nearly so much work as I have been able to accomplish. " So Dr. Donne, speaking of his illnesses, once said: "This advantage you and my other friends have by my frequent fevers is, that I am so much the oftener at the gates of Heaven; and by the solitude and close imprisonment they reduce me to, I am so much the oftener at my prayers, in which you and my other dear friends are not forgotten. "

Schiller produced his greatest tragedies in the midst of physical suffering almost amounting to torture. Handel was never greater than when, warned by palsy of the approach of death, and struggling with distress and suffering, he sat down to compose the great works which have made his name immortal in music. Mozart composed his great operas, and last of all his 'Requiem, ' when oppressed by debt, and struggling with a fatal disease. Beethoven produced his greatest works amidst gloomy sorrow, when oppressed by almost total deafness. And poor Schubert, after his short but brilliant life, laid it down at the early age of thirty-two; his sole property at his death consisting of his manuscripts, the clothes he wore, and sixty-three florins in money. Some of Lamb's finest writings were produced amidst deep sorrow, and Hood's apparent gaiety often sprang from a suffering heart. As he himself wrote,

"There's not a string attuned to mirth,
But has its chord in melancholy."

Again, in science, we have the noble instance of the suffering Wollaston, even in the last stages of the mortal disease which afflicted him, devoting his numbered hours to putting on record, by dictation, the various discoveries and improvements he had made, so that any knowledge he had acquired, calculated to benefit his fellow-creatures, might not be lost.

Afflictions often prove but blessings in disguise. "Fear not the darkness, " said the Persian sage; it "conceals perhaps the springs of the waters of life. " Experience is often bitter, but wholesome; only by its teaching can we learn to suffer and be strong. Character, in its highest forms, is disciplined by trial, and "made perfect through suffering. " Even from the deepest sorrow, the patient and thoughtful mind will gather richer wisdom than pleasure ever yielded.

"The soul's dark cottage, batter'd and decayed, Lets in new light through chinks that Time has made. "

"Consider, " said Jeremy Taylor, "that sad accidents, and a state of afflictions, is a school of virtue. It reduces our spirits to soberness, and our counsels to moderation; it corrects levity, and interrupts the confidence of sinning.... God, who in mercy and wisdom governs the world, would never have suffered so many sadnesses, and have sent them, especially, to the most virtuous and the wisest men, but that He intends they should be the seminary of comfort, the nursery of virtue, the exercise of wisdom, the trial of patience, the venturing for a crown, and the gate of glory. " (16)

And again: —"No man is more miserable than he that hath no adversity. That man is not tried, whether he be good or bad; and God never crowns those virtues which are only FACULTIES and

DISPOSITIONS; but every act of virtue is an ingredient unto reward." (17)

Prosperity and success of themselves do not confer happiness; indeed, it not unfrequently happens that the least successful in life have the greatest share of true joy in it. No man could have been more successful than Goethe—possessed of splendid health, honour, power, and sufficiency of this world's goods—and yet he confessed that he had not, in the course of his life, enjoyed five weeks of genuine pleasure. So the Caliph Abdalrahman, in surveying his successful reign of fifty years, found that he had enjoyed only fourteen days of pure and genuine happiness. (18) After this, might it not be said that the pursuit of mere happiness is an illusion?

Life, all sunshine without shade, all happiness without sorrow, all pleasure without pain, were not life at all—at least not human life. Take the lot of the happiest—it is a tangled yarn. It is made up of sorrows and joys; and the joys are all the sweeter because of the sorrows; bereavements and blessings, one following another, making us sad and blessed by turns. Even death itself makes life more loving; it binds us more closely together while here. Dr. Thomas Browne has argued that death is one of the necessary conditions of human happiness; and he supports his argument with great force and eloquence. But when death comes into a household, we do not philosophise—we only feel. The eyes that are full of tears do not see; though in course of time they come to see more clearly and brightly than those that have never known sorrow.

The wise person gradually learns not to expect too much from life. While he strives for success by worthy methods, he will be prepared for failures, he will keep his mind open to enjoyment, but submit patiently to suffering. Wailings and complainings of life are never of any use; only cheerful and continuous working in right paths are of real avail.

Nor will the wise man expect too much from those about him. If he would live at peace with others, he will bear and forbear. And even the best have often foibles of character which have to be endured, sympathised with, and perhaps pitied. Who is perfect? Who does not suffer from some thorn in the flesh? Who does not stand in need of toleration, of forbearance, of forgiveness? What the poor imprisoned Queen Caroline Matilda of Denmark wrote on her chapel-window ought to be the prayer of all, —"Oh! keep me innocent! make others great. "

Then, how much does the disposition of every human being depend upon their innate constitution and their early surroundings; the comfort or discomfort of the homes in which they have been brought up; their inherited characteristics; and the examples, good or bad, to which they have been exposed through life! Regard for such considerations should teach charity and forbearance to all men.

At the same time, life will always be to a large extent what we ourselves make it. Each mind makes its own little world. The cheerful mind makes it pleasant, and the discontented mind makes it miserable. "My mind to me a kingdom is, " applies alike to the peasant as to the monarch. The one may be in his heart a king, as the other may be a slave. Life is for the most part but the mirror of our own individual selves. Our mind gives to all situations, to all fortunes, high or low, their real characters. To the good, the world is good; to the bad, it is bad. If our views of life be elevated—if we regard it as a sphere of useful effort, of high living and high thinking, of working for others' good as well as our own—it will be joyful, hopeful, and blessed. If, on the contrary, we regard it merely as affording opportunities for self-seeking, pleasure, and aggrandisement, it will be full of toil, anxiety, and disappointment.

There is much in life that, while in this state, we can never comprehend. There is, indeed, a great deal of mystery in life— much that we see "as in a glass darkly. " But though we may not apprehend the full meaning of the discipline of trial through which the best have to pass, we must have faith in the completeness of the design of which our little individual lives form a part.

We have each to do our duty in that sphere of life in which we have been placed. Duty alone is true; there is no true action but in its accomplishment. Duty is the end and aim of the highest life; the truest pleasure of all is that derived from the consciousness of its fulfilment. Of all others, it is the one that is most thoroughly satisfying, and the least accompanied by regret and disappointment. In the words of George Herbert, the consciousness of duty performed "gives us music at midnight. "

And when we have done our work on earth—of necessity, of labour, of love, or of duty, —like the silkworm that spins its little cocoon and dies, we too depart. But, short though our stay in life may be, it is the appointed sphere in which each has to work out the great aim and end of his being to the best of his power; and when that is done, the accidents of the flesh will affect but little the immortality we shall at last put on:

> "Therefore we can go die as sleep, and trust
> Half that we have
> Unto an honest faithful grave;
> Making our pillows either down or dust!"

NOTES

(1) 'Calcutta Review, ' article on 'Romance and Reality of Indian Life.'

(2) Joseph Lancaster was only twenty years of age when (in 1798) he opened his first school in a spare room in his father's house, which was soon filled with the destitute children of the neighbourhood. The room was shortly found too small for the numbers seeking admission, and one place after another was hired, until at length Lancaster had a special building erected, capable of accommodating a thousand pupils; outside of which was placed the following notice:—"All that will, may send their children here, and have them educated freely; and those that do not wish to have education for nothing, may pay for it if they please. " Thus Joseph Lancaster was the precursor of our present system of National Education.

(3) A great musician once said of a promising but passionless cantatrice—"She sings well, but she wants something, and in that something everything. If I were single, I would court her; I would marry her; I would maltreat her; I would break her heart; and in six months she would be the greatest singer in Europe! "— BLACKWOOD'S MAGAZINE,

(4) Prescot's 'Essays, ' art. Cervantes.

(5) A cavalier, named Ruy de Camera, having called upon Camoens to furnish a poetical version of the seven penitential psalms, the poet, raising his head from his miserable pallet, and pointing to his faithful slave, exclaimed: "Alas! when I was a poet, I was young, and happy, and blest with the love of ladies; but now, I am a forlorn deserted wretch! See—there stands my poor Antonio, vainly

supplicating FOURPENCE to purchase a little coals. I have not them to give him! " The cavalier, Sousa quaintly relates, in his 'Life of Camoens, ' closed his heart and his purse, and quitted the room. Such were the grandees of Portugal! —Lord Strangford's REMARKS ON THE LIFE AND WRITINGS OF CAMOENS, 1824.

(6) See chapter v. p. 125.

(7) A Quaker called on Bunyan one day with "a message from the Lord, " saying he had been to half the gaols of England, and was glad at last to have found him. To which Bunyan replied: "If the Lord sent thee, you would not have needed to take so much trouble to find me out, for He knew that I have been in Bedford Gaol these seven years past. "

(8) Prynne, besides standing in the pillory and having his ears cut off, was imprisoned by turns in the Tower, Mont Orgueil (Jersey), Dunster Castle, Taunton Castle, and Pendennis Castle. He afterwards pleaded zealously for the Restoration, and was made Keeper of the Records by Charles II. It has been computed that Prynne wrote, compiled, and printed about eight quarto pages for every working-day of his life, from his reaching man's estate to the day of his death. Though his books were for the most part appropriated by the trunkmakers, they now command almost fabulous prices, chiefly because of their rarity.

(9) He also projected his 'Review' in prison—the first periodical of the kind, which pointed the way to the host of 'Tatlers, ' 'Guardians,' and 'Spectators, ' which followed it. The 'Review' consisted of 102 numbers, forming nine quarto volumes, all of which were written by De Foe himself, while engaged in other and various labours.

(10) A passage in the Earl of Carlisles Lecture on Pope—'Heaven was made for those who have failed in this world'—struck me very forcibly several years ago when I read it in a newspaper, and became a rich vein of thought, in which I often quarried, especially when the sentence was interpreted by the Cross, which was failure apparently."—LIFE AND LETTERS OF ROBERTSON (of Brighton), ii. 94.

(11) "Not all who seem to fail, have failed indeed;
    Not all who fail have therefore worked in vain:
    For all our acts to many issues lead;

And out of earnest purpose, pure and plain,
Enforced by honest toil of hand or brain,
The Lord will fashion, in His own good time,
(Be this the labourer's proudly-humble creed,)
Such ends as, to His wisdom, fitliest chime
With His vast love's eternal harmonies.
There is no failure for the good and wise:
What though thy seed should fall by the wayside
And the birds snatch it;—yet the birds are fed;
Or they may bear it far across the tide,
To give rich harvests after thou art dead."
POLITICS FOR THE PEOPLE, 1848.

(12) "What is it, " says Mr. Helps, "that promotes the most and the deepest thought in the human race? It is not learning; it is not the conduct of business; it is not even the impulse of the affections. It is suffering; and that, perhaps, is the reason why there is so much suffering in the world. The angel who went down to trouble the waters and to make them healing, was not, perhaps, entrusted with so great a boon as the angel who benevolently inflicted upon the sufferers the disease from which they suffered. "—BREVIA.

(13) These lines were written by Deckar, in a spirit of boldness equal to its piety. Hazlitt has or said of them, that they "ought to embalm his memory to every one who has a sense either of religion, or philosophy, or humanity, or true genius. "

(14) Reboul, originally a baker of Nismes, was the author of many beautiful poems—amongst others, of the exquisite piece known in this country by its English translation, entitled 'The Angel and the Child. '

(15) 'Cornhill Magazine, ' vol. xvi. p. 322.

(16) 'Holy Living and Dying, ' ch. ii. sect. 6.

(17) Ibid., ch. iii. sect. 6.

(18) Gibbon's 'Decline and Fall of the Roman Empire, ' vol. x. p. 40.

Lightning Source UK Ltd.
Milton Keynes UK
UKHW010638280121
377837UK00001B/82